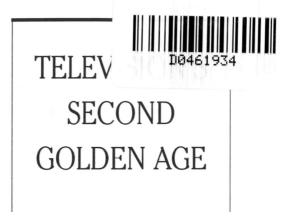

# TELEV[ISION'S]
# SECOND
# GOLDEN AGE

*The Television Series*
Robert J. Thompson, Series Editor

*Other titles in The Television Series*

**Bonfire of the Humanities**
*Television, Subliteracy, and Long-Term Memory Loss*
David Marc

**"Deny All Knowledge"**
*Reading* The X-Files
David Lavery, Angela Hague, *and* Marla Cartwright, *eds.*

**Dictionary of Teleliteracy**
*Television's 500 Biggest Hits, Misses, and Events*
David Bianculli

**Gen X TV**
The Brady Bunch *to* Melrose Place
Rob Owen

**Laughs, Luck . . . and Lucy**
*How I Came to Create the Most Popular Sitcom of All Time*
Jess Oppenheimer, *with* Gregg Oppenheimer

**Living-Room War**
Michael J. Arlen

**Lou Grant**
*The Making of TV's Top Newspaper Drama*
Douglass K. Daniel

**Prime Time, Prime Movers**
*From* I Love Lucy *to* L.A. Law—*America's Greatest TV Shows
and the People Who Created Them*
David Marc *and* Robert J. Thompson

**Storytellers to the Nation**
*A History of American Television Writing*
Tom Stempel

**The View from Highway I**
*Essays on Television*
Michael J. Arlen

# ROBERT · J · THOMPSON

# TELEVISION'S SECOND GOLDEN AGE

## From *Hill Street Blues* to *ER*

*Hill Street Blues* / *thirtysomething*
*St. Elsewhere* / *China Beach*
*Cagney & Lacey* / *Twin Peaks*
*Moonlighting* / *Northern Exposure*
*L. A. Law* / *Picket Fences*

■ ■ ■

WITH BRIEF REFLECTIONS ON
*Homicide, NYPD Blue, & Chicago Hope,*
AND OTHER QUALITY DRAMAS

SYRACUSE UNIVERSITY PRESS

First Syracuse University Press Edition 1997

97  98  99  00  01  02        6  5  4  3  2  1

Originally published in 1996. Published by arrangement
with The Continuum Publishing Company, New York.

Photographs are courtesy of Mark Dawidziak.

The paper used in this publication meets the minimum requirements of
American National Standard for Information Sciences—Permanence
of Paper for Printed Library Materials, ANSI Z39.48-1984. ∞™

**Library of Congress Cataloging-in-Publication Data**

Thompson, Robert J., 1959–
Television's second golden age : From Hill Street blues to ER :
Hill Street blues, Thirtysomething, St. Elsewhere, China Beach,
Cagney & Lacey, Twin Peaks, Moonlighting, Northern exposure, L.A.
law, Picket fences, with brief reflections on Homicide, NYPD blue &
Chicago hope, and other quality dramas  / Robert J. Thompson — 1st
Syracuse University Press ed.
p.    cm.
Originally published: New York : Continuum, 1996.
Includes bibliographical references and indexes.
ISBN 0-8156-0504-8 (alk. paper)
1. Television programs—United States—History and criticism.
I. Title.
PN1992.3.U5T49    1997
791.45'75'0973—dc21              97-17284

*Manufactured in the United States of America*

To Nancy
and Juliana

∎   ∎   ∎

# Contents

# Acknowledgments

I am grateful to many people for the help they gave to me while I was writing this book, including David Bianculli, Denise Bodah, Mary Deskiewicz, Laurel and Ted Fagenson, Tom Fontana, the Fulmers, Paul Furia, Sharon Hollenback, Doris Izuno, Takumi Izuno, Bill Lyon, Cynthia and Charles Macri, Rob Owen, Felicia Patinkin, Christopher Poulos, Cori Ranzer, Bob Roth, Mylinda Smith, Catherine Steele, Dorothy Swanson, Grant Tinker, Mark Tinker, Roy, Joan, Ken, and Barbara Thompson, Andres Versage, and Ramon Versage. Visiting lecturers at the NHSI Summer Institute, a program I directed at Northwestern University from 1986 to 1991, also provided me with invaluable ideas, especially these people: Ralph Daniels, Lewis Erlicht, Richard Gilbert, William Link, Garry Marshall, A. C. Nielsen, Jr., Jay Rosen, and Fred Silverman. Thanks also go to Ian Bruce and Petra Redchuck, my research assistants at the Newhouse School; Melanie Jackson, my agent; Joe Galuski and his listeners at WSYR radio; and my students at Syracuse University and Cornell.

I would like to offer special thanks to Ray B. Browne, J. Fred MacDonald, David Marc, and David Rubin for their ongoing help and support, and to my editors, Evander Lomke at Continuum, and Nancy Izuno, without whom this book wouldn't have been written.

*Note:*
Network schedules are referred to throughout the book using Eastern Standard Time.

# From "The Golden Age
of Television" to "Quality TV"

Ask anyone over fifty and they're likely to tell you that they just don't make television like they used to. Their eyes may glaze over as they recall the "Golden Age of Television"—a time stretching roughly from 1947 to 1960 when serious people could take TV seriously. Back then, the well-read could switch on the set on an average evening and find series with titles like *The Pulitzer Prize Playhouse*. Emily Brontë's *Wuthering Heights* alone rated six network adaptations during this period, and fans of Ibsen could have caught five stagings of *A Doll's House* and four of *Hedda Gabler*. The plays of Shakespeare were commonly seen on the networks during prime time. *Studio One* alone presented three live adaptations of *Julius Caesar* and one each of *The Taming of the Shrew, Coriolanus,* and *Macbeth*. Airing alongside the hundreds of classics were thoughtful original plays by writers like Rod Serling, Paddy Chayefsky, Gore Vidal, and Reginald Rose, that featured actors like James Dean, Grace Kelly, Paul Newman, and Lee Grant. Some of these were good enough to inspire stage and film adaptations. *Marty,* for example, the 1955 film that won Oscars for best picture, best director, best screenplay, and best actor was based on a 1953 episode of *The Goodyear TV Playhouse*.

It's always tempting to compare these early highbrow programs to a few outrageously silly later series and to find the latter sorely wanting. Shows like 1972's *Me and the Chimp* are often cited as proof that the evolution of artistic quality on network TV is going backwards. But this idea of a consistent aesthetic degeneration doesn't accurately describe the history of the television program. After all, from 1953 through 1957, right in the heart of television's golden age, *The Today Show* itself was cohosted by a chimpanzee.

The fact is that most of the programs during the golden age of the 1950s weren't very good. Although the same holds true of more recent times, the medium has significantly matured in the last decade and a half. Much of the best television ever to appear in this country was made after 1980. Some of the programs from this period were, and are, truly outstanding. "Don't tell me about the Golden Age of Television," Pulitzer Prize-winning critic Howard Rosenberg wrote in the *Los Angeles Times* in 1985. "[Don't tell me about] that late-1940s-to-late-1950s decade in which the raw, infant medium was said to have spilled over with greatness. The Golden Age of Television is now."[1] A few years later, David Bianculli wrote an entire book encouraging a new respect for the medium. "If the fifties were the Golden Age of Television," he wrote in *Teleliteracy: Taking Television Seriously* in 1992, "the quantity and quality of today's TV offerings make the modern era worthy of the appellation 'The Platinum Age of Television.'"[2] By the end of 1995, praising television had become almost as fashionable as trashing it.

Still, the TV of the 1950s continues to bask in the glow of selective recall. Most living Americans have no memory of what most TV was really like back then, and only the good stuff is ever seen in reruns and in montage sequences on Emmy Award shows and network anniversary specials. The big picture of the 1980s and 1990s, on the other hand, is still too fresh in our memories to support such respectful nostalgia. We remember the chaff along with the wheat. Could we seriously call "golden" an age that gave us *Manimal* and *Joanie Loves Chachi?* Nevertheless, a renaissance in American commercial television was beginning while these shows were on the air.

Though very few critics went so far as to see the 1980s as the start of a new "golden age," many did recognize that a new type of programming was emerging that they thought was better, more sophisticated, and more artistic than the usual network fare. They called it "quality television." This descriptive if unimaginative term started regularly appearing in the 1970s, but it really caught on after the debut of *Hill Street Blues* in 1981. By 1984, the British Film Institute had published a book called *MTM: Quality Television,* a critical history of MTM Enterprises, the company that made *Hill Street.*[3] That same year, a lobbying group protesting the cancellation of *Cagney & Lacey* called themselves Viewers for Quality Television. Journalists now use the term "quality TV" almost as regularly as they use programming neologisms like "sitcom," "infomercial," and "docudrama."

Yet even today, no one can say exactly what "quality television" means. There was, for that matter, never a definition of what made a program "golden" during the "golden age." *Studio One* clearly was; *Private Secretary* clearly was not. Like "quality TV," people just seemed to know it when they saw it. Nor does the word "quality," when referred to television, simply mean "excellence" or "superiority" as the dictionary suggests, although that certainly is part of it. Many people believe that *60 Minutes,* for example, is a show of high quality; it is seldom referred to, however, as "quality TV." On the other hand, *Entertainment Weekly's* Ken Tucker identified *Picket Fences* as a "quality drama"[4] while also including it on his list of the five *worst* shows of 1992.[5] Though it may have originally been used just to describe unusually good shows, the "quality" in "quality TV" has come to refer more to a generic style than to an aesthetic judgment.

So what is "quality TV?" The Viewers for Quality Television organization have a definition—

> A quality series enlightens, enriches, challenges, involves, and confronts. It dares to take risks, it's honest and illuminating, it appeals to the intellect and touches the emotions. It requires concentration and attention, and it provokes thought. Characterization is explored. And usually a quality comedy will touch the funny bone and the heart[6]—

but it's a hard one to apply with any degree of objectivity. And though TV critics regularly use the term to describe individual shows, they are usually no better at listing its specific defining characteristics. Some of the most helpful definitions have come from three academic critics. Jane Feuer and Susan Boyd-Bowman explored the history of "quality" in their essays about MTM Enterprises, as did Betsy Williams in hers about *Northern Exposure.*[7] Viewers, critics, and scholars alike, however, seem to agree a lot on what shows fit the category, and taken all together something approaching a profile of "quality television" begins to emerge:

1. Quality TV is best defined by what it is not. It is not "regular" TV. The worst insult you could give to Barney Rosenzweig, the executive producer of *Cagney & Lacey,* was to tell him that his work was "too TV."[8] *Twin Peaks* was universally praised by critics for being "unlike anything we'd ever seen on television." In a medium long considered artless, the only artful TV is that which isn't like all the rest of it. Quality TV breaks rules. It may do this by taking a traditional genre and transforming it, as *Hill Street Blues, St. Elsewhere,* and *Moonlighting* did to the cop show, the doctor show, and the detective show, respectively. Or it may defy standard generic parameters and define new narrative territory heretofore unexplored by television, as did *thirtysomething* and *Twin Peaks.*

2. Quality TV usually has a quality pedigree. Shows made by artists whose reputations were made in other, classier media, like film, are prime candidates. Furthermore, directors of small art films have a better chance of making quality TV than directors of blockbuster movies. John Sayles's *Shannon's Deal* and David Lynch's *Twin Peaks* both got the quality nod by most critics; Steven Spielberg's *SeaQuest DSV* did not. As the genre developed through the 1980s, a few creators who'd worked exclusively in TV also became associated with this designer label television. Since *Hill Street Blues,* for example, any show with Steven Bochco's name on it is presumed quality (*NYPD Blue*) until proven otherwise (*Capitol Critters*). In all of these cases, the creators usually insist upon and get a much greater degree of independence from network influence than is typical in the production process of commercial TV.

3. Quality TV attracts an audience with blue chip demographics. The upscale, well-educated, urban-dwelling, young viewers advertisers so desire to reach tend to make up a much larger percentage of the audience of these shows than of other kinds of programs.

4. Desirable demographics notwithstanding, quality shows must often undergo a noble struggle against profit-mongering networks and nonappreciative audiences. The hottest battles between Art and Commerce, between creative writer-producers and bottom-line-conscious executives are often played out during the runs of these series. With some obvious exceptions, these shows seldom become blockbusters and their survival is often tenuous, at least at the beginning. Their futures often hang in the balance between network noblesse oblige (the renewing and promoting of a low-rated show) and network stupidity (scheduling it in a deadly time slot). When a quality show does become a hit, it is often after a long struggle and some unusual circumstances. *Hill Street Blues* reached the top twenty-five only after it won a record-breaking batch of Emmy Awards; *Cagney & Lacey* was canceled three times on the way to ratings respectability; *NYPD Blue* debuted strongly after its forbidden language and nudity were reported in nearly every paper in America and a handful of stations refused to air the show.

5. Quality TV tends to have a large ensemble cast. The variety of characters allows for a variety of viewpoints since multiple plots must usually be employed to accommodate all of the characters.

6. Quality TV has a memory. Though it may or may not be serialized in continuing story lines, these shows tend to refer back to previous episodes. Characters develop and change as the series goes on. Events and details from previous episodes are often used or referred to in subsequent episodes.

7. Quality TV creates a new genre by mixing old ones. When describing *Northern Exposure*'s creolized generic heritage, for example, Betsy Williams says that while the show "is usually billed as a drama . . . it functions more as an hour-long ensemble comedy with a slight nod to the medical franchise, another to primetime melodrama, another to the fish-out-of-water sitcom, and still another to the sixties' 'magicom.'"[9] All quality shows integrate comedy and tragedy in a way Aristotle would never have approved.

8. Quality TV tends to be literary and writer-based. The writing is usually more complex than in other types of programming.

9. Quality TV is self-conscious. Oblique allusions are made to both high and popular culture, but mostly to TV itself. *Moonlighting*, for example, could bury an obscure reference to a play by Eugene O'Neill right alongside a direct address to the camera about the fact that *Moonlighting* had been airing a lot of reruns lately. Both the classier cultural references and the sly, knowing jabs at TV serve to distance these programs from the stigmatized medium and to announce that they are superior to the typical trash available on television.

10. The subject matter of quality TV tends toward the controversial. *St. Elsewhere* presented the first prime-time series story about AIDS, and other quality series frequently included some of television's earliest treatments of subjects like abortion, homosexuals, racism, and religion, to name a few. The overall message almost always tends toward liberal humanism. So consistent have these shows been in this regard that it is hard to imagine a right-wing "quality TV" series. "Quality TV is liberal TV," Jane Feuer, making no bones about it, wrote in *MTM: Quality Television*.[10]

11. Quality TV aspires toward "realism."

12. Series which exhibit the eleven characteristics listed above are usually enthusiastically showered with awards and critical acclaim. Since the 1980–1981 season, shows of the type described in this list have dominated the best drama category for most major entertainment awards. Emmy Awards for best drama went to *Hill Street Blues* and *L.A. Law* four times each, *Cagney & Lacey* and *Picket Fences* twice, and *thirtysomething* and *Northern Exposure* once each. Best Drama Golden Globes for the same period went to *Hill Street* twice, *L.A. Law* twice, *Northern Exposure* twice, and *thirtysomething*, *China Beach*, and *Twin Peaks* once each. Peabody Awards went to *Hill Street Blues*, *St. Elsewhere*, *L.A. Law*, *thirtysomething*, *China Beach*, *Twin Peaks*, and *Northern Exposure*. The award for best dramatic episode was given by the Writers' Guild of America three times to *Hill Street Blues* and *Moonlighting*, twice to *Cagney & Lacey* and *China Beach*, and once each to *Miami Vice*, *St. Elsewhere*, and *thirtysomething*. A survey of college professors and TV critics con-

ducted by the Siena Research Institute in 1990 named *Hill Street Blues* the best television drama ever,[11] and when the editors of *TV Guide* compiled an "All Time Best TV" list in 1993, the all-time best drama went to *St. Elsewhere* and the all-time best cop show to *Hill Street Blues*.[12] When this author asked TV critics from the 388 largest circulation daily newspapers to name the best prime-time TV shows of all time, *Hill Street Blues* came out on top.[13]

As this list suggests, when looked at all together, these "quality" programs all begin to look a lot alike. What emerges by the time we get to the 1990s is that "quality TV" has become a genre in itself, complete with its own set of formulaic characteristics. As is the case with any genre—the cop show, the western, the doctor show—we come to know what to expect. All of the innovative elements that have come to define "quality TV," even its unpredictability, have become more and more predictable. By 1992, you could recognize a "quality show" long before you could tell if it was any good. Quality television came to refer to shows with a particular set of characteristics that we normally associate with "good," "artsy," and "classy."

But we can say that of other media as well. The films that play in the city art houses also have a surprisingly lot in common with each other. Serious novels, paintings, and films have a distinct set of characteristics that distinguish them from bestsellers, K-Mart seascapes, and Hollywood blockbusters. "Quality TV" is simply television's version of the "art film." And while it is made with a definite formula in mind, it is a formula that has inspired the development of the medium in new and exciting ways. With the emergence of this new genre, made possible by major changes in the entertainment industry in the 1980s, American TV has truly entered a second Golden Age.

▪ ▪ ▪

A few words should be said at the outset about what will and won't be included in this book. First, I will be looking exclusively at prime-time series that aired on commercial television. This is not to say that excellent programs did not appear during the 1980s in other places and in different forms at different times. There were many made-for-TV movies, miniseries, nonfiction specials, and programs that played on cable or the Public Broadcasting Service that deserved and received critical acclaim. My project is not to examine all the good TV that has ever been made since 1980, but to examine one particular type of programming that flowered during this time. In spite of the vast array of programming choices that have been made available in recent years, the prime-time network series still earns the largest and most diverse audience and is still the closest thing we have to a national drama. That programs like the ones that will be discussed in this book developed at all on network TV, and the way in which they did, reveals a lot about the tensions between art and profit in a commercially supported medium. The very fact that "quality TV" acquired such a label suggests that most people don't expect quality on prime time. An art museum, of course, would never advertise a collection of "quality painting and sculpture." It's assumed that if it's in a museum it must be good. No such assumption has ever been made about television.

Next, the examinination will be limited to the hour-long dramatic form. No one, of course, will argue that there weren't quality comedies on TV during the period in question. *Cheers* is only the most obvious example. The "quality TV" phenomenon described above, however, was one that had its own unique development in the hour-long dramas. Although the term "quality TV" means different things to different people, it has come to be associated in the minds of many with the "quality drama," and that will be the area of concern in the following pages. Jane Feuer has argued that "from the standpoint of quality TV, the charge leveled against stereotyped characters has always been that they lack psychological realism and the potential for identification from the 'quality' audience. The sitcom remains forever on the far side of quality for this reason, since a certain amount of stereotyping is necessary to get laughs."[14]

Third, this is a book about quality dramas, not the much larger category of dramas of quality. Many might be surprised that such admittedly *good* shows as *Murder, She Wrote* and *Star Trek: The Next Generation* are not included here. Although these shows indeed had many merits, they fall into a different tradition from the kind of program we attempted to define above.

And finally, the very subject matter of this book may seem to reflect a certain degree of snobbery on the part of its author. I'd like to dispel that right from the start. I grew up watching and enjoying the likes of *The Andy Griffith Show, The Partridge Family,* and *CHiPS,* and I continue to acknowledge the important place such shows hold in the history of entertainment and popular art in this country. I am not so much arguing that the quality dramas of the 1980s were inherently better than anything else that has been aired through the years, than I am suggesting that the shows were different. The principal difference that distinguishes these programs is that one *could,* in fact, be a snob and still admit to watching them.

# The Golden Ages of Television

That Americans took early to calling the television set the boob
tube and the idiot box says a lot about what they thought of what
came out of it. The publicly voiced opinion of many thinking
adults still holds that entertainment TV in general is usually at best a
waste of time and at worst a toxic influence.[1] Yet in the very short
history of the medium, critics and serious viewers alike have identified
a surprising number of high points in what they agree, of course, is an
otherwise low medium. Some point to the anthology dramas of the
1950s, when legitimate theater was available at the flick of a switch.
Others remember the brief, shining moment in the early 1960s when
a handful of earnest but short-lived dramas reflected the hopeful sensi-
bilities of Kennedy's Camelot. Some dismiss current programming with
disgust as they remember that halcyon season in 1973 when *All in the
Family, M\*A\*S\*H,* and *The Mary Tyler Moore Show* could be seen one
after the other on Saturday nights on CBS. Still others think TV is
reaching its artistic peak at this very moment. Depending on who you
listen to, in less than half a century, television has already enjoyed at
least three renaissances.

"Although television as we know it today is, give or take a couple of
years, only forty-five years old," John J. O'Connor reminded us in the
*New York Times* in 1994, "talk about one golden age or another has
been bandied about for decades."[2] For all the stubborn resistance to
seeing television as a whole as anything more than a purveyor of mindless garbage, sober-minded people continue to watch it. Perhaps to
justify the time they log in front of the set, or perhaps in a sincere
desire to witness the maturation of the most pervasive of mass media,
they seem to perch on the sofa as in a crow's nest, eyes peeled for
something good, waiting for art to come out of a box.

Throughout television history there have been good shows and bad shows, as there is always good and bad in any medium at any time. Ironically enough, most of the shows considered good by critics and scholars are usually judged as such based on criteria established in older, more traditional arts. For the most part, whenever TV begins to resemble any other medium but itself—film, the stage, the novel— positive critical attention seems to follow. The common refrain that a show was "too good for TV" suggests a grudging respect for what was an obvious exception in a disdained medium. In the eyes of many serious viewers, TV can only aspire to art when it's pretending to be something else.

## "THE GOLDEN AGE OF TELEVISION"

Pretending to be something else wasn't too hard for television in the beginning. It started off, after all, not as an expressive form of its own but as nothing more than a transmission device. Musical performances, boxing matches, sermons, old films—anything was fair game in the search to fill air time. But within a few years an identity did emerge and much of it remains intact today. Based on formulas and styles plundered from radio and the movies, most of entertainment television's signature genres—sitcoms, doctor shows, cop shows, Westerns, adventures, game shows, soap operas—had been introduced by the early 1950s.

Also based in other media were two types of live programming, the comedy-variety show and the anthology drama, which have come to dominate our idea of national television in the 1940s and early 1950s. As victims of mass cultural natural selection, these programs tend to be remembered more fondly than those described above. Having for the most part disappeared from contemporary network schedules, these shows are now mourned as examples of what TV might have been.

The variety show brought vaudeville back from the brink of death, mixing songs, dances, comic sketches, jugglers, acrobats, and animal acts into one of the first major video genres. Shows hosted by Milton Berle, Arthur Godfrey, Ed Sullivan, Jackie Gleason, and Dean Martin and Jerry Lewis were among the most watched programs of the period. The low, physical humor characteristic of the vaudeville stage was often balanced by lofty flirtations with the finer arts, often within an individual episode of a single series. Berle, host of TV's first blockbuster hit, *The Texaco Star Theater*, once delivered an opening monologue dressed in a wedding gown and then yielded the stage to a concert violinist. In contrast to the pie-in-the-face raucousness of *Texaco Star Theater,* on the other hand, *Your Show of Shows* boasted a high-toned writing staff that included such future comic luminaries as Woody Allen, Mel Brooks, Larry Gelbart, and Neil Simon. Nevertheless, between the urbane wit of the sketches and the occasional operatic performance by a member of the New York Metropolitan Opera, Sid Caesar managed to drop his pants at least once during the series' four-and-a-half-year run.

It is the anthology drama, however, that is perhaps most associated with the Golden Age of television. Based not in radio and the movies but in the New York stage, these shows were bound to be darlings of the critics and the cognoscenti. Under a single weekly title, the anthology shows presented independent, self-contained plays on a weekly basis. Series like *Kraft Television Theater, Studio One, Philco TV Playhouse, Robert Montgomery Presents, Goodyear TV Playhouse, The U.S. Steel Hour,* and *Playhouse 90* are still remembered for their serious and thoughtful original dramas and adaptations. A classic canon by an emerging class of new writers began to form which included "Requiem for a Heavyweight" (Rod Serling, 1956), "Patterns" (Rod Serling, 1955), "Marty" (Paddy Chayefsky, 1953), "Bang the Drum Slowly" (Arnold Schulman, 1956), "No Time for Sergeants" (Mac Hyman, 1955), "Days of Wine and Roses" (JP Miller, 1958), "Twelve Angry Men" (Reginald Rose, 1954), and "Visit to a Small Planet" (Gore Vidal, 1955). Many of the scripts for these plays were collected and sold in book form, a distinction prime-time programs would not enjoy again for many years. Several were remade as motion pictures. Kinescope recordings of some of these live dramas even resurfaced in the 1980s on PBS under the umbrella title *The Golden Age of Television.*

Inspired by nostalgic retrospectives like these, it's often forgotten that most of the productions from this period never stood a chance of making it to PBS's video museum. "For every memorable dramatic success," media historian J. Fred MacDonald points out, "the medium offered hundreds—many hundreds—of shows that were average at best. Turned out according to familiar formulas of boy-meets-girl, good-triumphant-over-evil, love-conquers-all, and the like, these productions filled the great showcases. . . . In the Golden Age of well-remembered giants . . . there were many creative pygmies at work."[3] But many hold that bad Shakespeare on network prime-time television was better than no Shakespeare at all, and that 1951's sixteen weekly live anthologies of classic and original theater was better than 1981's thirty weekly sitcoms.[4]

Conditions were just right for a healthy teletheater in the late 1940s and the 1950s, but they soon changed and when they did the anthologies all but disappeared.

The theatrical model was a natural one for the new medium to turn to for programming. Plays unfold live and they're performed in a confined space, both made-to-order features for early television. Furthermore, most of network programming was made in New York, a city teeming with writers, actors, directors, and staff with the ability and/or the desire to work in the theater. But television's manifest destiny lay to the west. After years of isolating themselves from the medium that threatened to put them out of business, the major motion picture studios realized that, unable to beat television, they may as well join in on the bonanza. Disney went first, supplying a series to ABC, which, as the newest kid on the block, was in dire need of competitive programming. It changed titles and networks over the years, but Disney's series stayed on the air for a record-breaking thirty-four seasons. Warner Brothers followed in 1955, providing a long string of Westerns and adventures, also for ABC. After that, TV pretty much loaded up the truck and moved to Beverly Hills, leaving behind its New York-based theatrical aesthetic and all the respectability that went with it. Once a workable videotape system was introduced in 1957, yet another bell had tolled for live TV. In 1953, 80 percent of network television was broadcast live. In 1960, the figure was at 36 percent and falling like a rock.[5] Filmed Westerns and adventures filled much of the programming void. In the 1958–59 season, seven of the ten top-rated shows, including the top four, were Westerns. With the Westerns and adventures came complaints that TV content had become too violent, a charge that hasn't let up to this day.

Although a few anthologies held on for years, the series with a consistent set of characters took over as the dominant form. Even before TV went Hollywood, these types of filmed series were attracting large audiences. *I Love Lucy* and *Dragnet,* both L.A.-produced, were the number one and two shows of the 1953–54 season. Episodic series made good business sense. Whereas viewers never knew if they'd like the play of the week on an anthology show, they knew exactly what they were getting into with each installment of an episodic series. These were predictable, each episode in effect a promotion for the next. Furthermore, they could be a lot cheaper to produce. The same sets could be used over and over, and the consistent format made the jobs of cast, crew, writers, and directors easier. Instead of launching a unique play week after week, these series were assembly-line productions.

Another argument for the temporary prominence of the theatrical anthologies is that most of the families who could afford television in the earlier years were wealthier and better educated and therefore more predisposed to watching classy legitimate drama.[6] In 1950, a television set cost several weeks' salary for the average worker.[7] Along the same elitist lines, it has been argued that the predominance of urban Northeasterners in the early TV audience helped support a higher form of programming than did the wider mass audience that came along a little later. Whether the classy TV of the 1950s was determined by the class of set owners is debatable. Media professor Lynn Spigel argues that TV was considered lowbrow right from the start and that "by the 1950s television might well have been less a status symbol than a sign of 'bad taste.' Although television had been a rich person's toy in the 1930s and 1940s," she concedes, "its rapid dissemination to the middle and even lower classes after 1948 transformed it into a poor person's luxury."[8]

Nevertheless, it is true that at about the same time as TV was heading west it was also becoming a truly national mass medium. Television was finally reaching the majority of American households (55.7 percent) by 1954,[9] the same year TV historian Erik Barnouw marks as the "fall of the anthology"[10] and the end of the golden age.

The relationship between programs and advertisers might also have helped nurture the anthology form. Prior to the quiz show scandal, which started making news in 1958, it was common for a single advertiser to sponsor an entire series that would often bear the sponsor's name. Up to a third of the programs broadcast on the network during this time were produced by advertisers and their agencies.[11] This arrangement led to some legendary stories of sponsor interference. Alcoa, manufacturers of aluminum, for example, would not let Reginald Rose set a tragic event in his episode of *The Alcoa Hour* in a trailer park, where most of the homes are made of aluminum. The Mars company, which sponsored *Circus Boy*, made it known to those making the show that they didn't appreciate references in the program to ice cream, cookies, or other treats that competed with Mars's candy products for the sweet tooth of America's youth.[12] In "Judgment at Nuremberg," an episode of *Playhouse 90* about the trials of Nazi war criminals, a reference to "gas chambers" was deleted by the sponsor, the American Gas Association.[13]

But single sponsorship also had advantages. R. D. Heldenfels, TV critic and author of *Television's Greatest Year: 1954*, points out that, "Unlike the current system, where a terribly low-rated show is pulled after one or two telecasts, a single sponsor willing to wait for good numbers—or to settle for lower numbers because the show increased the sponsor's prestige—could keep a show going."[14] Since networks made money as long as the show remained sponsored, the only reason for them to cancel a sponsored series was if the ratings were so low that they threatened to reduce the size of the potential audience for the next show on the schedule. Indeed, many companies were more concerned with prestige than they were with numbers. If not for prestige, why would a company like U.S. Steel have sponsored an anthology? There were no raw U.S. Steel products that a mass audience could buy over the counter and most viewers had no idea where the steel in their automobiles came from. It was even possible that a show would continue to be sponsored based on the tastes of a single executive or company owner. The classical music on *The Voice of Firestone* played for five years on NBC and another five on ABC to comparatively small audiences because the Firestone family was more concerned with attaching their name to a cultural show than they were with ratings.[15]

As with New York-based production, this system also didn't last long. After the quiz show scandals left egg on the faces of the networks who had relinquished programming to sponsors now implicated in the rigging of the quizzes, networks moved quickly to take control. CBS President Frank Stanton announced that, "We will be masters in our own house,"[16] and soon a variety of different sponsors were buying spots on shows that were made by the networks themselves or for the networks by independent producers. Quiz show scandal or not, the single-sponsor model would probably have been replaced by a la carte spots anyway. Networks profited from making their own programming and many sponsors could not long have afforded to produce the increasingly expensive programs all by themselves. With networks selling each show to a multitude of advertisers, maximizing rates by maximizing audience size became the order of the day.

Heldenfels, in a chapter describing the years 1955 through 1961 entitled "TV Goes to Hell," eulogizes his favorite year in television as follows:

> When 1954 came to an end, television had not merely reached a crossroads. It faced a simultaneity of courses more like a freeway cloverleaf—this way to New York, that way to Hollywood, film on this off-ramp, live TV around the bend, culture here, crassness there . . . In just about every case, the medium took the wrong turn.[17]

## FLOWERS IN THE WASTELAND

That the Golden Age had given way to the Dark Ages was the cry heard from many corners. The slow fade of the live dramas, the game show scandal, the flap over violence in Westerns and action series like *The Untouchables,* and even the loss of the venerable CBS newsgod Edward R. Murrow from the weekly schedule in 1955 were among the many symptoms that seemed to mark television's fall from art-form-in-training to three-ring circus.

It was the federal government itself that declared the Golden Age of television to be officially over on May 9, 1961. That's when Kennedy's newly appointed Federal Communications Commission chair, Newton Minow, described the state of the industry in a speech to broadcasters from across the nation. According to his description, TV had been far from golden for quite some time. He acknowledged that some "eminently worthwhile" programming was still to be seen, even since "the much-bemoaned good old days of *Playhouse 90* [which had only just left the air that past September] and *Studio One*." He even went so far as to acknowledge that "When television is good, nothing—not the theater, not the magazines or newspapers—nothing is better." But, of course, he went on to add that when it is bad, "nothing is worse." And to him it was almost always bad.

Then he called TV "a vast wasteland" and issued his famous and often-quoted challenge to the station owners in the audience to watch their own programming for an entire day:

> You will see a procession of game shows, violence, audience participation shows, formula comedies about totally unbelievable families, blood and thunder, mayhem, violence, sadism, murder, Western bad men, Western good men, private eyes, gangsters, more violence and cartoons. And, endlessly, commercials—many screaming, cajoling and offending. And most of all boredom. True, you will see a few things you enjoy. But they will be very, very few.[18]

Redundancy and judgmentalism aside, it wasn't a bad catalog summary of the state of the art. Minow didn't like what he saw, but apparently many viewers did. In 1961, 88.8 percent of American households had TV sets and they were on for over five hours a day,[19] much of that time tuned to the very types of programming Minow described. Minow's feelings, however, echoed those of many critics, educators, and community leaders. But another, albeit isolated, bright spot was just around the corner.

It became increasingly clear after May of 1961 that government pressure could affect programming. Since Minow and his FCC controlled the licensing of all television stations and could therefore potentially wreak havoc on the livelihoods of broadcasters, it should come as no surprise that yet another little period of serious programming followed the "vast wasteland" speech. A spate of public affairs and nonfiction shows was the first reaction, but some dramatic entertainment programming also got in on the act. Even the anthology form, which Minow had praised, got a temporary new lease on life.

Socially relevant series like *Dr. Kildare, Ben Casey, The Defenders,* and the filmed anthology *Alcoa Premiere,* that had already been in development when Minow went on the rampage, were put on the networks' front burners and debuted the following fall. Herbert Hirschman, the producer of *Dr. Kildare,* defended his new project by saying that it "fulfills all of Mr. Minow's requirements: it is adult, literate, free of sadism and violence—a distinguished and at the same time, dramatically engrossing drama."[20]

Similar shows were quickly developed and a new programming trend that media professor Mary Ann Watson calls "New Frontier character dramas"[21] emerged. *Mr. Novak* followed an idealistic and dedicated high school English teacher; *East Side/West Side* starred George C. Scott as a social worker dealing with everything from child abuse to drugs on New York's mean streets; *Slattery's People* was about a state legislator trying to pass social programs over the objections of the evil Speaker of the House; *Channing* was a sincere drama set on a fictional university campus; *The Great Adventure* presented a series of careful docudramas about American history; *The Richard Boone Show* featured a repertory company and an occasional script by Clifford Odets in an anthology drama as good as anything done in the 1950s; and *Profiles in Courage* presented weekly dramatized biographies in the spirit of the book by John F. Kennedy, who had given script approval on all episodes before his death.[22] When *Dr. Kildare* and *Ben Casey* both landed in the Nielsen top twenty in their first season, the medical show suggested a possible way to satisfy both Minow and the bottom line. *The Breaking Point* and *The Eleventh Hour,* which were set amidst the psychiatric profession, and *Nurses* were introduced over the next two seasons.

The preponderance of liberal social themes was in fact something new to television. Though Golden Age dramas had dabbled in issues like prejudice, such subjects were often compromised when done at all. Reginald Rose's "Thunder on Sycamore Street," an installment of the anthology *Studio One,* was originally based on an actual incident in which a group of white homeowners had formed to get an African-American family to move out of their neighborhood. Both sponsor and network agreed to give the go-ahead only after the black man was changed to a white ex-convict. This situation changed significantly in the early 1960s. "Whereas social criticism appeared rarely in the early dramatic showcases," J. Fred MacDonald points out, "now entire series were fashioned around pressing issues."[23]

Two series debuted the fall after Minow's speech, however, that are most remembered as the crowning achievements of this period. David Marc called *The Dick Van Dyke Show* "the only emphatically New Frontier sitcom ever produced."[24] It not only carried the spirit of the Kennedy era, right down to the first-family haircuts of the main couple, but it was also financed by Kennedy money. Actor Peter Lawford was married to the soon-to-be-President's sister Patricia when Carl Reiner was searching to finance the pilot episode of what would become *The Dick Van Dyke Show*. Lawford agreed to put up money for the pilot, but only after he had shown the script to and gotten the approval of the family patriarch, Joseph P. Kennedy.[25] Arguably one of the finest sitcoms ever made, *The Dick Van Dyke Show* won fifteen Emmy Awards and can still be seen regularly in reruns.

*The Defenders,* the apex of the New Frontier dramas, might never have made it onto the CBS schedule had it not been for Minow. Starring E. G. Marshall and Robert Reed as father and son lawyers, the show dealt with such issues as blacklisting, mercy killing, capital punishment, and abortion. The project had reportedly been on indefinite hold at CBS until network chairman William Paley personally resuscitated it after being called to testify before the FCC.[26] With a creative staff that included people with 24-carat golden age credentials like Reginald Rose, Herbert Brodkin, and Ernest Kinoy, *The Defenders* was in many ways a throwback to the live dramas of the 1950s. Not only was the series staffed by Golden Age alumni, it was based on a two-part 1957 installment of *Studio One,* and it was filmed in New York. It wasn't live and it did have continuing characters, but the heritage of the anthology drama was certainly obvious here.

Although *Doctor Kildare, Ben Casey,* and *The Defenders* were hits, most of the New Frontier dramas didn't last very long. In addition to these dramas and the new nonfiction programming of the period, Minow had accidentally created another more lasting legacy: *The Beverly Hillbillies.* The rural sitcom—*The Real McCoys; The Andy Griffith Show; The Beverly Hillbillies; Green Acres; Gomer Pyle, U.S.M.C; Petticoat Junction; Mayberry, R.F.D.*—and its comedy-variety counterpart, *Hee Haw,* were among the very most popular series of the turbulent decade. These weren't all Minow's fault, of course. Both *The Real McCoys* and *The Andy Griffith Show* had debuted before he began his tenure at the FCC. But Minow did complain about violence more than anything else in his speech, and Senator Thomas Dodd, as head of the Senate Subcommittee to Investigate Juvenile Delinquency, had followed up a month later by strongly suggesting a relationship between televised violence and youth crime. Comedy was a natural place for the networks to turn, and *The Andy Griffith Show*'s Andy Taylor, a pacifist to the point of lethargy who was known in the show as "the sheriff without a gun," provided, if nothing else, a model for nonviolent programming.

When Minow resigned from the FCC in May of 1963, Kennedy replaced him with E. William Henry, a former campaign aide to Robert Kennedy and someone fully committed to Minow's agenda. But when Lyndon Johnson took over the presidency upon Kennedy's death that November, the regulatory climate changed considerably. Johnson was himself a broadcaster with properties worth millions. He made it clear that controlling and harassing a thriving business like television was not something his administration was interested in doing.[27] The New Frontier dramas were soon gone; *The Beverly Hillbillies* went on to become one of the most popular series of all time.

## "THE SITCOM AT LITERATE PEAK"

*New York Times* critic John J. O'Connor picked the mid-1970s as his candidate for television's golden age. He cited an active and blossoming PBS, the maturing of the made-for-TV movie and the miniseries, the innovative treatments of old genres on new shows like *Columbo, Kojak,* and *The Waltons,* and a number of news specials as some of the reasons for his choice. He also saw this as a time when, as in the 1950s, "classy drama became almost commonplace on the networks":

> Laurence Olivier in "Long Day's Journey Into Night" and Katherine Hepburn in "The Glass Menagerie" were on ABC. Joseph Papp's Broadway production of "Much Ado about Nothing" and Lewis Freedman's "Playhouse 90" resurrection were on CBS. The latter showed Brian Moore's "Catholics," with Trevor Howard and Martin Sheen, and Ingmar Bergman's play "The Lie" with George Segal and Shirley Knight. On NBC, Jack Lemmon starred in John Osborne's "Entertainer." If not an entire age, certainly a golden year or two.[28]

Also figuring prominently in O'Connor's assessment of the period, however, was the sitcom, a form unused to critical acclaim at the time. CBS, in an effort to appeal to a younger audience made socially conscious by the turbulent 1960s, had dumped its hit rural comedies in the first years of the 1970s while their aging audiences were still placing them in Nielsen's top twenty-five. Critics, who for the most part had loathed the likes of *Petticoat Junction* and *Gomer Pyle,* loved some of what replaced them. By 1973 the network was offering one of the most memorable lineups in the medium's history, Saturday's *All in the Family, M*A*S*H, The Mary Tyler Moore Show, The Bob Newhart Show,* and the comedy-variety remnant, *The Carol Burnett Show.* Combining timely subject matter with meticulously written scripts in what had become the medium's most popular genre, the sitcom had came of age.

O'Connor's high opinion of mid-1970s comedy reflected that of nearly all media critics. Scholars also responded positively. When writing of the early and mid-1970s, pioneering television studies professor Horace Newcomb and his coauthor Robert S. Alley observed that "In the area of television comedy it is fair to say . . . that these were television's 'Golden Years.'"[29] In his history of television comedy, David Marc decribed *The Mary Tyler Moore Show, All in the Family,* and *M\*A\*S\*H* as "a kind of period triptych of seventies America, constituting the sitcom at its literate peak during the last days of three-network hegemony. There was a sense while watching these shows," he went on, "that whether one liked them or not, somehow they could not be goofed on in the same way as virtually all the sitcoms that preceded them. . . . Sitting on an aesthetic cusp between pre-cable innocence and postcable cynicism, these three series drove the sitcom to the brink of respectability as an art form."[30]

The television industry itself showed its support of these series by showering them with Emmy Awards: twenty-seven for *Mary Tyler Moore,* twenty-one for *All in the Family,* and twelve for *M\*A\*S\*H.*

Most significantly, however, was the fact that viewers liked these shows as much as the critics, scholars, and ballot casters. Never before had the cultural elite been more in agreement with the ratings box. *All in the Family* spent five years at the top of the Nielsens, an achievement tied only by *The Cosby Show. The Mary Tyler Moore Show* was in the top twenty-five for all but its final season, and in the top ten for three years running. *M\*A\*S\*H* was still in third place when it voluntarily left the air in 1983 after ranking in the top ten for nine of its eleven seasons.

Both *All in the Family* and *The Mary Tyler Moore Show* would breed a host of spin-offs, and producers, writers, and directors who graduated from these shows would dominate television for years to come. But "though their commercial and artistic success was astounding," Marc wrote, "it did not bring about the sitcom millennium."[31]

Though *All in the Family, Mary Tyler Moore, M\*A\*S\*H,* and the shows they inspired continued to perform very well through the 1970s, the top of the ratings became dominated by ABC toward the end of the decade. Prior to the mid-1970s, ABC had always ranked behind CBS and NBC in the ratings. With cable and VCRs still in the future for most Americans, and with the three networks still attracting over 90 percent of the viewing audience during prime time, network executives could afford to be brave. Both *All in the Family* and *M\*A\*S\*H* debuted to weak ratings and strong controversy, but the network stayed the course and let them develop an audience. But when ABC came from the back of the pack and knocked CBS into second place, the delicate balance that allowed such patience was disturbed.

Fred Silverman left CBS in 1975 to become president of ABC Entertainment. The aggressive and innovative strategies he employed toward ratings supremacy were so successful that CBS and NBC were forced to imitate them. Patience with a good but struggling show, among other policies, was a luxury that could no longer be afforded in this take-no-prisoners competitive environment. ABC's rise was greatly facilitated by the one-two punch of producers Garry Marshall and Aaron Spelling, who introduced some of the most commercially successful and critically abhorred television in American history. Marshall's retro sit-coms, *Happy Days* and *Laverne & Shirley*, dominated the ratings in the late 1970s. Along with *Mork & Mindy* and *Angie*, Marshall held four of the top five slots in the Nielsens in the 1978–79 season. The fifth slot went to second-place *Three's Company*, the anchor program in what became known as "jiggle" or "T&A" television. Spelling's *Charlie's Angels*, *The Love Boat*, and *Fantasy Island*, the latter two lowbrow co-optings of the anthology form, also became big and lasting hits in this disclaimed new genre.

## THE SECOND GOLDEN AGE

The increased competition brought on by ABC in the mid-1970s was nothing compared to that introduced by cable in the 1980s, but for reasons that will be discussed in the next chapter, the result was, at times, quite different. Pressed into the deployment of target marketing strategies by the proliferation of cable services, network TV began to introduce a new type of complex and sophisticated programming aimed directly at an upscale audience. Not only was the writing artistry exhibited in shows like *Hill Street Blues* and *Cheers* reminiscent of the Golden Age, but other remnants of the 1950s also began to resurface at this time on a small but significant scale. The decade's biggest hit, *The Cosby Show*, for example, was shot in New York. And the anthology form returned very briefly to prime time with series like *Amazing Stories*, *Alfred Hitchcock Presents*, and *The Twilight Zone*, the last two of which were remakes of now-classic anthologies from the 1950s and early 1960s.

Most prominent, however, was the return of the serious, literary, writer-based drama. *Hill Street Blues* debuted in January 1981 and set an entirely new standard for television drama. Over the next few years, critics went into paroxysms of praise as shows like *St. Elsewhere*, *Cagney & Lacey*, *Moonlighting*, *L.A. Law*, *thirtysomething*, and *China Beach* were introduced. Though not nearly as popular with the mass audience as the literary sitcoms of the early 1970s, all of these series were retained by the networks for at least three seasons, mostly because those who were watching could command a high price from advertisers. By the 1990s, the "quality drama" had settled in as a small but viable part of the network schedule.

The prime-time dramatic series was perhaps one of the last places we might have expected an aesthetic flowering in 1981. The form (the weekly series), the venue (commercially supported TV), and even the genres (cop shows, lawyer shows, doctor shows, detective shows) had all been relegated to the cultural trash heap in the minds of most serious people by that time. The three hour-long series that ranked in the Nielsen top five for the 1980–81 season were *Dallas*, *The Dukes of Hazzard*, and *The Love Boat*—hardly a movable feast for the aesthete. Although *Lou Grant*, *The White Shadow*, and *Magnum, P.I.*, were breaking some new ground, the current state of the cop show, the medical drama, and the detective show were represented by *CHiPs*, *Trapper John, M.D.*, and *Hart to Hart*. But herein lies what was monumental about the quality dramas of the 1980s. Within the great limitations of a critically disclaimed medium, sow's ears became silk purses. In 1981, a cop show, complete with car chases, commercial interruptions, and a requirement that every installment be exactly forty-eight minutes, twenty seconds long, became what many saw as the apotheosis of the world's most pervasive storytelling medium. Featuring complex characters and narratives, and a rich mix of symbols and allusions, an old, even moribund, form was suddenly made honorable.

One of the most important things about these stories was that they employed, to one degree or another, the serial form. They continued from episode to episode. The Golden Age of the 1950s had really been a golden age of mass-distributed theater. Adaptations of established plays were a programming staple during this time, and even the plays made especially for TV fell more into the traditions of the stage than of the small screen. Broadcast live from small studios, these shows were not yet able to take advantage of the medium's unique ability to play fast and easy with time and space, an ability TV now shares with film. The cameras were indoors, bound to stage sets. Furthermore, because they were anthologies, the jewels in the crown of the Golden Age never developed the most distinct aesthetic feature of broadcasting, the series format.

In his seminal book, *TV: The Most Popular Art*, Horace Newcomb saw that television's

> real relationship with other media lies not in movies or radio, but in the novel. Television, like the literary form, can offer a far greater

sense of density. Details take on importance slowly, and within repeated patterns of action, rather than with the immediacy of other
visual forms. It is this sense of density, built over a continuing period
of time, that offers us a fuller sense of a world fully created by the
artist.[32]

The series is, indeed, broadcasting's unique aesthetic contribution to
Western art. Unlike any other medium but old-time radio and the
comic strip, television presents stories that can go on forever. In soap
operas and long-running series, we can see characters age and develop
both physically and narratively in a way that even Wagner's longest
operas or Dickens's most extended novels didn't allow. Even serialized
comics and movies, which may be released over long periods of time,
lack the regularity of the television series. Only the newspaper comic
strip can also boast the weekly told eternal story, but the installments
are so small that development and detail is slow and limited.

*Guiding Light,* on the other hand, continues to supply five weekly
hours of a drama that has been being continuously told for well over
half a century, starting on the radio in 1937 and moving to television
in 1952. Patriarch Papa Bauer was portrayed by Theo Goetz from 1949
until his death in 1973, and Charita Bauer (her last name in art as in
life) put in thirty-two years as Papa's daughter-in-law, Bertha, before
she and her character succumbed in 1985. Television can, and in this
case does, tell a story *in real time* that goes on for generations.

For many years, though, most TV programming didn't take advantage of this unique dramatic possibility. For the most part, daytime
soap operas like the *Guiding Light* were the only places in which TV's
most distinct characteristic was being demonstrated. Series turnover in
the competitive prime-time hours has always been much greater than
in daytime, and evening programs seldom ever approach the longevity
of the soaps. But even in the exceptions, like *My Three Sons,* a series
that lasted for twelve seasons and showed us the development of characters from childhood, through adolescence, and ultimately to marriage
and parenthood, the prime-time series prior to the 1980s didn't so
much develop continuing stories as they just showed signs of aging.
Each episode of *My Three Sons* was, as were most prime-time episodes,
an independent and self-contained story. Unlike an installment of a
soap opera or a chapter in a novel, it made very little difference
whether or not you saw what came before or after it.

So until fairly recently, only the soap opera could be legitimately
compared to the novel. The traditional series—even the long-running
one—was more like a collection of short stories. Although they all were
based on the same premise, individual episodes were independent of

all the rest. By the end of each installment, everything had returned to where it was before the episode began, hardly true of a chapter in a novel. Beaver Cleaver seldom if ever cited a lesson he'd learned in a previous episode as the basis for how he should behave in this one. No matter how many homilies about tolerance Archie Bunker was at the center of, he never really got the message. For most of its history, prime time's collective memory was erased every seven days.

Given the irregular viewing habits of the audience, this narrative philosophy made perfect sense. Evening series were self-contained and it was OK if you missed a few episodes, as most people did. The premise of the show itself usually supplied all the background you needed: "Here's the story of a lovely lady . . . ," "the ship set ground on the shore of this uncharted desert isle . . . ," "Come and listen to a story 'bout a man named Jed. . . . "[33] A viewer sitting down to watch the twentieth episode of *Gilligan's Island* needed no knowledge of the first nineteen to understand it.

Surprisingly, network TV's very first soap opera, *Faraway Hill*, was introduced in 1946 as an evening series. As they had been in radio, however, soaps were aired on television almost exclusively in the daytime. *Peyton Place* was the most obvious exception, a very successful experiment by ABC that brought the daytime soap opera model back to prime time in 1964. Other than the airtime, *Peyton Place* followed the conventions of the day, not of the night. In its first seasons it aired twice and sometimes even three times per week, its cast was enormous, numbering over a hundred regular characters, and there were no reruns, even in the summer. What was unusual about *Peyton Place* was not its commercial success, which might have been expected given the popularity of soaps in the afternoon, but the fact that it wasn't effectively imitated. In its first season, both the Tuesday and Thursday installments of *Peyton Place* ended the year in the Nielsen top twenty. Though those ratings were not sustained for long, it still seems strange that more attempts weren't made to bring the soap out after dark.

Fourteen years passed after the debut of *Peyton Place* before the nighttime soap emerged as a viable series form. Two years before that, the miniseries began preparing the way. The British had been making limited series for years, some of which had played here on PBS, and the six-and-a-quarter-hour TV movie *QBVII* was broadcast on two consecutive nights in 1974. But the real breakthrough was ABC's *Rich Man, Poor Man*, based on Irwin Shaw's 1970 book of the same title. Appropriately advertised by the network as a "Novel for Television," eight "chapters" were watched weekly by an enormous audience in the winter of 1976, proving that the American public could remember story elements from week to week. Two years later *Dallas* adapted the idea to the continuing series. Though serialized like the daytime soaps, however, this was something different. Unlike *Peyton Place, Dallas* had the characteristics of a prime-time series, airing only once a week and going into reruns with the rest of the lineup during the summer.

It was this latter feature of the show that helped establish the soap in prime time. Introduced at the end of the 1977–78 season, *Dallas* came onto the scene without a lot of fanfare. By the end of its first full season, the show had not yet cracked the top twenty. By the end of the 1979–80 season, though, things had changed. Already in sixth place, the final episode of the season would make television history and pro-pel *Dallas* to the top of the ratings for years to come. In the episode's final moments, the show's principal character, J. R. Ewing (Larry Hag-man), was shot down by an unknown assailant. Because it was the last episode before going into reruns, the question of "Who Shot J.R.?" lingered all summer long. It popped up on bumper stickers, buttons, T-shirts, and radio contests, and became one of the most talked-about events in the popular culture. The secret was finally revealed the follow-ing November in what was then the highest-rated series episode of all time.

The soap opera form is what made *Dallas* the success it was. The fact that viewers *cared* who shot J.R. was established by the fact that his story was a continuing one. J.R.'s despicabilty was allowed to develop over the course of two-and-a-half seasons. As details accrued, viewers really came to know him and to hate him. The fact that the show had a very large cast, another element borrowed from daytime soaps, made his attempted murder a real mystery. Any of almost twenty characters might have wanted J.R. dead.

The "cliff-hanger," a device that had been used in B-movie serials, comics, and daytime soaps for years, had finally been discovered to be an amazingly effective marketing tool in prime-time television as well. The cliff-hanger worked best, of course, in a continuing story. People had tuned in to their favorite series in the past because they enjoyed seeing the characters go through their formulaic motions. Now they also tuned in because they actually wanted to see what was going to happen next.

The nighttime soap began to propagate across the schedule. Before J.R. was shot, *Dallas* begat a spin-off, *Knots Landing*. Afterwards, every network grabbed for a piece of the action with series like *Secrets of Midland Heights, Flamingo Road, Dynasty,* and *Falcon Crest.* But *Dallas's* success did more than just inspire spin-offs and rip-offs. It gave a mem-ory to the entire medium. Soon many dramatic shows—even those that weren't exactly soaps—began employing ongoing story lines. The same went for the sitcom. The relationship between *Cheers's* Sam and Diane, for example, took on distinct serialized features as it developed across episodic and seasonal lines and brought the season-ending cliff-hanger to a comedy series. Even commercials jumped on the bandwagon, from "Bud Bowls" to the glacially developing romance between those two who like Taster's Choice coffee so much.

The "quality dramas" of the 1980s, though, were perhaps the greatest beneficiaries of *Dallas* and its imitators. As the Golden Age of television was rooted in the legitimate stage, quality dramas were rooted in the soap opera. *Hill Street Blues, St. Elsewhere, thirtysomething,* and *L.A. Law* all employed continuing story lines, and, though less like soap operas, *Cagney & Lacey, Moonlighting,* and *China Beach* still built heavily on previous episodes.

Careful attention to detail has been one of the most celebrated characteristics of the quality drama. The complexities of these shows that are so praised by critics, scholars, and serious viewers come from the slow layering of events, character traits, and other visual and dramatic details over the entire run of the series. *Hill Street Blues*'s leisurely portrayal of the slow turning of the wheels of justice, illustrated when a suspect arrested at the beginning of the second season is finally executed in the fourth, or the long and treacherous evolution of a marriage explored in *thirtysomething:* these are things that could not have been done in a genre where the world had to return by the end of the episode to where it was at the beginning. These slowly accruing stories could only be told in the serial form. More importantly, they could only be told on television. Waylon Green, the coexecutive producer of *NYPD Blue,* observed in 1995 that many leading dramatic writers had been abandoning the theater and movies for television because, "You can get a lot more information into television, and play things out in natural, dramatic order. If you try some of those things in movies, you are usually dead."[34]

But there was also a lot about the quality drama that defied the traditions of commercial television. The large casts, complicated story lines, and often grim and thought-provoking subject matter clashed with the simple and happy world presented on most TV. In 1981, shows started appearing that would never have made the lineup just a few years earlier. Almost overnight, the rules of prime time had changed dramatically.

# The Causes of Quality

The artistic heights that TV drama began to achieve in 1981 were not reached by mere coincidence. At the dawn of the new decade, television as we knew it was on the eve of the greatest crisis it had ever encountered. About to be expelled from the oligopolistic Eden that they had so happily and profitably occupied for their entire history, the networks were now faced with a horde of new contenders for the American consciousness. Unused to competition from anyone but each other, ABC, CBS, and NBC were profoundly unprepared for what was about to happen to their medium. Amid the ensuing chaos, a crack in the door opened just widely enough to admit a few new ideas and a spirit of experimentation atypical of network TV in more prosperous times.

First, their bad news. In 1970, only 8 percent of American households were receiving basic cable. By 1980, that number had climbed to 23 percent and it doubled over the next five years. Just as important, 12 percent of homes were receiving pay channels like HBO and Showtime by 1980.[1] Though no single cable service's audience even approached the size of any major network's, the combined rating of all cable channels was beginning to make quite a dent, and all indications showed that things were only going to get worse. In the late 1970s, over 90 percent of the prime-time viewing audience was tuned to one of the three networks; by the end of 1989, that number was down to 67 percent and still heading south.[2]

Other elements were also complicating the picture. Independent stations, those over-the-air channels that don't play network programming, became much more aggressive competitors in the 1980s. Added all together, independent stations lost money until 1975, but after that they began, like cable, to peck away at the networks' share of the audience. Between 1975 and 1980, advertiser dollars spent on independent stations climbed 25 percent.[3] The fortunes of these stations had started to change in 1971, when the FCC passed the Prime-Time Access Rule, which forbade the networks from providing programming during the heavily viewed hour from 7:00 to 8:00 P.M. on Mondays through Saturdays, but the advent of cable also provided a big boost to the independents. Aired over UHF stations (channels 14–83) in many cities, the independents were often harder to find and harder to tune in than the network affiliated stations, which were more often broadcast on the VHF band (channels 2–13). Cable made the signal quality of all stations equal, rendering the independents suddenly just as clear and sometimes just as attractive as their network-affiliated competitors.

While cable and independent stations were changing what people were watching on television, VCRs and remote-control devices were changing the way they watched it. Through the 1980s, household ownership of VCRs grew from 1 percent to 68 percent, a pace matched by the wireless remote.[4] The VCR allowed viewers to turn off television entirely while they played Hollywood movies on their sets. The remote control allowed facile and visceral travel through the landscape of competing services.

For the most part, the networks were slow to respond to this new state of affairs, grudgingly refusing to acknowledge the wolf at the door in much the same way Hollywood had pretended TV didn't exist in the hopes that it might just go away. A common response to the plummeting ratings was to close ranks and play it safe, introducing new shows that resembled the tried-and-true formulas that had worked before. But giving the audience more of what it was already rejecting in droves wasn't always the best way to go. Like the other networks, NBC tried this approach. Among the series they introduced in the fall of 1981 were *Father Murphy,* a historical drama inspired by the aging chestnut, *Little House on the Prairie; McClain's Law,* an old-fashioned cop show featuring an even more old-fashioned star, *Gunsmoke's* James Arness; and *Nashville Palace,* a remake of the late-1960s hit *Hee Haw.* Old formulas and old stars didn't serve them very well, however, and none of these series lasted more than a season and a half.

But NBC had simultaneously come up with an alternative tactic. Rather than always attempting to please everybody in the audience, which was getting harder to do now that so many people had so many choices, the network executives decided to aim some of their programs directly at a smaller group. All three networks had, of course, been sensitive to the demographic makeup of their audiences for years. It was that sensitivity that had prompted CBS to cancel many of its hit shows in 1970 because it felt the audience was getting too old. NBC, however, was about to focus in on a much more specific target. If television was to become a house divided into many pieces, they reasoned, why not go after, at least occasionally, the piece that advertisers would pay the most for: young, upscale, well-educated viewers? As a media-savvy group that had grown up and grown tired with network TV, these viewers had been among the most enthusiastic defectors to cable and prerecorded videotapes. It was unlikely that they were going to be lured back to the network fold with the likes of *Father Murphy*. For them, NBC had something else in mind. Something different and more sophisticated. Stuck in third place and fresh out of ideas, NBC executives were formulating a notion that was shockingly uncharacteristic for people of their profession: critical acclaim, they began to speculate, might be their quickest way to commercial success.

The strategy was logical enough. While flipping through the channels, viewers were much more likely to be caught by the high-budget, cinematic look and sound of HBO or Showtime than the flatly lit, sanitarily written TV series episode. This was especially true of the demographic class that was about to be named the "yuppie" and in which NBC was increasingly interested. With advertisers willing to pay premium prices for the attention spans of these liberally educated and conspicuously consuming viewers who were now being lured by uncut and recently released movies on cable, the introduction of "quality TV" seemed tantamount to good business sense. *Hill Street Blues,* the first serious attempt at this new type of programming, was literary, visually dense, and filled with language that sounded more like the movies than television.

NBC concentrated its high-end product on Thursday nights. By the fall of 1982, they had assembled an impressive lineup that consisted of the first full season of *Fame,* an unusual generic hybrid that the critics had applauded when it had been introduced in January; the first season of *Cheers,* a brainy sitcom that wouldn't catch on with a larger, more diverse audience until two years later; *Taxi,* a three-time winner of the Emmy for best comedy series that ABC had canceled in the spring; and *Hill Street Blues,* which had swept the Emmy Awards the previous year. Although they were still losing the ratings race, the "proud as a peacock" network had announced its commitment to quality and boasted about it in their promotional advertisements that crowned Thursdays "the best night of television on television." For one night a week at least, NBC had substituted class appeal for mass appeal.

This strategy marked an important moment in TV history. Not that many years ago, from 1977 to 1979, NBC was being guided by the philosophies of Paul Klein, their vice-president of programming who was applying his notorious "LOP" theory. LOP stood for "least objectionable programming," and the theory held that people switched through the channels and settled not on what they liked but on what they least disliked. Klein described the idea in print on several occasions:

> We exist with a known television audience, and all a show has to be is least objectionable among a segment of the audience. When you put on a show, then, you immediately start with your fair share. You get your 32-share . . . that's about ⅓ of the network audience, and the other networks get their 32 shares. We all start equally. Then we can add to that by our competitors' failure—they become objectionable so people turn to us if we're less objectionable. Or, we could lose audience by inserting little "tricks" that cause the loss of audience. . . . Thought, that's tune-out, education, tune-out. Melodrama's good, you know, a little tear here and there, a little morality tale, that's good. Positive. That's least objectionable. It's my job to keep my 32, not to cause any tune-out *a priori* in terms of ads or concepts, to make sure that there's no tune-out in the shows vis-à-vis the competition.[5]

These comments, which appeared in a book entitled *Inside the TV Business* in 1979, were based on two assumptions that NBC would begin to question only a year later. That a network could continue to expect to start out with one-third of the total viewing audience was nothing but a pipe dream by the 1980s. The idea of least objectionability had become no less archaic. Once audiences had specialized program services supplying them with what they really wanted—sports on ESPN, kids' shows on Nickelodeon, music videos on MTV—they no longer needed to tolerate shows that they merely disliked less than the other two or three choices. NBC, the network at which LOP was coined, was now programming portions of prime time not for the entire mass audience but for specialized segments of that audience.

All of this was potentially good news for quality television. A commitment to attracting a serious, upscale audience would most likely be followed by the scheduling of serious, upscale programming. Besides, the shrinking network share of the audience had made the survival of such shows much more likely, even without the added benefit of their premium demographics. In the good old days, a series was likely to be canceled if it dipped too far below the magical thirty-two share. The number of people in the audience willing to watch a complex and thoughtful series was usually not big enough to make such a show competitive. In the cable era, when the audience was divided into many more than three pieces, the cutoff point for cancellation fell considerably. No more people were tuning in to quality shows in the 1980s than they were in the 1960s, but in the 1980s those same numbers were enough to keep a show on the air. A quality program like *East Side/West Side,* for example, was canceled in 1964 after a single season because it had only earned a twenty-six share;[6] *St. Elsewhere,* on the other hand, ran for six years from 1982 through 1988 with an annual share that ranged from only nineteen to twenty-two.

Not since the 1950s could a show survive with such a small audience. Coast to coast saturation of broadcast television had made network TV a truly mass medium and moved it from the Golden Age to the age of the lowest common denominator; coast-to-coast saturation of cable, by making TV a medium of many specialized services, was threatening to bring it back again.

▪    ▪    ▪

In many ways, network TV was simply experiencing what the movies had gone through several years earlier. Slowly but surely film had given up its status as the reigning mass medium to television. After an initial plunge during TV's introductory years, the number of weekly filmgoers had stablized by 1953 at somewhere between forty and fifty million. In 1965, weekly attendance began another drop, from forty-four million that year to a mere 17.5 million by 1969.[7] This second decline was no doubt in part due to the final phase of television's usurpation of the mass audience. Color TV had finally begun to make significant inroads by this time. In the fall of 1965, all three networks had adopted color, and by December of 1966 color set sales exceeded those of black-and-white ones for the first time.[8] Between 1960 and 1965, the average number of daily viewing hours went up twenty-three minutes per TV household, the largest jump in any five-year period to that date.[9] The fall of 1965 was also a watershed in television's transition to the commercial aesthetic so many intellectuals would come to know and hate. The last of the holdout anthology dramas, *Alfred Hitchcock Presents* and *The Kraft Suspense Theater,* failed to return to the schedules that year, and in their place were introduced some of the standard series that would help define the post-Golden Age medium, including *Gidget, Green Acres, Please Don't Eat the Daisies, F Troop, Lost in Space, Hogan's Heroes, I Dream of Jeannie,* and *My Mother the Car.*

By 1965 television was firmly established as the most popular storytelling medium. Since it was watched by everybody, it also became the reigning source of entertainment for the entire family. If it couldn't always please everyone, at least it tried not to offend anyone. Skittish sponsors and the eternal threat of government regulation tended further to guarantee that not much would spill into the living room that wasn't appropriate for viewers of all ages.

Hollywood, on the other hand, was now occasionally free to concentrate on less traditional, less mainstream product. In 1966, the movie industry trashed the Hays Production Code, a self-regulating policy that had been in effect since 1930 and that limited the content of the movies. Rules controlling language and the presentation of sex, violence, and other "offensive" material were lifted, and in their place came a rating system that measured each film's appropriateness for younger viewers. With TV firmly established as the purveyor of popular "fluff," many filmmakers had designs on more eclectic projects. Some argued, in fact, that the very survival of the movies depended upon their providing material that audiences couldn't get on TV. Once the content restrictions had been eliminated, Hollywood started releasing "art" films that could have never been made a few years earlier, including *Bonnie and Clyde* (1967), *Easy Rider* (1969), *MASH* (1970), *Five Easy Pieces* (1970), *A Clockwork Orange* (1971), and *The Godfather* (1972). The serious film community responded positively. *MASH* was the first American movie to take the top prize at Cannes in thirteen years, and over the next decade the award also went to *The Conversation* (1974), *Taxi Driver* (1976), *Apocalypse Now* (1979), and *All That Jazz* (1980), all films that flagrantly broke the rules of the defunct Hays Production Code. In 1965 the Oscar for Best Picture had gone to *The Sound of Music,* a wholesome and very conventional musical about a nun; in 1969 it went to *Midnight Cowboy,* a difficult *X-rated* film about a male prostitute.

Just as television, by taking over as the dominant mass medium, had allowed Hollywood to pursue some more specialized audiences, so cable, by shattering the mass audience into many pieces, invited TV to do the same. Television broadcasters, like the moviemakers, abandoned their own production code just as their audiences began shrinking. The National Association of Broadcasters had adopted the Television Code in 1952, which, like the Hays Production Code, was a voluntary set of content restrictions. The Television Code put limits on the number of commercials that could be aired each hour, and it restricted program content, with special emphasis on language, sex, and violence. Arguing that limits on advertising time deprived advertisers of free and open competition, the Department of Justice dismantled the code in 1982, just in time for many of the quality shows that would defy it.[10] Following in this spirit, the in-house network standards and practices departments—the "censors"—had been significantly curtailed by the end of the 1980s. TV, of course, didn't open things up as much as the movies had. The specter of government regulation and the fear advertisers had of boycotts organized by offended viewers provided unstated limits on how far things could go. But a comparison of television before and after the early 1980s reveals that things could and did go pretty far. *NYPD Blue* is only the most extreme case of a major change in TV content that had begun in earnest over a decade earlier. Steven Bochco defended his controversial series with the claim that the only way to compete with cable was to "paint with some of the same colors that you can paint with when you're making movies."[11]

Sex and violence are often the first elements cited in attacks on the products of popular culture. Together they are seen as sleazy standbys employed by unscrupulous executives in an effort to grab a larger audience. It is interesting to note, however, that in the case of both movies and television, greater artistic freedom led to products that featured these elements very prominently. Indeed, sex and violence play a very important role in serious modern art across the media. One need only look at the degree of violence in *Pulp Fiction,* the critically adored winner of Cannes's 1994 Palme d'Or, or the sexual material in some of the art once deemed fundable by the National Endowment of the Humanities, to see this. This may have something to do with contemporary definitions of art that hold serious work to be what goes against the grain, what challenges the status quo. Since both movies and television spent much of their history in a state of institutional sanitization, the most obvious way to break the mold was to present previously forbidden material. Sexy and violent films and television defied old conventions of these media, and in some cases that very defiance earned them admittance to a higher aesthetic realm.

Nearly all the critically acclaimed television dramas of the past fifteen years have depended heavily upon subjects of a sexual nature and the earthy language such subject matter invites. This isn't to say that sex wasn't also being used in more mainstream productions. *Nightingales,* a salacious 1989 drama about nurses with lingering locker-room scenes that looked like they had been torn right from the Frederick's of Hollywood catalog, is only one of the more glaring examples. But by far the most explicit discussions and portrayals of sexual material were going on in critically applauded series. Dolled up with social consciousness, sex is a principal ingredient of quality television. *St. Elsewhere, thirtysomething, L.A. Law, China Beach,* and *Picket Fences* were all lauded for their sensitive and frank portrayals of abortion and/or homosexuality and/or AIDS, for example. *Picket Fences,* a two-time winner in the best drama category at the Emmy Awards, has run a gamut of sexual subjects that might make even Oprah blush. *NYPD Blue,* another favorite among critics, has received kudos and a best drama Emmy for breaking the obscenity and nudity barriers on network TV. Graphic violence, though usually less tolerated by critics than sex, is certainly a crucial element in many of the crime shows that have also been praised and awarded.

The old argument that sex and violence are used only to sell tickets and detergent is a problematic one. Some of the highest-grossing movies have been G-rated, and Michael Medved makes a persuasive argument that the loss of "family values" in movies in favor of sex and violence was the cause, not the effect, of Hollywood's loss of a big chunk of its weekly audience. (Indeed, weekly film attendance has never regained the levels it enjoyed before the Production Code was abandoned.) On TV, the major envelope pushers in language and sex—*St. Elsewhere, thirtysomething, Civil Wars*—did well in the ratings only among the loftier demographic groups. Even hits like *Hill Street Blues, L.A. Law,* and *NYPD Blue* didn't quite reach the ratings heights of more old-fashioned series like *The Cosby Show* and *Family Ties.*

▪ ▪ ▪

Another possible cause of the rise of the quality drama might be the fact that by 1981 a general malaise had descended over prime time. Perhaps after thirty years of virtually the same dramatic formulas, many viewers were simply getting tired of network TV. Not only had they been watching it on the networks, but now it was available in reruns on both cable and independent stations. At the height of Hollywood's prosperous studio era, most adults saw no more than one or two movies per week. Books and plays were consumed at a considerably lower weekly rate throughout American history. Television, on the other hand, had been on in the average household for over six hours per *day* throughout the 1970s,[12] and the same old same old was getting old.

The 1980s arrived during a particularly arid period of TV programming. The "jiggle" series of Aaron Spelling (*Charlie's Angels, The Love Boat, Fantasy Island*), and the pubescent, nostalgic sitcoms of Garry Marshall (*Happy Days, Laverne & Shirley, Mork & Mindy*) that had been such hits a few years earlier were really starting to show their age. Classics like *M*A*S*H* and *All in the Family* were also getting pretty long in the tooth. *All in the Family* would mutate to *Archie Bunker's Place* in 1981, and in 1983 both it and *M*A*S*H* left the air.

By the 1983–84 season, only one sitcom appeared in the Nielsen top ten, proving that even the most venerable genre of the medium was susceptible to overkill. Although sitcoms were about to make a triumphant comeback, the top ten that year was dominated by new or not over-used genres like the nighttime soap (*Dallas, Dynasty, Falcon Crest*), the cartoonlike comedy-drama (*The A-Team*), the pseudoanthology (*Hotel*), the yet-to-be-over-imitated newsmagazine (*60 Minutes*), and the quality drama (*Cagney & Lacey*).

Daily household viewership continued to climb through the 1980s,[13] but not as much as might have been expected given the explosion of new viewing options. It could be speculated that the network audience size might have dropped even if cable and VCRs had never been introduced. As it was, people were continuing to watch TV, but many of them were looking for something different and finding it off the beaten network track.

The mandate was clearly for something different, but two of the three networks were reluctant to react. Though their audience size might have been tumbling, CBS and ABC were at least doing well in the much-publicized three-network race. Fearing to lose at least this competitive edge, they both tended to stick with what was working. But for NBC, nothing was working and they had nothing to lose.

Being in third place has proved to be a powerful catalyst for the quality drama ever since. These shows, after all, are innovative, and innovation in a popular medium is always dangerous. With no place to go but up, floundering networks are better positioned than leading ones to try new things and stick with them when they don't catch on right away. While in third place, NBC introduced unique and slow-starting series like *Hill Street, St. Elsewhere,* and *Cheers,* but once the network had climbed into first place, its output of innovative programming slowed considerably. By 1990, producers with struggling shows on NBC were dreaming of the good old days. Producer Andrew Susskind assessed the imminent cancellation of his acclaimed series *Parenthood* by claiming that NBC was caught "in real short-term thinking. . . . They're number one," he pointed out, "but their lead is shrinking. I'm not sure they have the confidence they had when they were number three and shooting for number one, which was to give quality shows a chance."[14]

After NBC's climb to the top of the ratings, ABC fell into third, and shortly thereafter it picked up the quality baton, offering up a string of inventive and original series like *Moonlighting, thirtysomething, China Beach,* and *Twin Peaks.* "Ironically or not," Tom Shales said in his review of *China Beach* in 1988, "as network television draws smaller and smaller percentages of the total viewing audience, TV programming gets better. . . . Network executives seem inclined to give writers and producers more leeway to pursue a vision, and slowly, prime time is becoming less smothered with standardization than it used to be."[15]

This is not to say that being in third place guarantees quality or that being in first place guarantees the lack thereof. NBC was in third when it gave the world *Manimal;* it was in first when *L.A. Law* was introduced. The diverse state of all network programming in the 1980s might be best represented by the NBC career of actor William Daniels, who was simultaneously winning Emmy Awards on *St. Elsewhere,* which arguably was the best prime-time series ever, and supplying the voice of a talking car on *Knight Rider,* which arguably was not.

Both NBC and ABC benefited from their third-place attempts to provide something new to the television audience. Younger viewers especially appreciated the direct challenge to traditional programming genres that the hip, in-joke-heavy quality dramas provided. As it turned out, though, most of the most successful shows of the 1980s were quite traditional. One of the oldest formulas in the medium, the nuclear family sitcom, proved more resilient than the ratings were indicating just a few years earlier. *Cosby, Family Ties,* and *Roseanne* became three of the biggest hits of the decade. Before that happened, however, the networks' uncertainty had caused them to cast around for some alternative programming as insurance for the future, and in doing so they had invented the contemporary quality drama.

■   ■   ■

In 1981, smaller network audiences promised the potential for better network programs, and one network in particular was floundering just badly enough to provide a welcome home to innovative shows. These facts seemed like ironies, but together they helped serious television drama to flourish. But there was still one major ingredient missing.

# 3

# The Quality Factory

A lthough the political, social, and industrial environments may have been just right for an explosion of quality drama on network television in the early 1980s, that explosion could never have happened had there not been a group of writers, producers, and actors ready and waiting to set it off. Without MTM Enterprises, an independent production company formed in 1970, there would likely have been no second Golden Age of television. Formed around *The Mary Tyler Moore Show*, MTM went on to define the standard of quality in the television industry. Of the ten shows most closely examined in this book, two—*Hill Street Blues* and *St. Elsewhere*—were made at MTM, five—*Moonlighting, L.A. Law, Twin Peaks, thirtysomething,* and *Northern Exposure*—were conceived by people who had cut their creative teeth there, and one—*Picket Fences,* was created by someone who learned the trade from one of MTM's most notorious ex-employees.

Former MTM employees have in fact been dominating television since the mid-1970s, playing key creative roles in many critical, and often commercial, triumphs, including *Taxi, Cagney & Lacey, Cheers, Family Ties, Buffalo Bill, The Cosby Show, Miami Vice, The Days and Nights of Molly Dodd, The Tracey Ullman Show, Frank's Place, A Year in the Life, China Beach, The Simpsons, Equal Justice, Law & Order, I'll Fly Away, Brooklyn Bridge, Civil Wars, Homicide: Life on the Street, Frasier, NYPD Blue, Friends, ER, Chicago Hope* and *Murder One.* Half the Emmy Awards given in the categories for both best comedy and best drama from 1971 through 1994 went to shows produced by MTM or its alumni.

The company was like a college where the writing, producing, and directing of quality TV was taught, learned, and executed by such graduates as James Brooks, Allan Burns, James Burrows, Glen and Les

Charles, Jay Sandrich, Gary David Goldberg, Ed. Weinberger, David Lloyd, Hugh Wilson, Jay Tarses, Tom Patchett, Stan Daniels, Michele Gallery, Steven Bochco, Bruce Paltrow, Dick Wolf, Kevin Hooks, Thomas Carter, Eric Laneuville, John Tinker, Mark Tinker, Tom Fontana, Lydia Woodward, Anthony Yerkovich, Glen Gordon Caron, David Milch, Robert Butler, and Marshall Herskovitz.[1] Though some of these are hardly household names, the people on this list went on to work on some of the most distinguished television of the past two decades. Even David Letterman got some of his earliest TV experience at MTM on *Mary*, a 1978 comedy-variety show starring M.T.M. herself.

At the heart of the company was Grant Tinker, who cofounded MTM with Moore, his wife at the time, and her manager, Arthur Price. A former executive at an assortment of advertising agencies, NBC, Universal, and Twentieth Century-Fox, Tinker openly acknowledges that he himself is not a creative person. Celebrated as one of the giants in television history, Tinker's principal contribution to the medium was to do what few executives have had the courage to do: to gather together talented creative people and to leave them alone. "From my earliest days around and about television," he recalled in his 1994 autobiography, "it's been clear to me that good shows can be made only by good writers. That's why I asked two fine writers, [James Brooks and Allan Burns], to create and produce a show for Mary. . . ."

> What I didn't realize at the time was that I had found the ingredients that were to make MTM a *writer's* company. Before Mary's show had run its seven-year course, Jim and Allan, through their work, would attract dozens of first-rate writing contributors, a number of whom would stay with MTM to produce other wonderful programs. . . . MTM quickly became known as a production company that allowed its creative people almost limitless independence and authority. I respect such people and feel privileged simply to watch them perform their magic. I don't try to do it for them, which I assuredly could not, and I've never understood the gall of executives who think they can. Not only did MTM give good creative people the freedom to do their work, but I became justly famous for throwing my body between our producers and network bureaucrats who sought to oversupervise or meddle in their efforts.[2]

One MTM staffer, Gary David Goldberg, who had started out in television on MTM's *The Bob Newhart Show* and who went on to create *Family Ties* and *Brooklyn Bridge*, called MTM a "Camelot for writers."[3] Another, Bruce Paltrow, who produced *The White Shadow* and *St. Elsewhere* for MTM, called it an "all-pro" company that was a haven for television artists. "You just knew good work was being done all around you by good people," Paltrow said. "And no one ever interfered with who you hired, on what basis you hired them, or what you did with them."[4]

By letting his writers and producers do what they wanted to do and by protecting them from the network interference that was a fact of life for most other writers and producers, Tinker created a situation from which a very different kind of television could emerge. When a CBS executive forbade Jim Brooks and Allan Burns from shooting one of their scripts as written, for example, the writers took the script to Tinker, who read it, liked it, and told them "The hell with him . . . Go ahead and shoot it."[5] Later, low ratings on *Lou Grant* inspired a crowd of CBS staffers to come up with a list of changes in the show that they thought would increase the size of its audience. In what would become a common strategy, Tinker simply told them to back off. "You're sitting here with three of the best producers in television," he said in a meeting with the network. "They are making the show you bought and the one you want to make. If you're that unhappy with it, then cancel it now and let them get on with other projects."[6]

The above examples weren't exceptions either. They illustrate what was the standard operating procedure of the company. In her essay on "The MTM Style," Jane Feuer argues that "the central component in MTM's image is its reputation for giving its creative staff an unusual amount of freedom," a condition that "enabled MTM to develop an individualized 'quality' style."[7]

The programming history of MTM Enterprises can roughly be divided into four phases. The first phase included such notable sitcoms as *The Mary Tyler Moore Show, The Bob Newhart Show,* and *Rhoda.* Although the company continued to make comedies throughout its history, by 1977 it had begun to specialize in hour-long social dramas. The best known of these Phase Two series included *Lou Grant,* the pseudospin-off of *The Mary Tyler Moore Show* that ripped headlines from the real newspapers and put them in Lou's fictional one. Some of the more controversial episodes explored nursing home care, the plight of the homeless and Vietnam veterans, sexual harassment in the office, and toxic waste disposal. *Lou Grant's* sister show was *The White Shadow,* which followed the exploits of a young, white, professional basketball player who becomes a coach at a racially mixed inner-city high school in South Los Angeles. During its third phase, which began in 1981 as Tinker was about to leave the company to become president of NBC, MTM introduced the gritty, serialized drama-comedies best exemplified by *Hill Street Blues* and *St. Elsewhere.* MTM's final phase began in the summer of 1988 when it was sold to the British company, TVS Entertainment. *St. Elsewhere* had left the air that spring, and

*Newhart,* the last of the series from the old regime, would be gone two years later. In December of 1992 Pat Robertson bought TVS and, ironically, acquired along with it MTM, the company that had made history by breaking most of the very rules Robertson held sacred. Among the series now bearing the famous MTM logo (a meowing kitten) are the bizarre children's series *Xuxa* and a new version of *The Galloping Gourmet.* "The talented writer/producers who made MTM the cat's meow have long since departed," Tinker laments. "Now the logo signs off product the original company would not have watched, much less made."[8]

During the first three phases between 1970 and 1988, however, that meowing kitten had become synonymous with quality television. MTM had, in fact, virtually invented the genre, and most its twelve defining characteristics (see the preface) were already present in the company's first series. *The Mary Tyler Moore Show* provided the blueprint not only for future MTM shows but for quality TV in general. Two distinct themes are worth special mention.

The first was the idea of the "workplace family." Though there had been sitcoms set in the workplace before, most notably the military comedies, the nuclear family had been the dominant model of the genre from the very beginning. *The Mary Tyler Moore Show* changed that. Unlike most contemporary sitcoms, this one wasn't always confined to the living room, and when it was it was the living room of a single woman, not a family. Mary's bachelorette pad was not populated by a spouse, kids, and a pet, but by a visiting neighbor and landlord. Most often, however, the show took place in the WJM-TV newsroom where Mary worked, and the "family" she found there was united by institutional ties, not biological ones. The workplace family, whether it was in a police station, a hospital, or a Vermont inn, became a defining characteristic of nearly all of MTM's subsequent series.

Although the very premise of *The Mary Tyler Moore Show,* by featuring an intelligent, professional woman, was seen as quite progressive in 1970, it has been argued that the workplace setting itself also carried a liberal message. "At a time when the nuclear family was under attack ouside the institution of television," Jane Feuer has written, "MTM pioneered a different kind of family, one that retained certain residual ideologies of family life while doing away with the more oppressive aspects of the nuclear family. The MTM work-family," she went on, "both reproduces the wholesome norms of family life on TV and presents us with a Utopian variation of the nuclear family more palatable to a new generation and to the quality audience," an audience she described as "a liberal, sophisticated group of upwardly mobile professionals."[9]

A second theme that became part of the MTM corporate aesthetic was self-reflexivity, a creative device often associated with modern "high art" in 1970, but seldom with such consistent subtlety and sophistication in a popular form like television. *The Mary Tyler Moore Show* was, after all, a TV show about a TV show, and its final episode was about a final episode. Many later MTM series would be set directly in mass media institutions: *The Betty White Show* was about the behind-the-scenes life of the star (White) of a police drama; *Lou Grant* took place in a major L.A. daily newspaper; *WKRP in Cincinnati* was about a radio station; *The Mary Tyler Moore Hour* was a variety show about the making of a variety show; *The Duck Factory* followed the employees of a film animation company; *Mary* was set in a tabloid newspaper; and *FM* took place at a public radio station. Several other shows were about related "entertainment" industries, such as sports (*The White Shadow* and the short-lived *Bay City Blues*), or included little self-conscious details (the title character of *Rhoda,* for example, made a living as a window dresser who, like a television maker, organizes things in a frame to appeal to potential customers). Within each series, it was very common for individual episodes to go off on hyper self-conscious jags. In *The White Shadow,* for example, one of the student's schoolwork, values, and friendships suffer when he is "discovered" and given a starring role in a TV series called "Downtown High." The premise of "Downtown High"—a caring white principal gets involved in the lives of his black students—sounded an awful lot like the premise of *The White Shadow* itself. "In aligning itself with the modernist self-conscious mode," Feuer points out, "the MTM style makes yet another claim to quality status."[10]

Related to self-reflexivity, nearly every MTM show featured competent, qualified characters trying to work and survive within environments that were collapsing and filled with incompetent people. WJM's news show, on which Mary Richards works, is a joke; WKRP is near the bottom of Cincinnati's ratings and even the call letters say it's "crap"; *The White Shadow*'s Carver High is in a ghetto, as are the police station and the hospital in *Hill Street Blues* and *St. Elsewhere.* The principal characters—Mary, Andy Travis, Coach Reeves, most of the cops and doctors—do their best amid the chaos. Many of the MTM writers and producers undoubtedly saw themselves in much the same way. Members of the MTM staff have, over the years, boasted some pretty fancy résumés. David Milch of *Hill Street Blues,* for example, taught writing at Yale before he joined the show. As a group, these people saw the work they did as better than most of what was on TV. They went on to create characters who, like themselves, might have been perceived as highly talented people working in a world run by idiots. MTM's constant uphill struggle against network interference perhaps best illustrates this phenomenon. "The kind of creative people who gravitated to MTM were not the kind to brook much network interference," Grant Tinker said, clearly singling out his employees as a special breed. "They brought real meaning to the term *independent production*."[11]

By the time MTM was sold to TVS Entertainment in 1988, most of what it had been doing for the past eighteen years had become almost commonplace. Former MTM employees were working throughout the industry and many had taken the quality formula with them. Others who hadn't worked for MTM but had grown up watching its products were also borrowing the company style. From the workplace families of *Cheers* and *Murphy Brown* to the self-conscious dramas of *Picket Fences* and *Homicide*, the MTM style had become a recognizable television formula.

■   ■   ■

All of MTM's programming, as well as many series made by other companies after 1970, bear the distinct set of styles, themes, and characters developed in *The Mary Tyler Moore Show*. But that series itself was not without its creative forebearers. Much of the foundation upon which *Mary Tyler Moore* was built had been established by *The Dick Van Dyke Show* nearly a decade earlier.

The literate writing, the occasional descents into the playfully bizarre, and the sophisticated performances by an extended ensemble cast were all features that *Mary Tyler Moore* would borrow from *Dick Van Dyke*. Both of the MTM themes discussed above were also already present on *The Dick Van Dyke Show*. While the earlier series had one foot in the traditional nuclear family sitcom, the other was firmly planted in the workplace. Half the action was set, as were so many contemporary sitcoms, in the living room, which was complete with a wife, a child, and a set of wacky visiting neighbors. But the other half took place where Rob Petrie (Van Dyke) worked. Here we found yet another family, consisting of siblingesque coworkers Buddy Sorrell (Morey Amsterdam) and Sally Rogers (Rose Marie) and parental bosses Mel Cooley (Richard Deacon) and Alan Brady (series creator Carl Reiner). The other theme MTM would later develop was also clearly observable. With Rob as the head writer of "The Alan Brady Show,"[12] *Dick Van Dyke* was in essence a TV series about a TV series, and the competent writing of Rob, Sally, and Buddy was often questioned by the incompetent Mel and the tyrannical Alan. The MTM formula that would be employed from the first episode of *The Mary Tyler Moore Show* in 1970 through the final episode of *St. Elsewhere* in 1988 was without question already being established by the time Rob Petrie took his first tumble over that inconveniently placed ottoman in October of 1961.

The clearest link between the two shows was Mary Tyler Moore herself, who costarred in *The Dick Van Dyke Show* as Rob's wife, Laura. But the connection between the shows goes even deeper. Grant Tinker had been an ad executive representing the sponsors of *Dick Van Dyke*. He met Moore as the show was being developed and married her at the end of its first season.[13] "From the start of the 1962–63 season," Tinker remembers, "three months after Mary and I were married, I was the most faithful audience member of *The Dick Van Dyke Show*. I attended the Tuesday night filming of nearly every episode."[14] In his definitive history of the series, Vince Waldron writes that Tinker "has long acknowledged that he kept the creative framework of the old Van Dyke show in the forefront of his mind when he assembled the creative team of actors, writers, and directors who would eventually sustain *The Mary Tyler Moore Show* through seven critically acclaimed seasons."[15] Allan Burns, one of the creators and writers of *The Mary Tyler Moore Show* had, in fact, been such an avid admirer of *The Dick Van Dyke Show* that he had applied to Carl Reiner for a spot on the writing staff.[16] Though he never got the job, his familiarity with the show's formula, style, and characters would serve him well a few years later.

With two Emmy awards on her mantel, Mary Tyler Moore was a star when *The Dick Van Dyke Show* ended its run in 1966. Her subsequent work in feature films and on Broadway, however, didn't meet with the success she had achieved on television. By 1969, when Dick Van Dyke invited her to appear on a TV special with him, she was ready to return to the scene of her triumph. *Dick Van Dyke and the Other Woman* reintroduced Moore to CBS executives, who immediately became interested in putting her in a series of her own. Tinker and Moore agreed to a deal but only if CBS would give them a series commitment and a degree of creative control atypical at the time but characteristic of what MTM would demand of the networks in the future.[17] The final formal link between MTM and *The Dick Van Dyke Show* came, incidently, ten years later when Moore returned Van Dyke's favor and brought him on as a guest on her short-lived variety series, *The Mary Tyler Moore Hour*. In a short comic sketch, Van Dyke reprised the Rob Petrie role for the first and to date only time.[18]

Though the evolution from *The Dick Van Dyke Show* to *The Mary Tyler Moore Show* is fairly clear, there is an important missing link between the two. By the time discussions had begun about a series for Moore, Grant Tinker had become an executive at Twentieth Century-Fox. He had arrived in 1969 during the first season of a new series, *Room 222*, which was set in an integrated Los Angeles high school. A year and a half before the debut of *All in the Family*, *Room 222* was dealing with contemporary issues like racial prejudice and drug abuse in the context of a half-hour comedy. An early example of the workplace sitcom, nearly all of the action on *Room 222* took place among the family of administrators, teachers, and students at Walt Whitman High. "It may not have been the first television show to mix comedy with substantial issues," Grant Tinker recalls, "but I can't remember any prior program that accomplished that difficult trick as well."[19]

MTM would ultimately borrow both ideas and staff from *Room 222*. The setting and theme of the show heavily influenced *The White Shadow*, for example, and the mixture of comedy and drama would become an MTM staple on such shows as *Hill Street Blues* and *St. Elsewhere*. Gene Reynolds, one of the show's producers, would later serve as executive producer of *Lou Grant*, and Eric Laneuville, who played a student for two seasons on *Room 222*, would become a star and director of *St. Elsewhere*. Most importantly, however, it was on *Room 222* that Tinker discovered James Brooks and Allan Burns. Brooks had created the show and was serving as one of its producers. When the other producer, Gene Reynolds, had left, Brooks promoted Burns, one of his writers, to take Reynolds's place. Tinker liked their work and hired them to create and produce Moore's new show for CBS. Together with Tinker, Moore, and Arthur Price, Brooks and Burns completed what was then a company of five. By 1974, MTM would be employing as many as five hundred.

Brooks and Burns were starting from square one. The CBS series commitment had been made on the strength of Mary Tyler Moore's drawing power. There was no title, no pilot script, not even an idea of what the show would be about. "Obviously we didn't want to put Mary in a domestic situation comedy," Brooks told TV professors Robert Alley and Irby Brown, "because she had just done probably the most successful such comedy of all time with Dick Van Dyke."

> We didn't want to repeat that and that sort of limited us. We said, "Okay, here we have a woman thirty years old." In 1970 we felt we had to explain why a woman was thirty and unmarried. In a way that demonstrated how limited our own thinking was at the time with respect to women. Our explanation—she probably has to be divorced.[20]

Burns felt the divorce idea was consistent with the kind of work he and Brooks had already been doing. "Remember that Jim and I had just come off *Room 222*, which was a reality-based comedy," he said. "We didn't want to go and do typical sitcom sort of stuff. CBS kept telling us Lucy was never divorced, Doris Day was never divorced, and we're saying, we can't do that kind of show."[21]

Though one might be hard-pressed to find anyone in Hollywood who admits to doing "typical sitcom sort of stuff," this attitude that they were going to make TV that wasn't like other TV would become the most clearly defining characteristic of MTM and the quality movement in general. Right from the start, Brooks and Burns were defining themselves and their company as classy Mary Richardses trying to make a go of it in an industry filled with Ted Baxters.

Tinker himself was the greatest embodiment of this attitude. Looking more like a professor than a TV executive, Tinker holds an Ivy League degree in English literature from Dartmouth. In describing the aesthetic predecessors to the MTM series, he employs the lingo not of show biz but of literary criticism. Citing that he wrote his senior thesis on Richard Brinsley Sheridan (1751–1816), the Irish playwright who wrote *The Rivals, The School for Scandal,* and *The Critic,* Tinker goes on to point out that "Sheridan's wit, his ability to involve the audience quickly, his gift for dialogue, and his sharply drawn characters gave me a standard by which to judge literate comedy designed for a mass audience. Sheridan's style was very close to that of the best three-camera comedies on television, the kind on which MTM would later be founded. To me, he was a creative forerunner of Jim Brooks and Alan Burns."[22]

▪    ▪    ▪

*The Mary Tyler Moore Show* was introduced during an especially rich and innovative period in prime-time programming. It and *All in the Family* were both freshman series in the 1970–71 season and, along with *M\*A\*S\*H,* which debuted in 1972, these shows were among the most celebrated of the decade.

*All in the Family* came onto the scene with the most racket. Its premise, the domestic life of a family, and its setting, the American living room, were nothing new, but any similarity to previous prime-time TV stopped there. The strident, aggressive, and noisy sound of the show was matched by its in-your-face look, partly the result of its being shot on videotape, a medium most viewers knew of only from the news. In its early years, the show explored thematic new territory previously nearly unknown to prime-time comedy, including homosexuality, the antiwar movement, impotence, menopause, and explicit racial prejudice, and in doing so it used language that had never come out of the TV set before.

There had, of course, been rumblings in the TV industry that a change was in the air before *All in the Family.* The year 1968's *Julia,* for example, was a sitcom all about a woman(!) who was single(!!) and black(!!!), and who, unlike *Our Miss Brooks,* did not spend every episode trying to snag a husband. Series like the new *Dragnet* and *The Mod Squad* had managed at least to recognize the counterculture before it had disappeared, and *The Smothers Brothers Comedy Hour* and *Rowan & Martin's Laugh-In* were occasionally downright feisty in their topical humor. But *Julia* was an anomaly that couldn't maintain its first-year hit status, *The Mod Squad* and Sergeant Friday and Officer Gannon were defenders of the old order, and the controversies surrounding *The Smothers Brothers* eventually forced it off the air.

*All in the Family*'s influence, on the other hand, was stronger and more enduring. By fitting comparatively revolutionary ideas into the tried-and-true form of the family sitcom, it provided a formula that could be emulated again and again. And by climbing to the top of the ratings in its second season and staying there for five consecutive years, social "relevance" had suddenly become the hottest ticket in town. The effect on TV programming was almost immediate. *All in the Family* itself spawned a family of spin-offs and similar series, including shows like *Sanford and Son* and *The Jeffersons*, which brought back the predominantly African-American cast to series TV for the first time since *Amos 'n' Andy*. Other producers responded as well. *Gomer Pyle, U.S.M.C.*, a CBS sitcom set in the Marine Corps from 1964 to 1970 that never mentioned the Vietnam War, was the second highest-rated show of the 1968–69 season; by 1972, *M\*A\*S\*H* was using the Korean War as a setting in which to tell critical tales of Vietnam, albeit to an audience by then already disenchanted with the war.

The formula developed by Tandem Productions, which was headed up by *All in the Family*'s creators, Norman Lear and Bud Yorkin, became one of the anchors of 1970s prime-time TV. By the 1974–75 season, five of the top ten series on the air were Lear's—*All in the Family, Sanford and Son, The Jeffersons, Good Times*, and *Maude*—and a sixth, *Chico and the Man*, had been created in the Lear style. Lear's *One Day at a Time* would be in the list two years later, and his protégés were adapting his style as well. Susan Harris, who'd written the episodes of *Maude* in which Maude decides to have an abortion, had moved on to create her own controversial hit series, *Soap*, and would later create *Benson, The Golden Girls*, and *Empty Nest*.

Though *All in the Family* had come on with Sturm und Drang in January of 1971, however, the kinder, gentler, and quieter *Mary Tyler Moore Show* had beat it to the punch by half a season. When it debuted the previous September, it caused much less of a fuss. While *All in the Family* took many of its ideas from the TV news, *The Mary Tyler Moore Show* took place in the TV newsroom. But the news itself was strikingly absent from the show. WJM never seemed to broadcast stories about the war, for example. Mary never got pregnant (although it was sneakily revealed in one episode that she was taking birth control pills), she was never sexually assaulted, and she never contemplated getting an abortion, all events that had punctuated the lives of Lear's female characters. *All in the Family* had concentrated on issues and controversy; *Mary Tyler Moore* concentrated on characters. *All in the Family* may have provided overt discussions of the equality of the sexes, but *The Mary Tyler Moore Show,* by its very premise, foregrounded the women's movement without a lot of talk about it.

Brooks and Burns, in fact, didn't even succeed in making Mary Richards a recently divorced woman, as they had originally planned. Providing the TV industry with one of its favorite legends, a CBS researcher allegedly produced a list of four types of people that viewers would not tolerate as the leading character in a series: divorced people, Jews, New Yorkers, and people with mustaches.[23] For Mary Richards, a Protestant from the Midwest with no discernible facial hair, three out of four wasn't good enough, and the producers were forced to change Mary from a divorcee to a woman who has just broken off a long relationship.

Divorce or not, though, as a professional woman with no love interest and no immediate desire to obtain one, Mary Richards made television history. And the success of *The Mary Tyler Moore Show* almost immediately began to break down the anachronistic network attitudes that had refused to grant her a divorce. Before the decade was over, divorced women on television had become commonplace. Four years after the debut of *The Mary Tyler Moore Show,* in fact, the spin-off series *Rhoda* became a hit for CBS. Rhoda Morgenstern was Jewish, she lived in New York, and she divorced her husband in a special two-part episode.

▪    ▪    ▪

Tandem and MTM were both powerhouses of the 1970s, but Norman Lear's company failed to evolve with the times. Tandem never fully escaped the constraining confines of the socially "relevant" sitcom, and what had once been revolutionary soon became old news. Although Lear flirted with the hour-long form in *Palmerstown, U.S.A.,* a Depression-era drama set in the South, he stuck mostly to the half-hour comedy. By the 1980s, the formula just wasn't working anymore. He tried a series about a Mexican-American family (*A.K.A. Pablo*), a political satire (*The Powers That Be*), and a sitcom that explored religion (*Sunday Dinner*), but none lasted longer than a season. *Archie Bunker's Place,* which left the air in 1983, remains Lear's last hit, and even the venerable *All in the Family* franchise has proven no longer able to deliver. *Gloria,* a sitcom featuring Sally Struthers as Archie's daughter living life after Meathead, lasted only a season in 1982, and, most recently, *704 Howser Street,* a series about the African-American family living in the Bunkers' old house, proved that though Lear might have been able to go home again, he'd have to leave after only a few episodes.

*M\*A\*S\*H,* the third of the breakthrough series of the early 1970s, left a surprisingly limited legacy. Although it was an extraordinary hit, ending its run in third place in the ratings and leaving the air in a final episode blaze of record-breaking glory, its overall influence never reached that of *All in the Family.* Larry Gelbart, who had developed the show for television, left the series early, took a brief stab at experimental TV as creator of *United States,* then abandoned television entirely for film and the theater. Gene Reynolds, one of the show's principal producers, was absorbed into the MTM company when he left *M\*A\*S\*H* to become the executive producer of *Lou Grant. M\*A\*S\*H* engendered only two spin-offs, *Trapper John, M.D.,* a show very different from its parent, and *AfterM\*A\*S\*H,* a notorious disappointment. Though *M\*A\*S\*H* might be credited with being the forerunner of the "dramedy," its unique blend of comedy and grimness was never really imitated successfully in the half-hour format. After *M\*A\*S\*H,* series about the military were reabsorbed into serious dramas like *China Beach* and *Tour of Duty* or straight comedies like *Private Benjamin.*

Unlike Lear and the producers of *M\*A\*S\*H,* however, MTM still had its best trick up its sleeve when the 1980s rolled around. By 1975, the company had began experimenting with the hour-long drama. Within a few years, series like *Lou Grant, The White Shadow,* and *Paris,* and a string of made-for-TV movies had firmly established MTM as a supplier of quality dramatic programming. This diversification served them well when the sitcom went into a slump in the early 1980s. The diversifying tactic was to some extent just a practical response to the fact that MTM's best comedy writers were either being stolen by Paramount or starting their own production companies at the same time that highly talented dramatic writers like Bruce Paltrow and Steven Bochco were joining MTM.[24] Still, MTM was adapting its programming to the new decade. While the company continued to make comedies, it also came up with a recipe for a new type of programming that is still visible today. By integrating its own sitcom style with the new content areas and language usage that the Lear shows had brought to television, and then putting it all together into a soap opera format, MTM came up with *Hill Street Blues.*

▪ ▪ ▪

After eleven years of building MTM into the classiest act around and a few months after the debut of *Hill Street Blues,* Grant Tinker himself joined the network bureaucrats when he became chairman and CEO of NBC in the summer of 1981. Acknowledging that "MTM had grown and prospered by *not* trying to do the producers' jobs for them," Tinker reasoned that "the only way to ensure that NBC would enjoy the same kind of results would be to behave, as a network, in a similar manner."[25] Taking his hands-off philosophy with him, Tinker made NBC the "quality conscious" place where producers most wanted to do business. "Tinker altered the culture at NBC," Ken Auletta reported in *Three Blind Mice.* "Employees came to feel that the network was special, a place that defied the tyranny of Nielsen's ratings, a place with the swagger to trust its gut instincts."[26] Midway through his tenure at NBC, *American Film* magazine had dubbed Tinker "Mr. Quality Television."[27]

To be sure, Tinker, along with his programming chief Brandon Tartikoff, didn't run NBC as though it were PBS. *The A-Team,* for example, was one of the earliest series he scheduled, and one that would start NBC on the road to ratings recovery. But Tinker's managerial style also gave time and creative latitude to good but marginally performing series—most of them from his former colleagues at MTM—that would have quickly met cancellation at the other networks, if they'd ever been aired at all. "What earned NBC its reputation for quality was its willingness to air good shows even though the initial research and then the Nielsen numbers were dismal," Auletta claimed. "Bolstered by Tinker, the talented Tartikoff began to err on the side of more quality series, to boast of challenging the audience rather than giving it what it wanted."[28] Assuming, as he had at MTM, that quality could bring profits and that the same shows could please both Nielsen and the critics, Tinker led NBC on its quest for upscale demographics discussed in the last chapter, and under his stewardship, the network went from third place to first. Tinker still holds that "the collegial approach that was the essence of the MTM style played a real part in resuscitating NBC."[29]

Having provided a place where writers and producers could do their best work, Tinker was now providing a place where they could sell it. Having presided over MTM during the creation and launching of *Hill Street Blues,* a series that could have been made no place else, he was now protectively presiding over the network that aired it. Prime time television would never be the same.

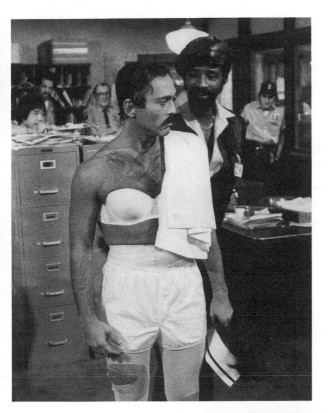

1.
*Hill Street Blues.*
Bruce Weitz (left)
and Taurean Blacque.

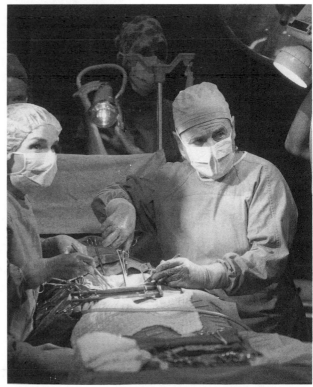

2.
*St. Elsewhere.*
Sagan Lewis (left)
and William Daniels.

3.
*Cagney & Lacey.*
Tyne Daly (left)
and Sharon Glass.

4.
*Moonlighting.*
Bruce Willis and
Cybill Shepherd.

5. *L.A. Law.* Susan Dey and Harry Hamlin.

6. *thirtysomething*. From left: Rachel Nagler, Timothy Busfield, Patricia Wettig, Jason Nagler, Polly Draper, Mel Harris, Brittany Craven, Ken Olin, Melanie Mayron, and Peter Horton.

7. *China Beach*. Robert Picardo and Dana Delany.

8.
*Twin Peaks.*
Kyle MacLachlan (left)
and Michael Ontkean.

9. *Northern Exposure.* From left: John Cullum, Rob Morrow, Cynthia Geary, Barry Corbin, Yvonne Suhor, John Corbett, Jo Anderson, Darren E. Burrows.

10. *Picket Fences.* Tom Skerritt and Kathy Baker.

# 4

# *Hill Street Blues:*
# The Quality Revolution

Sometime in the 1980s, TV became Art. Anthologies of television scripts started appearing in the drama sections at B. Dalton; college English departments began offering courses with titles like "The Analysis of the Televisual Image"; and well-known writers and directors based in the novel, the cinema, and the legitimate stage started clamoring to work in the once despised medium. The quality dramas were mostly responsible for this new respect, and it was *Hill Street Blues* that had first convinced many serious artists that television had finally come of age.

One of America's most prominent and prolific novelists, Joyce Carol Oates, enthusiastically celebrated the series in a 1985 cover story of *TV Guide*, calling it the only TV show she watched regularly. "[It is] one of the few television programs watched by a fair percentage of my Princeton colleagues," she went on to reveal, "arguably because it is one of the few current television programs that is as intellectually and emotionally provocative as a good book. In fact, from the very first, *Hill Street Blues* struck me as Dickensian in its superb character studies, its energy, its variety; above all, its audacity."[1] Princeton? Dickens? As good as a book? TELEVISION?! What was becoming of the vast wasteland? Pulitzer Prize-winning playwright David Mamet was also a great admirer of the show, and he went Oates one better by even writing an episode for *Hill Street*'s final season.

The literary résumés of the regular staff of *Hill Street Blues* were as surprising as those of some of the people watching it. Michael Kozoll, the show's co-creator, had published stories in literary journals, done graduate work in linguistics at the Sorbonne, and taught English in colleges in the San Francisco area;[2] Jeffrey Lewis had written poetry while at Yale and had taught expository writing at Harvard, where he'd also received his law degree; David Milch graduated Phi Beta Kappa from Yale and received a master's degree from the prestigious Iowa Writers' Workshop before returning to Yale to teach creative writing; Roger Director had a masters degree in English literature from Columbia and had contributed to the *New Yorker;* Mark Frost had been a Literary Associate at the Guthrie Theater in Minneapolis.[3] Clearly this was not your average collection of hacks.

Much about *Hill Street Blues,* in fact, wasn't average. Created and overseen by a producer who was determined to defy network television standards, made at a production company that had grown powerful on a string of critical and commercial successes, and aired on a network in a tailspin, *Hill Street Blues* brought something truly different to prime-time television. That it ever got, much less stayed, on the air was the result, as Kozoll said, of "a long series of flukes."[4] In a definitive chapter about the series in his book *Inside Prime Time,* Todd Gitlin argued that:

> *If* a producer gets on the inside track; *if* he or she has strong ideas and fights for them intelligently; *if* they appear somewhat compatible with the networks' conventional wisdom about what a show ought to be at a particular moment; *if* the producer is willing to give ground here and there; *if* he or she is protected by a powerhouse production company that the network is loath to kick around; *if* the network has the right niche for the show; *if* the product catches the eye of the right executive at the right time, and doesn't get lost in the shuffle when the guardian executive changes jobs . . . then the system that cranks out mind candy occasionally proves hospitable to something else.[5]

Needless to say, it is rare for all these "ifs" to be satisfied. When they finally were, *Hill Street Blues* was the result.

The conception and very early development of the show was not all that unusual. Fred Silverman, then head of the NBC network, reportedly had either seen or heard about the yet-to-be released feature film *Fort Apache, The Bronx* (1981) and decided that what NBC needed was a realistic, gritty, urban police series. Although Silverman had nurtured such acclaimed shows as *The Mary Tyler Moore Show* and *All in the Family* when he was chief programmer at CBS, he was more well-known for helping to usher in the "jiggle" era by introducing series like *Three's Company* and *Charlie's Angels* to ABC during his tenure there in the mid-1970s. His not entirely deserved reputation as a programmer of exclusively schlocky shows followed him when he became the head of

NBC, where he developed such programs as *The Misadventures of Sheriff Lobo* and *Real People.*

NBC was not known for prestige programming in 1980, and Silverman's original idea for *Hill Street Blues* didn't seem to be consciously aiming at anything especially classy. As is often the case with TV series, this one was being conceived in terms of other films and television shows. Though his idea had been inspired by some admittedly well-respected precedents, what Silverman was essentially looking for was another cop show. "The sort of mixture that Silverman and his fellow executives had in mind," TV culture scholar Paul Kerr said as he tried to parse *Hill Street*'s aesthetic heritage, "included such ingredients as the film *Hospital* [1971],[6] for its ragged style and generic parody, *MASH,* for its tragicomic tone, and *Fort Apache, The Bronx* for its ghetto precinct settings and protagonists. Also mentioned," Kerr goes on, "were such [TV] series as *Police Story* for its focus on the private lives of its police protagonists and on the consequences of their professional public duties on those lives, *Barney Miller,* for its ethnic mix and precinct comedy, and the TV spin-off series *M\*A\*S\*H* for its televisual version of a cinematic style."[7] Along with this promising heap of raw material, Silverman had even gone so far as to suggest that the show feature an ensemble of actors rather than the usual cop-and-sidekick combination.

It was Michael Zinberg who took the project to an important new level. Zinberg had been a producer at MTM during its heyday as a supplier of character comedies, but by 1980 he was serving as the vice-president of comedy development at NBC. When he heard of Silverman's sketchy idea for an urban police drama, he suggested MTM's Steven Bochco and Michael Kozoll as the guys to do it. From that point forward the die had been cast for a truly unique new television form. For as it turned out neither Bochco nor Kozoll had any desire to make a cop show, and their unmitigated disinterest would ultimately lead to new frontiers of creative autonomy.

In January of 1980 Silverman sent Zinberg and NBC's head programmer Brandon Tartikoff off to a lunch meeting with Bochco, Kozoll and MTM executive Stu Erwin. The two writers made it clear that they didn't like Silverman's idea. They wanted to do an anthology drama, a sort of "*Love Boat* set in a San Francisco hotel,"[8] as Brandon Tartikoff remembers it. Though *The Love Boat*'s Aaron Spelling would eventually make just such a show, right down to the San Francisco setting, Silverman was fishing for urban cops, and Bochco and Kozoll weren't biting.

The reason for their reluctance had something to do with the fact that they were already sick of the cop show format. Born in New York in 1943 and educated as a drama major at Carnegie Tech, Bochco had secured himself a job as a writer at Universal Television three days after graduation,[9] and he'd been writing crime stories ever since. Universal in the 1960s was the classic sausage factory, grinding out a prodigious amount of product every season. In his more than twelve years there, Bochco rose through the ranks as a writer, a story editor, a producer, and a creator-producer on series like *The Name of the Game; Columbo; McMillan and Wife; Banacek; Griff; Richie Brockelman, Private Eye;* and a handful of made-for-TV movies and pilots.

One of Bochco's last efforts at Universal was as producer and writer of *Delvecchio,* which starred Judd Hirsch as a tough police detective working the big-city streets of Los Angeles. This was to be one of two major dress rehearsals for *Hill Street Blues.* Among the supporting cast of *Delvecchio* were Michael Conrad, Charles Haid, and Kiel Martin, all of whom would become part of *Hill Street*'s ensemble. The story editor of the series was Michael Kozoll, a graduate of the University of Wisconsin. Although his reputation was not as established as Bochco's, Kozoll himself had done his fair share of writing in the detective and police genres, also at Universal. By the time he and Bochco met on *Delvecchio,* he'd already logged in time at *Quincy, McCloud, Switch,* and *Kojak. Delvecchio* would last only a season, but the pairing of Bochco and Kozoll would prove to be an auspicious one.

After a few more projects at Universal, Bochco joined MTM just as the company was making a transition from comedy to dramatic program production. As executive producer of the MTM made-for-TV movie *Vampire,* Bochco brought Kozoll over as his cowriter. Kozoll also helped out on *Paris,* Bochco's first series at MTM.[10] *Paris* turned out to be the next step up the quality food chain toward *Hill Street.* Woody Paris (James Earl Jones) was a cerebral police captain who enforced the law by day and taught criminology at a nearby university by night. Though Captain Paris was still a long way from Captain Furillo, Bochco has pointed out, the show "fed into what *Hill Street* finally became, because what I began to do in *Paris,* to an even greater degree than what we had done on *Delvecchio,* was to try and frame the thing in the context of a man's personal life. Woody Paris was a police captain with an enormous amount of responsibility and very little authority. He was a true kind of middle-management guy."[11] No fewer than six of the future thirteen regular cast members of *Hill Street Blues* appeared in *Paris.* Michael Warren played a regular role, and Kiel Martin, Joe Spano, Taurean Blacque, James P. Sikking, and Michael Conrad all made guest appearances.

*Paris* received some strong critical notices, but it left the air after only ten episodes on January 15, 1980, exactly one year before the debut of *Hill Street Blues* and two weeks after Bochco and Kozoll had met with Tartikoff and Zinberg. Neither writer talks very fondly about the experience of *Paris*. Kozoll remembered the show as "a strange combination of *Columbo* and *Delvecchio* with a black cop lead. . . . The demise of *Paris*, I think, we can credit to the fact that it wasn't very good."[12] Bochco told Todd Gitlin that he was "personally so dismayed" with *Paris*. "I wasn't happy with what I did at all. And so I sure wasn't looking to do another cop show."[13] After the short runs of *Delvecchio* and *Paris*, both Bochco and Kozoll were ready to give the genre a rest. The very fact that both writers knew the cop show formula so well, and that they had grown to disdain it, however, rendered them perfectly poised to transform it completely. Once they realized this, Silverman's offer became too tempting to refuse. "We . . . did not approach it from the point of view of wanting to do something that had never been done before," Bochco said of their thought process after they agreed to the NBC deal, "but from the point of view of *not* wanting to do a whole bunch of things that we'd been doing for the last six or seven years in television."[14]

▪ ▪ ▪

No one in 1980, in fact, was better positioned than Steven Bochco to make television that was different. Among other things, his dislike of network broadcast standards departments, whose staff members were referred to by creative people as "the censors," was already notorious, and it became positively legendary during the run of *Hill Street*. Each of the three networks maintained their own standards office that served as a voluntary mechanism of content regulation. These offices are, of course, concerned with more than just regulating the presence in programming of strong language, sex, and violence, although these are the areas for which they are best known. As the name of the office implies, these people are charged with making sure that all shows aired by the network adhere to a certain set of company standards. The creative limitations guaranteed by this institutionalized standardization made Bochco crazy and gave him a purpose in life. "I actually have been put on this earth for one primary reason," Bochco told Todd Gitlin, "and that is to torment network broadcast standards people."[15]

As far back as 1977, when he was writing and producing *Delvecchio*, Bochco himself had contributed an essay on in-house network censorship to an anthology on the history and inner workings of the medium. In it he clearly shows his combative attitudes toward the entire process:

> It is my responsibility to submit each of my scripts to the network's Broadcast Standards Department before it is shot. The representa-

tive I work with from that department is a very nice lady performing a difficult task. She has, however, several powerful weapons at her disposal: an elaborate set of ground rules that have been established by higher-ups in her department; the ultimate authority to deny me the right to make any given episode if it does not meet certain broadcast standards as set forth in the aforementioned elaborate ground rules; and the ability to cry at me over the phone any time I raise my voice at her. But these weapons are offset by some weaponry of my own: I'm older than she is, I shout louder, I am not intimidated by cheap trickery (such as crying on the phone), and, ultimately, I am a better negotiator. For that is what censorship, in the real world, is all about—negotiating.[16]

Bochco continues the essay with a few selectively ridiculous examples of this negotiation process—the networks insisted that "rat do-do," for example, had to be changed to "rat-do" in a *Delvecchio* script—and tells the old saw about how writers include twice the number of "hells" and "damns" that they actually want to use because they know that they will always be asked to reduce them by half.

If a network television show was ever to stop looking like all other network television, someone was going to have to insist upon breaking the ground rules that kept everything so standardized. In 1980, Bochco and Kozoll seemed perfect candidates for this job. Their disinterested, demanding, sometimes even belligerent attitude toward the network that was offering them a series commitment seemed to say that this really was a project that they could take or leave. But when they refused to do a cop show in their first meeting with NBC executives, the network seemed to want them all the more. Their blasé attitude, combined with the fact that they'd be doing the show at Grant Tinker's MTM, a company celebrated for protecting the creative interests of its writers and producers against the intrusions of network "input" and a company that NBC wanted to keep on its good side, Bochco and Kozoll were clearly coming to the table from a position of strength.

Within a few years, Bochco would become something of a star in his own right, playing the role of the quintessential maverick TV producer who was always ready with a good sound bite when speaking out against anything that stood in the way of letting television artists like him do what they wanted to do. An articulate spokesperson for quality TV as well as a producer of hits, Bochco's role in the proliferation of quality series was a significant one.

■    ■    ■

As discussions of *Hill Street Blues* developed, it turned out that NBC seemed sincerely interested in letting Bochco and Kozoll do something truly different. "They were talking about giving us carte blanche to do whatever we wanted within that genre," Bochco said, "the likes of which I had never heard from a network before."[17] Before agreeing to do the show, the two producers extracted an agreement from Brandon Tartikoff that the network, within reasonable limits, would leave them alone. They also asked for a meeting with Broadcast Standards against whom they launched an aggressive preemptive strike before a word of the script had been written.[18] "We had an hour-and-a-half meeting with [Broadcast Standards]," Bochco told *TV Guide* after the first season of the series, "in which we screamed and hollered. They kept saying: how can we give you assurances about something that doesn't exist? And we kept saying: You have to give us something or we ain't gonna do it. . . . We let them know right away that we were going to be rude and feisty and antagonistic to everything they represent."[19] Right from the start, Bochco had put Broadcast Standards on notice that he wasn't going to take any rat-do.

A quick look at *Hill Street Blues* reveals that all that fussing indeed had some effect. In both its style and its content, the series got away with things that other shows didn't. Surprisingly, the network did for the most part live up to its promise of remaining out of the creative loop. It helped that the show was backed by MTM, an established and dependable company, and that ex-MTMer Michael Zinberg was now an NBC executive pulling for the show. Furthermore, commercial concerns aside, the tastes of network executives do occasionally figure into the decision-making process, and both Fred Silverman and Brandon Tartikoff liked how the show was shaping up.[20] Most importantly, however, NBC had been in a big hurry for a pilot, and they knew that they wouldn't get one unless they agreed to the creators' demands.

Other evidence suggests, however, that NBC executives didn't just sit back and let Bochco and Kozoll do whatever they wanted. When the network screened the pilot to a test audience in May of 1980, they sent a memo to MTM reporting the results. Members of the test audience, they said, found the show too confusing, too violent, and too depressing. There were too many subplots and the main characters' personalities were too flawed. They suggested that perhaps the cast "should be successful in dealing with most of their cases both inside and outside the station house, and that personal problems be introduced gradually and over a period of time and perhaps not to all members of the cast." In commenting on the memo, Grant Tinker said that "The network saw every one of the elements that were to make *Hill Street Blues* an enduring and memorable show as a problem to be overcome. The subtext of the NBC memo: Make it look like all those other programs."[21] But not only did the producers, with the support of Tinker, essentially ignore this memo, the success they achieved in doing so went some distance in changing network attitudes. By the time *Twin Peaks* was in development nine years later, network executives were screaming for programming that was different, not for more of the same.

Bochco himself told a reporter for the *Los Angeles Times* that making *Hill Street* was a constant battle with the Broadcast Standards people. "All those things that you look at on *Hill Street* and you say, 'Holy mackerel! Boy, I haven't seen that before!' represent maybe an hour or a day or a week of trench warfare," he said. "And that's an hour or a day or a week I should have been spending on a hundred other things relevant to the creative sensibility of the show."[22] "I think that what *Hill Street* started out to be—and evolved into—was partially the result of my almost daily warfare with network Broadcast Standards,"[23] he later revealed in a 1986 interview.

For all NBC's skittishness, the idea Bochco and Kozoll had developed was realized, reasonably intact, in the fifteen episodes of the abbreviated first season. Although the network was willing to go out on a limb and air the show, however, they were not so committed to wasting a good time slot on it. Like so many quality dramas after it, *Hill Street Blues* was buried in an undesirable part of the schedule and it was moved around frequently. Though Silverman was perhaps making a sincere effort to find a good spot for the show, the first fifteen episodes were aired in no fewer than five different time slots, including Saturday night, traditionally the lowest-rated night of the week when the very people who might be most interested in a show like *Hill Street* were out having dinner or watching a movie. Even when it settled into its regular Thursday night time slot in the second season, it spent the entire year airing after the incompatible lead-in series *Diff'rent Strokes* and *Gimme a Break.*

Not surprisingly, the ratings for the first season were very low, ranking eighty-third out of a total of ninety-seven series. When Fred Silverman renewed it in May, it was widely reported to be the lowest-rated series ever to be invited to return for another season. The decision wasn't all that miraculous, though. For one thing, NBC in general and Silverman in particular were both in need of some good press, and the critics were supplying it with raves for *Hill Street*. Furthermore, as the third-place network, NBC's schedule was full of holes and they didn't have a lot of confidence that what they would replace *Hill Street* with would do any better than it had. Both Silverman[24] and Bochco[25] agree that only a third-place network, one that wasn't flush with hits and successful formulas, would likely have aired a show as different as *Hill Street* in the first place. Finally, the prime demographics the series was earning were beginning to register as dollar signs in the eyes of network executives. While its overall rating was low, the show did very well among affluent eighteen-to-forty-nine-year-olds whose viewership could be sold to advertisers at inflated prices. All indications were suggesting that network audience shares would plummet as cable and VCRs penetrated the country, and NBC began to realize that programs like *Hill Street* rated higher in homes with cable than those without. The idea of occasionally programming for a smaller, "quality audience" became more focused here. As television-shy companies like Mercedes-Benz began buying time on *Hill Street Blues,* it became clear that NBC was rethinking the idea of "lowest common denominator" programming. By the 1982–83 season, the network had come up with their Thursday night "best night of television on television" lineup that would be a principal ingredient in a new type of target programming and a complete reversal of their fortunes. "As long as the rules dictated that each network seek one-third of the mass audience, there was no chance any would break the lockstep and adopt a higher standard," Michael Pollan wrote that year in an analysis of NBC's new strategies. "But the environment is changing in ways that could transform 'quality' from a moral to a commercial imperative."[26]

Once Silverman renewed the series in May of 1981, the future of *Hill Street Blues* was much more secure. In July of that year, Grant Tinker himself left MTM to take over Silverman's job as president of NBC. He would institutionalize the philosophy of reserving some slots in the schedule for upscale programming like *Hill Street,* and he was clearly predisposed to protect the show he had played such an important role in developing. Later that summer the show would be nominated for twenty-one Emmy Awards, more than any other series in history, including *all five* nominations in the dramatic writing category. It would go on to win eight. Between the praise in the press and the triumph at the Emmys, *Hill Street*'s ratings climbed substantially in its second season, and by its third it was a bona fide hit.

■   ■   ■

Anyone stumbling upon a rerun of *Hill Street Blues* today might be surprised at how tame it looks now. Much of what *Hill Street* did that was so new at the time has now been done to a greater degree by other shows that have adapted the *Hill Street* style. The shaking, frantic hand-held camerawork that was so jarring when it opened each *Hill Street* episode, for example, now seems steady and calm compared to the jumping and swishing camera of *Homicide: Life on the Street. Hill Street*'s "realism" has been outdone by reality shows like *Cops,* and when it comes to language and sex, *NYPD Blue* has upped the ante considerably.

But when it first appeared, *Hill Street Blues* was like nothing else before it on prime time. The audio-visual style was the first thing to strike the new viewer. Each episode opened with a scene of the morning roll call at Hill Street station, the law enforcement center of a ghetto precinct in a big unnamed city. Unlike the clean, steady, beautifully lit scenes of other network television, however, this one had the look of a low-budget documentary. Shaking cameras seemed to be roaming around the room in search of subjects, sometimes correcting their focus right before our eyes. The sound track was just as chaotic. Overlapping conversations in a style that would be compared to the movies of Robert Altman could be heard under and around the main dialogue of the roll call sergeant's recitations of the crimes *du jour*. Music wasn't incorporated at all in the roll-call scenes and only sparingly throughout the episodes, contributing to the sense that this show didn't sound like all the rest.

Robert Butler established *Hill Street*'s visual and aural styles as the director of the first five episodes of the series. His idea was to give the show a sense of urgency and realism by shooting it in a manner that was as ragtag as its principal characters and as unpredictable as the jobs they were trying to perform. This was clearly supposed to look like a documentary, not a prime-time cop show, and both the dialogue and camera movement of the roll-call scene seemed to be trying to suggest that there was no script here. ABC had, in fact, broadcast a gritty documentary a few years before that featured a similar roll-call scene. "We really stole the style of *Hill Street Blues* from something called *The Police Tapes*, which was shot in the South Bronx—Fort Apache, in fact—in black and white," Bochco remembered in a 1988 interview with *American Film:*

> The crew just followed a bunch of cops around—domestic violence, crime, street-gang murders, whatever—and put together a remarkable couple of hours of stuff that was very stark and all hand-held. It was one of the most arresting things I'd ever seen in my life. We said, "This is the feeling we want. We want to create something that gives the illusion of random event."[27]

Butler and his colleagues had, in fact, discussed shooting the entire show with hand-held cameras, in black-and-white, and on 16-millimeter film,[28] but there were limits as to how different this series would be allowed to be. As it turned out, between the occasional hand-held sequences and the confusingly noisy overlapping dialogue, the rest of each episode was much more conventional in its directorial style. Still, it didn't look like an episode of a TV show. Standard TV establishing shots were seldom used, action would pass from one group to another without a cut, extras would occasionally walk between the camera and the principal subjects, and every now and then a strikingly artsy composition would punctuate a scene. From the very start of every episode, *Hill Street*'s creators were flaunting their disregard for the standard ideas of how a TV show ought to look and sound.

The opening credits that played right after the weekly roll-call scene also indicated that something different was afoot. The cast was enormous compared to most other prime-time shows, featuring thirteen principal actors in the opening credit sequence of the first season and fourteen the following year. The typical MTM workplace family was still the model here, but the family had gotten a lot bigger. The proliferation of these characters across the screen defied the rule that TV was supposed to be easy to watch. In the early episodes, just keeping all those characters straight required a concerted and conscious effort not usually associated with watching television.

Furthermore, the characters in this crowd didn't fit the usual television profile. Captain Frank Furillo (Daniel J. Travanti) was no Starsky, Hutch, or even Columbo. Disposed to neither waving weapons, screeching tires, nor making brilliant deductions, Furillo wasn't a typical TV cop hero. A dedicated middle-aged, middle-management executive in a cheap suit, Furillo stoically went about his job, which consisted not of eliminating crime—that was presented as an impossibility—but merely of maintaining enough order that would allow him to return to fight another day. Furillo's adversary in court and occasional companion in bed and in the tub was public defender Joyce Davenport (Veronica Hamel), a professional woman with a strength and depth that was atypical of female characters on contemporary television. Patrolling the Hill was a motley collection of not-made-for-TV cops that included Officer Andy Renko (Charles Haid), a Rabelaisian redneck who talked a lot about the state of his bowels; Detective J. D. LaRue (Kiel Martin), an alcoholic on the verge of self-destruction; Mick Belker (Bruce Weitz), a misanthropic undercover detective who growled like a dog and was rumored to have once bitten the nose off a suspect, but who was also something of a Mama's boy; Phil Esterhaus (Michael Conrad), a fiftysomething Sergeant who was dating a high school girl; and Lieutenant Howard Hunter (James B. Sikking), a SWAT team leader whose near-fascist views on social management were often thrown in for comic relief.

Although *Hill Street Blues* was ostensibly a cop show, it resisted generic classification. At times, as in the roll call scenes, it was a mock documentary. At other times it borrowed the conventions of the sitcom, generating laughs by placing its characters in potentially funny situations: Officer Bobby Hill (Michael Warren) suffers through the work day with a huge boil on his butt, Lieutenant Ray Calletano (Rene Enriquez) gets audited by the IRS, Officer Lucy Bates (Betty Thomas) competes in the interdepartmental poker finals.

Perhaps most importantly, however, *Hill Street Blues* was an example of a new genre that was emerging at the time, the prime-time soap opera. Among the show's most influential innovations was its complex intertwining of many different story lines that continued from episode to episode.

*Hill Street* took the soap format in a different direction from *Dallas*. Whereas the characters on that earlier soap switched romantic partners, became embroiled in one scandal after another, and saw their fortunes made, lost, and made again, actual character development was somewhat limited. Particular stories stretched over a number of episodes, but the series as a whole seemed not to have a strong sense of artistic unity. As Joyce Carol Oates pointed out, *Hill Street* used the serial form in a way more akin to the novel. Characters really grew, changed, and developed over time.

*Hill Street* was also a lot denser and less viewer-friendly than *Dallas*. It was not uncommon for a single episode to follow threads from over a dozen stories. Eventually some of these threads would be tied up, but some of them would lead nowhere, or would finally be picked up many episodes or even many seasons later. This narrative method provided a way of finally breaking free of one of episodic television's greatest constraints: the need to tell a story from beginning to end in each episode, returning everything back to where it came from by the final credits.

Needless to say, NBC executives had a lot of trouble with *Hill Street*'s narrative density. The industry rule of thumb held that viewers could not handle more than three different stories in their heads per episode.[29] While they didn't demand paring the show down to three stories, network executives did ask that each episode have at least one story in it with a beginning, middle, and end, a request that was more or less adhered to starting in the second season.

The fact that *Hill Street Blues* was being conceived during all the frenzy surrounding the "Who shot J.R.?" phenomenon and the attendant rise of *Dallas* and the night-time soap certainly had some influence on Bochco and Kozoll. When casting around for ideas to make their cop show different from all the rest, the serial format would have obviously suggested itself. One can't help but wonder if Bochco and Kozoll would have come up with the idea of continuing stories, or if NBC would have accepted it, if they had not been developing the show on the heels of *Dallas*'s success. Without the soap opera structure, of course, *Hill Street Blues* would have been a very different series.

Besides being entangled and continuing, the stories were also unique in their content. Each character was saddled with a set of problems and vulnerabilities that were explored and played out in excruciating detail. And the final act platitudes so common to television crime shows gave way in *Hill Street* to a resigned hopelessness that led Michael Pollan to characterize the show as "post-liberal, shading to neoconservative":

> The Blues are well-intentioned men who have earned the melancholy wisdom that comes only after idealism has given way to experience; they are undeluded. All around them things fall apart: Squad cars break down; paint flakes off the precinct walls; boilers go berserk. The program shares the neoconservative nightmare of a society in which authority is rapidly yielding to anomie. In better times men might strive for justice; for now stability will have to do.[30]

Along with the style, structure, and story content that made *Hill Street Blues* unusual, there was also the flood of mischievously placed scatological and sexual references that would become one of Steven Bochco's calling cards.[31] He and his writers scattered such references throughout their scripts as markers that announced that they were breaking the rules, and getting them on the air became a kind of comic game that they played with the network's standards department. Whereas *All in the Family* had broken ground ten years ago by acknowledging that its characters used the bathroom, *Hill Street Blues* actually showed them doing it, employing the station's men's room as a principal site of action. It was not uncommon for two or more characters to advance the plot of the episode while standing side-by-side at the urinals. Fairly overt visual and verbal references to feces, urine, flatulence, vomit, saliva, sweat, pus, nasal discharges, vaginal discharges, and semen were made frequently. Fay Furillo's shoes were puked upon by a vagrant and her living-room carpet defecated upon by burglars. Howard Hunter was peed on by his own dog and the governor's dog, and he lost one of his few love interests when she left him for a urologist. In one episode, entitled "Ewe and Me, Babe," a routine call revealed a man who had been living with a female sheep. In another a prostitute was arrested who bore the allegorical name "Lotta Gue."

Such material served a number of purposes. For one thing, the unsanitized inclusion of all these gross details added to the veneer of realism that the show so carefully strived for. When describing the show to James B. Sikking, Bochco had said, "It's a western and we're gonna leave all the horseshit on the street."[32] The material also served a nice metaphoric function, letting the leaking, flatulating, puking human bodies represent the equally unhealthy body politic of the precinct. But most of all it represented Bochco's unabashed pushing at the traditional boundaries of commercial television. "Part of my job as I see it," he said while making the show, "is to expand those boundaries."[33]

Bochco was at his best when fighting for the right to tell the story of a man and his sheep. These fights made good copy, and this kind of material provided an easy standard by which to measure whose side was winning. Every time another outrageous moment appeared on *Hill Street*, the old television order crumbled a little more. "Little by little, we've chipped away [at network censorship rules]," Bochco claimed in a *Playboy* interview with the entire *Hill Street* cast.[34] By 1983, Bochco had managed a concession from NBC which allowed him to show, very briefly, naked buttocks in the players' locker room of his short-lived baseball drama *Bay City Blues*. Ten years later on *NYPD Blue*, of course, such shots would not be so brief, and *Hill Street*'s standby street euphemisms like "dirt-bag" and "scuz-ball" had been replaced with more authentic hyphenated street patois.

∎ ∎ ∎

As many times as they had threatened to quit over network practices, neither Bochco nor Kozoll left *Hill Street Blues* as the result of their relationship with NBC. Kozoll was seriously not interested in doing episodic television, and he stepped down as *Hill Street*'s coexecutive producer at the end of the first season and left the show entirely the following year. He went on to write the script for *First Blood* (1982), the first of the "Rambo" movies. Bochco left under less peaceful circumstances after the fifth season, fired by MTM for refusing to adhere to cost containment requests made by the company. With Tinker no longer at the helm, with production budgets rising much faster than network licensing fees, and with MTM's new status as a much larger, less personal operation, Bochco began to fight with them as he had with the network. Shortly after they had a hundred episodes of *Hill Street* in the can, the magic number for a potentially good syndication deal, the bosses at MTM decided they could afford to lose the man who had been the soul of the show.

Bochco got the last laugh, however. Some critics began to turn on *Hill Street* during its sixth season, attributing its slide in quality to Bochco's departure. Bochco meanwhile signed a deal with Twentieth Century-Fox and created *L.A. Law*. In its seventh and final season, *Hill Street* was yanked from its legendary Thursday nighttime slot on NBC and replaced with *L.A. Law,* which went on to become a bigger hit than *Hill Street.* In 1987, Laurence Tisch and William Paley invited Bochco to be the president of CBS Entertainment.[35] Though he didn't take the job, the offer was evidence of how much network attitudes had changed since the debut of *Hill Street.* Bochco's program philosophy hadn't changed at all; in fact, *L.A. Law* was often feistier than *Hill Street* had been. That a trouble-making maverick like Bochco would be offered the keys to the candy store showed the directions in which network television was willing to go in the complicated new marketplace.

After six months in Tuesday night exile, *Hill Street Blues* was canceled. The *Washington Post's* Tom Shales, who had been a cheerleader for the show from the very start, mourned its passing by saying: "We usually think of a masterpiece as something that hangs from a wall or rests between covers or occupies a couple of hours on a stage or a screen, not something that unfolds over the course of 146 installments. But put them all together and masterpiece is just about what you've got."[36]

In the final episode of *The Mary Tyler Moore Show* the station changes managers; in the final episode of *Hill Street Blues* the station burns up. In the self-conscious style so typical of all MTM productions, one of the final lines of the series seemed to be saying as much about *Hill Street Blues* as it was about the Hill Street station. "This building came through like a champ," the fire marshal says as he inspects the gutted structure. "They don't build 'em like this anymore." But he was wrong. Thanks to *Hill Street,* they were building more of 'em like that than ever before.

▪   ▪   ▪

Todd Gitlin saw *Hill Street Blues* as the exception that proved the rules of American commercial television. He saw it as an innovative, at times even brilliant show that was just lucky enough to emerge "at the end of a chain of ifs."[37] It was, he said, "commercial television banging up against its limitations, revealing at the moment of its triumph just how powerful are the pressures and formulas that keep prime time so close to dead center."[38] Indeed, he was right that a lot of unusual circumstances had to come together before a show like *Hill Street* would ever have made it onto a network schedule—circumstances that didn't present themselves very often. Given the commercial success of the show, however, those once rare and anomalous circumstances became institutionalized as a recipe for a promising new programming form. Many of the standard limitations of television had given way to all that banging, and the way many executives thought about prime time had been significantly changed. The idea of giving a strong, intelligent producer the freedom to develop his or her vision, and then giving the resulting show a chance to find a select audience had become a new network strategy thanks to *Hill Street Blues.* For years to come, network executives would develop new programs with the *Hill Street* model in mind.

Gitlin was right when he said that "breakthroughs in form soon become fossilized as formula,"[39] but this wasn't necessarily a bad thing. Sure, as in any long-running series, the innovations *Hill Street* introduced in 1981 had become quite familiar by 1983. "By definition, once you are a known quantity, you don't surprise," Bochco observed. "The reality of network television is that you can't surprise. The truth is, we never started out to surprise people. We simply were, I guess, surprising. But it's never been a motivation."[40] Constant innovation isn't a prerequisite of good programming, and the formula that had become fossilized was a good one that would inspire more than a decade of quality series.

As evidence of *Hill Street*'s eventual loss of novelty, Gitlin dismisses *St. Elsewhere* in a single sentence as a copycat hospital show "that aped *Hill Street*'s texture if nothing else."[41] *St. Elsewhere,* however, was more than just "*Hill Street* in a hospital." It took many of *Hill Street*'s innovations and brought them to an even higher, more mature level. *Hill Street Blues* had done more than establish a formula. It had provided a workable model whereby literate and complex drama could be made for prime-time television. Without *Hill Street*'s success, *St. Elsewhere* would never have been made. Without the memory of *Hill Street*'s slow start in the ratings, *St. Elsewhere* would never have been renewed. *Hill Street* provided a map whereby that long chain of ifs could be negotiated again and again. Without that map, the nine other shows discussed in this book might never have existed. In each case those shows were influenced and inspired by *Hill Street,* but they weren't mindless copies of it.

# 5

# Quality—The Next Generation:
## *St. Elsewhere*

Michael Kozoll, the co-creator of *Hill Street Blues*, called his program the product of "a long series of flukes."[1] Tom Fontana, one of the producers of *St. Elsewhere*, called his show "an aberration" resulting from a set of circumstances that "I don't think . . . will ever happen again."[2] By the mid-1980s, though, flukes and aberrations had become an important part of a new network product line. The "quality drama," as it had been defined by *Hill Street Blues*, depended upon its aberrant nature for its elevated artistic status. A new luxury line had been established that boasted of being different from and better than the rest of television's offerings. The well-publicized low ratings and near cancellations of these shows, combined with the regularly reported battles between their producers and the network executives, provided an effective promotional campaign that announced to upscale audiences that these shows were too good for a mass medium like television and therefore good enough for them.

Though *Hill Street Blues* ultimately became a modest hit even by regular network standards, NBC was already developing a copycat series while *Hill Street* was still in its very low-rated first season. Shortly after CBS canceled MTM's *The White Shadow* in the middle of the 1980–81 season, NBC's Fred Silverman offered Grant Tinker a thirteen-episode order for an hour-long drama based on an idea that had been floating around at MTM and that Tinker had been calling "*Hill Street Blues* in a hospital." It clearly wasn't *Hill Street*'s ratings that had sold the idea for *St. Elsewhere*, Tinker claimed. "It was the nature of the show: the multiple stories, the ensemble cast. I was already proud of *Hill Street* before it was a success, so I used that for a selling point."[3] In buying *St. Elsewhere*, NBC had given the go-ahead to a show that was being modeled after one of their lowest-rated series of the season. "They really believed in the *Hill Street* concept," said Mark Tinker, Grant Tinker's son and one of *St. Elsewhere*'s producers. "They thought it was different and exciting and they were comparing *St. Elsewhere* to it before it had caught on."[4] That Silverman was already nurturing its clone in the spring of 1981 suggests that his subsequent renewal of *Hill Street Blues* was part of a larger plan to attract a demographic elite with a new type of programming.

Many have argued that the trick didn't work quite as well the second time around. With its production offices located tellingly one floor below *Hill Street*'s in the MTM building, *St. Elsewhere* spent most of its prime-time life in the shadow of its precocious older sibling. It didn't win as many awards, its ratings never climbed as high, and most critics, though they showered the show with accolades, never quite accorded it the historical significance of *Hill Street*. Unlike Steven Bochco, *St. Elsewhere*'s executive producer Bruce Paltrow didn't become a household name during the run of his series. And the "*Hill Street Blues* in a hospital" designation proved to be a hard one to live down.

But the notion that *St. Elsewhere* evolved out of *Hill Street* is an oversimplified one. Both NBC and MTM had in fact come up with the basic idea that would become *St. Elsewhere* before they started toying with the concept that would become *Hill Street*. In 1979, Silverman had ordered a pilot from MTM called *Operating Room*, which followed the professional and personal lives of three doctors who worked in a Los Angeles hospital. With its large cast, its "realistic" feel, and its facile blending of comedy and drama, *Operating Room* began experimenting with some of the characteristics that *Hill Street* would later employ so much more effectively. Two of the show's actors, in fact, would become members of the *Hill Street* cast. The pilot was produced by Mark Tinker and directed by Bruce Paltrow, both of whom would go on to make *St. Elsewhere*, and it was cowritten by Paltrow and Steven Bochco. Silverman ultimately decided not to order a series based on *Operating Room*, claiming that the audience wouldn't accept such an irreverent portrayal of doctors. "Let's try it as a cop show first," he suggested, "and if it works we'll do it with doctors."[5] Less than a year after cowriting *Operating Room*, Bochco began developing *Hill Street*. In his autobiography, Brandon Tartikoff, Silverman's chief programmer at NBC, claimed that "*St. Elsewhere* was our second and much more successful attempt to execute *Operating Room*, a pilot that . . . was actually the predecessor to *Hill Street*."[6] At some basic level, then, *St. Elsewhere* wasn't so much "*Hill Street* in a hospital" as *Hill Street* was "*Operating Room* in a police station."

The most important creative impetus behind the early development of *St. Elsewhere*, however, came from Joshua Brand. Brand had been working on the writing staff of *The White Shadow* in 1980, when his ex-college roommate began calling him and telling him about his experiences as an intern at the Cleveland Clinic. Brand had not worked on *Operating Room* and had never even seen *Hill Street Blues*[7] when he began to concoct an idea for a medical drama that would take place in a once elite but now run-down institution like Boston City Hospital. When he told Grant Tinker about the idea, Tinker thought immediately of *Hill Street* and encouraged Brand to develop the show in the same style.[8] Brand turned to John Falsey, his *White Shadow* writing partner, for help with the project.

By April 1981, *The White Shadow* was history, NBC was committed to thirteen episodes of a series from MTM, and Grant Tinker had put most of *The White Shadow*'s creative staff to work on the development of *St. Elsewhere*. As executive producer, Bruce Paltrow was the boss, as he had been on *The White Shadow*. With a made-for-TV movie, a few pilots, and a reasonably successful series under his belt, Paltrow was considered a bankable and dependable producer, and NBC had made it a condition of the deal that he oversee the series. Under him were four writer-producers with classy credentials and not a lot of TV experience. Brand had graduated magna cum laude from the City College of New York in 1972 with Phi Beta Kappa honors and a B.A. in English literature. He continued his studies on a fellowship at Columbia, where he earned a master's degree with honors in 1974, and he was just beginning to gain some notoriety as a playwright when he took the job on *The White Shadow*. Falsey had also been an English major, a 1975 graduate of Hampshire College who went on to get a Master of Fine Arts degree in creative writing from the renowned University of Iowa Writer's Workshop and who had written for the *New Yorker*. John Masius also got his first job in television on *The White Shadow*. Prior to that he had been an aspiring playwright with a B.A. in economics from the University of Pennsylvania and an M.B.A. from U.C.L.A. Of the four, Mark Tinker, a graduate of Syracuse University's television, radio, and film department, was the only one with experience in the medium that went beyond *The White Shadow*. He'd been directing and producing on various MTM shows since 1975, and his directing of *St. Elsewhere* would provide the show with its unique visual identity.

In addition to these four producers, Paltrow hired a writer early in the first season who, along with John Masius, would provide the narrative heart and soul of *St. Elsewhere* by its second season. Tom Fontana had not been part of *The White Shadow* team. In fact, he'd never been part of any television team. A theater-arts major from Buffalo State University, he had been a playwright in residence at the Williamstown

Theater Festival in Western Massachusetts when Paltrow met him and invited him to write a script for the new series.

Whereas *Hill Street Blues* deviated from the traditional cop show because its creators had grown sick and tired of the formula they had been working in for so long, *St. Elsewhere* deviated from the traditional doctor show because most of its creative staff didn't know much about the formula in the first place. They had, of course, seen *Ben Casey, Dr. Kildare, Marcus Welby,* and *Trapper John,* and they intended, as *Hill Street*'s producers had, to go against the traditional generic grain. As neophytes in the medium, however, many of *St. Elsewhere*'s principal staff may have found it easier to break rules that they never really knew very well. And break them they did. Their doctors struggled with an assortment of complex personal problems, and their patients were as likely as not to leave the hospital with a sheet pulled over their faces.

St. Eligius Hospital, like the Hill Street station, was a collapsing old institution in a collapsing old neighborhood, and its hallways were often the site of chaos and confusion. A comparison between the two shows was both appropriate and inevitable, but there were some important differences. *St. Elsewhere*'s cameras, though they were often hand-held, didn't shake as much as *Hill Street*'s, for one thing. Instead, they lyrically flowed from scene to scene, often without a cut, as the action moved through hallways and up and down staircases, from the nurses' station to a patient's room to the hospital cafeteria. And the lighting, though dark and at times even gothic, was softer than it was on *Hill Street.*

Instead of a single narrative center of authority, as Captain Furillo had been, *St. Elsewhere* offered three, each an established doctor with his own personal cross to bear. Daniel Aushlander (Norman Lloyd), the administrative head of the hospital, was a distinguished liver specialist who was himself fighting cancer of the liver; Donald Westphall (Ed Flanders), the chief of staff, was a widower who played father not only to the hospital's residents but to his own teenaged daughter and preteen autistic son; and Mark Craig (William Daniels) was a brilliant but intolerant surgeon who expertly repaired and replaced the hearts of his patients while heartlessly bullying his colleagues and family. The core of the large ensemble was made up of a collection of young resident doctors, specialists, nurses, and orderlies.

In a pattern that would become pro forma for the quality drama, the ratings were prodigiously terrible. Throughout its first season, *St. Elsewhere* managed twice to hit the very bottom of the weekly Nielsen barrel, and overall it ranked eighty-sixth out of ninety-eight series. The soon to be familiar story then began to play itself out. By the spring of 1983, the show's cancellation was a foregone conclusion. "I'd give it a seventy-five to one shot," producer Mark Tinker told authors Mark

Christensen and Cameron Stauth in April. "And that's because I'm an optimist. *Hill Street,* however radical, was still within the timeworn genre of cops and robbers. People still want to see their doctors as mythically infallible."[9] Shortly thereafter, NBC told MTM not to expect a renewal, and the *St. Elsewhere* staff had dispersed. Executive producer Paltrow had gone to London, writer John Masius was in Hawaii, and both Falsey and Brand had already left the show as the result of creative differences with the other producers over its style and tone. Mark Tinker was the only one left in Los Angeles to take the call, which reported that the show had, after all, been renewed. "It was like a call from the governor," he claims of the unexpected reprieve.[10] Astonished reporters across the country expressed pleased amazement over the renewal, offering a variety of theories to explain it.

Most accounts give credit for saving the show to Grant Tinker, who'd left MTM to become the head of NBC in July of 1981. "My contribution to *St. Elsewhere* was playing a decisive role in getting it picked up after its first season," Tinker himself recalls. "But for me, as Chairman and head guy, and a programmer by trade, it would have bitten the dust. People in our trade are not known for their patience, and *Elsewhere* was floundering more than most."[11] Though the renewal may have been unheard of a few years ago, however, all the surprise was uncalled for in 1983. After the experience with *Hill Street Blues,* NBC had gotten the hang of dealing with programs that had low ratings, great demographics, and good critical notices. *St. Elsewhere's* modus operandi was much like *Hill Street's* had been in its first season, and now *Hill Street* was one of NBC's only hits. By the time *St. Elsewhere's* renewal came up, the network already had a strategy in place that allowed them to show patience with such a show. While they were programming mass-audience hits like *The A-Team* and *Knight Rider,* they were also doing well with more upscale fare like *Cheers* and *Hill Street.*

Upon renewal NBC did make a few "suggestions," all of which also sounded pretty familiar. The show was too depressing, they claimed, and it needed at least one story line tied up in every episode. Most of all, it needed a romance like the one between Frank Furillo and Joyce Davenport on *Hill Street.*[12] The producers took some pieces of network advice, ignored others, and went on to make six full seasons' worth of episodes. The show's average seasonal rating never placed it above forty-ninth place out of around a hundred series, but it made lots of money for the network, proving the efficacy of NBC's theory that going after a smaller audience of select viewers could be very good business. Anxious to reach the relatively wealthy audience that *St. Elsewhere* was attracting, advertisers made the show the fourth best-selling program on the network by its third season.[13]

By the time it was all over, the series had racked up sixty-three Emmy nominations and thirteen wins, a Peabody, a Humanitas, and an assortment of other awards. More importantly, it had launched a number of significant careers. Within a few years, *Newsday*'s TV critic Marvin Kitman remarked that "There are more creators/writers of *St. Elsewhere* floating around these days than people who came over on the Mayflower. [They], along with writers for *Cosby* and *M\*A\*S\*H*, are the three leading cash crops in Southern California."[14] At the start of the 1992–93 season, Falsey and Brand had a critically acclaimed show on each of the three major networks: *Northern Exposure* (CBS), *I'll Fly Away* (NBC), and *Going to Extremes* (ABC). Tom Fontana went on to coexecutive-produce *Homicide: Life on the Street* with Baltimore film auteur Barry Levinson. Other members of the *St. Elsewhere* staff went on to work on series like *Moonlighting*, *China Beach*, *L.A. Law*, *Civil Wars*, *NYPD Blue*, *ER*, and *Chicago Hope*. Denzel Washington, of course, who had been unknown when he started in his role as Dr. Phillip Chandler, was on the brink of superstardom when the show ended.

■　■　■

Though it may have been inspired by the innovations of *Hill Street Blues*, *St. Elsewhere* often strayed even further from traditional television conventions than its predecessor had. In its quieter, more anonymous way—the show never made the cover of *TV Guide*—*St. Elsewhere* did some truly shocking things. It was the first prime-time drama to tell a story about an AIDS patient, for example, which it did in December 1983. In the 1987–88 season, six years before the debut of *NYPD Blue*, network TV's first full moon shot was launched on *St. Elsewhere* when Dr. Westphall dropped his trousers in front of his supervisor just before he resigned from the hospital.

　　*St. Elsewhere* also broke a long-standing television rule that said that main characters aren't supposed to die. There had, of course, been several exceptions to this rule on other series over the years, but they tended to be on very special episodes, and they were usually the result of an actor's actual death or resignation from the show. Even *Hill Street Blues*, for all its innovation, remained fairly traditional on this front. Officers Hill and Renko were gunned down at the end of the pilot, but they were resurrected in the second episode. Lieutenant Howard Hunter, in a striking moment at the end of one episode, put his service revolver to his head and fired just after the final fade to black. But it turned out that one of his colleagues, having sensed Howard's depression, had substituted his bullets with blanks, and Howard sported nothing worse than a bandaged powder burn in the next episode. Sergeant Esterhaus was revealed to have died in flagrante in the clutches of

Grace Gardner only after the real-life death of actor Michael Conrad, and Officer Joe Coffey was killed only after it became known that Ed Marinaro was leaving the show.

St. Eligus, on the other hand, was a much more unpredictably dangerous place for its regular cast. Just because your name and face appeared during the opening theme song did not necessarily mean you'd make it through the episode. Resident Wendy Armstrong (Kim Miyori) quite unexpectedly committed suicide in the second season; her telegenic but incompetent colleague Peter White (Terence Knox) turned out to be a rapist and was shot and killed by yet another major character, nurse Shirley Daniels (Ellen Bry), who was subsequently sent to prison; Dr. Bobby Caldwell (Mark Harmon), the show's romantic leading man, left the hospital after contracting AIDS and was eventually revealed to have died of the disease; Elliot Axelrod (Stephen Furst) died in the final season when he disconnected himself from his life support machine after bypass surgery; and Dr. Daniel Aushlander succumbed to a stroke in the final episode. No one was safe, and the actors knew it. Howie Mandel, who played resident clown Wayne Fiscus and managed to survive the entire series, claimed that the lives of the characters in the show were as tenuous and vulnerable as the lives of real people. "I could get hit by a car and killed on my way to work," he said, "and so could Fiscus. You always felt they could've killed anybody off. It wasn't past what they would do on *St. Elsewhere*."[15]

Nor was *St. Elsewhere* to be outdone in the areas of sex, scatology, and forbidden language, all trademarks of *Hill Street Blues*. NBC Standards and Practices executive Ralph Daniels claimed that *Hill Street*'s Bochco and *St. Elsehwere*'s Paltrow actually competed to see who could slip the most outrageous stuff past the "censors" who worked in Daniels' office.[16] Given the nature of a hospital, with its ample narrative opportunities to feature a whole catalog of bodily fluids and functions, Paltrow had a distinct advantage in this competition. From testicular cancer to excessive flatulence, the writers of *St. Elsewhere* used the guise of clinical jargon to talk about parts and dysfunctions of the human body that could never have gotten by the standards department in any other context.

Many of the ailments and medical procedures on *St. Elsewhere* were aggressively made-*not*-for-TV, and their presence was yet another proclamation that the show was groundbreaking and daring. Various patients suffered from prostate cancer, hemorrhoids, hernias, infertility, impotence, premature ejaculation, an inability to urinate, and an inability to defecate. Doctors performed mastectomies, hysterectomies, vasetomies, sex change operations, colostomies, foreskin reconstructions, and once they even had to treat a colleague whose penis was stuck in his zipper. Sometimes these stories were very serious; sometimes they were irreverently funny.

And sometimes they provided the context for some of the dirtiest jokes ever told on television. The content of these jokes might have been bawdy and obvious, but their form was extremely subtle. Often only the most discerning viewer could even catch them. In one episode, for example, a semiregular patient has come in for an inflatable penile prosthesis that he needs after prostate surgery has left him impotent. In one scene, we hear the patient behind the curtain of his hospital bed trying out the device for the first time. After a good deal of progressively more excited pumping, we hear a loud pop, followed by the patient's "Oh-oh." In the very next scene, the carefully listening viewer could have heard a name being called over the hospital intercom system: "Paging Mr. Rise, Mr. Peter Rise." In another episode, Dr. Craig is dictating his novel to his assistant: "Chapter Ten. She came in from the garden, cheeks flushed, arms filled with flowers. I sat playing the Wurlitzer. She said wistfully, 'Where would you like these?' I smiled. 'Put roses on the piano and tulips on the organ.'" Having slipped a reference to one variety of oral sex into a network TV show, the writers went for two in the same scene. Stumped on a plot point in his novel, Dr. Craig's assistant helps him "think about what happens to Constance, the daughter, after the Lingus family reunion." In yet another episode, a doctor who learns, in an exchange that is barely audible above the din of the hospital hallway, that one of his patients has "acute angina," responds, "A good thing. She's got ugly legs."

There were hundreds of these jokes, some much filthier and more graphic than the examples above and nearly all of which required very close attention to catch.[17] Too disguised to offend the general public, these dirty little secrets gave great pleasure and pride to dedicated fans of the show as they carefully identified and chortled over them. "I have a tremendous respect for my audience," Paltrow said when describing the "just for sport" nature of these games. "They are so hip and bright. The people who get it aren't offended."[18]

*St. Elsewhere* was at its hippest, however, when it was making sly references to itself and other popular entertainments. Whereas the "in-joke" is told with tiresome frequency on television today, it was quite uncommon only a dozen years ago. *Hill Street's* writers seldom indulged in the practice, but after *St. Elsewhere* these self-conscious narrative devices became one of the calling cards of "quality" television. In her 1984 essay on the history of MTM, Jane Feuer told us why, and the reason was similar to the one that explained the profusion of dirty jokes as well:

> "Intertextuality," a literary term, refers in its broadest sense to the ways in which texts incorporate previous texts. Sometimes this takes

the form of "self-reflexivity," when a text refers in self-conscious fashion back to itself . . . . It has been argued that these self-conscious strategies distinguish "high-art" from the unselfconscious popular arts—such as TV series. . . . Intertextuality and self-reflexivity operate . . . as a way of distinguishing the "quality" from the everyday product.[19]

As we saw in chapter 3, MTM's writers and producers had been playing intertextual games since 1970, but in *St. Elsewhere* they went crazy.

After its eleventh-hour renewal at the end of its first season, producers and network executives alike agreed that what the new *St. Elsewhere* needed was a few good yuks. Although a hospital, especially one in a decaying urban neighborhood, hardly seems the ideal location for pies in the face or seltzer down the pants, it made sense that perhaps a little humor was just what the show needed to take the edge off the funereal setting. Furthermore, what the series premise lacked in comedic opportunity was made up for by the comic abilities of the cast. Howie Mandel, after all, had been a stand-up comedian before he joined the series, and Ed Begley, Jr., who portrayed resident doctor Victor Ehrlich, seemed to be at his best when playing a dignified clown reminiscent of Edward Everett Horton. Even such sedate actors as William Daniels and Norman Lloyd, both firmly grounded in the dramatic tradition, would go on to prove that they could play a room with considerable aplomb.

After the first season, Brandon Tartikoff and Grant Tinker met with Paltrow and told him that they expected a cheerier atmosphere to go along with the intense drama in the subsequent season. Tinker specifically asked if the hospital could be made a "lighter, brighter place."[20] On the first episode of the second season, there was an immediate sign of the production team's good intentions on both fronts. In an early scene in the first act, Dr. Chandler asks Dr. Westphall why the hospital halls are filled with scaffolding. Westphall responds that a new paint job is under way as "a gift from the Chairman of the Board" who "thinks brighter walls will let our patients live longer." This scene reveals that not only had the *St. Elsewhere* staff acceded to Grant Tinker's dictum by physically lightening the place up, they'd also initiated a new comic philosophy. The fact that only a limited number of viewers would ever catch this knavish dig at what they thought was "Chairman" Tinker's obsession with "lighter and brighter" was part of the fun and added to the show's air of exclusivity. Though these kinds of jokes had been present a little during the first season, the new, more humorous *St. Elsewhere* would now rely much more heavily upon them as a major source of comic material. From the obvious to the obscure, self-conscious stabs at television and at *St. Elsewhere* itself would soon punctuate nearly every script.

Along with the entertainment category in the blockbuster adult board-game Trivial Pursuit, *St. Elsewhere* provided a forum where tele-literate viewers could test and strut their familiarity with the popular mass media. In other categories of knowledge during the 1980s, Americans in general and young Americans in particular, were often reminded about how stupid they were. Though at least some college education had become commonplace for many segments of the population, best-selling books like Allan Bloom's *The Closing of the American Mind* (1987) and E. D. Hirsch's *Cultural Literacy* (1987) argued that we entered the educational system with our heads full of mush and left it in much the same state. Many didn't score very well on Hirsch's cultural literacy test—a sixty-three-page list of "what literate Americans know"—but maybe it was just because he wasn't asking the right questions.

While Hirsch's list asked readers to identify Currier & Ives and the Punic Wars, *St. Elsewhere* was more likely to ask them who shot J.R. or where the beef was. Truly "successful" viewing of *St. Elsewhere* often depended upon how many of the obscure media references one could find in each episode. The best and the brightest of the TV generation would delight in explicating examples like the following to less scholarly viewers:

• In one episode, a trio of hospital staffers named Charles, Burrows, and Charles are offhandedly mentioned by a nurse as having reserved a meeting room. (Glen Charles, James Burrows, and Les Charles were the executive producers of *Cheers.*) In another, Dr. Craig takes attendance in a gathering of new residents, calling out the names "Weinberger, Brooks, Allan, and Burns." (Ed. Weinberger, James Brooks, and Allan Burns were all writers on MTM's first series, *The Mary Tyler Moore Show.*)

• Throughout the series, quick off-the-cuff lines laced with hidden media references were commonly made in St. Eligius's morgue. Once a doctor mentions that "the Douglas family wants to see [the body of] their Uncle Bub." (Uncle Bub was the crusty pre-Uncle Charlie mother-substitute to the Douglases in *My Three Sons.*) In another morgue scene a request is made for the report on "the Hasselhoff car wreck." (David Hasselhoff was currently starring in *Knight Rider,* an NBC action-adventure about a futuristic car whose voice was supplied by William Daniels, one of *St. Elsewhere*'s stars.) Casual mentions were made of autopsy reports on patients named "Spelling," "Sagansky," and "Nielsen." (Aaron Spelling presided over *Hart to Hart, Dynasty,* and *Hotel,* all of which were series that at one time had aired on ABC during *St. Elsewhere*'s time-slot, and all of which trounced *St. Elsewhere* in the ratings. Jeff Sagansky had been a programming chief at NBC during much of *St. Elsewhere*'s run. In the last example, the entire Nielsen family had apparently died while watching TV.)

• In the one-hundredth episode, a patient named Cindy Kayshun is reported to still be going strong after a hundred episodes of angina. (An industry rule of thumb at the time was that a series needed a hundred episodes to assure a lucrative syndication deal. Of Cindy's prognosis, a doctor says he "hopes she lives forever.")

Never delivered with rim shots or knowing glances at the camera, these jokes were always intricately woven into the narrative, often as part of very serious and emotional scenes. E. D. Hirsch might have let these quickie references go by without batting a well-read eye; those familiar with the traditions of American television, however, were laughing their heads off.

The in-jokes came in several varieties. One commonly used device was to revive old TV characters. This would happen in one of three ways. The first was to introduce characters with the same name and profession of a well-known TV character from another show, but to have them played by a different actor from the original or to have them mentioned only in passing. Various episodes of *St. Elsewhere* included or referred to a barber named Floyd (*The Andy Griffith Show*); doctors named Kiley (*Marcus Welby, M.D.*), Gannon (*Medical Center*), Steiner (*Medic*), and B. J. Hunnicut (*M\*A\*S\*H*); a nurse named Consuelo Lopez (*Marcus Welby, M.D.*); cops named Pete Malloy (*Adam-12*), Mike Stone (*The Streets of San Francisco*), and Detective Zito (*Miami Vice*); and a Russian nanny named Natasha who had moved to Boston from Frostbite Falls, Minnesota (*Rocky and His Friends, The Bullwinkle Show*).

The second method was to have TV characters from past series appear in the show as their original characters and played by their original stars. Byron Stewart reprised his role as *The White Shadow*'s Warren Coolidge in four seasons of *St. Elsewhere*, and Jack Riley came back in an episode playing the neurotically antisocial Mr. Carlin, the same role he played in *The Bob Newhart Show*.

Finally, stars of classic series were brought back in new incarnations. Among them were Alan Young (*Mr. Ed*), Jane Wyatt (*Father Knows Best*), Ray Walston (*My Favorite Martian*), Jack Dodson (*The Andy Griffith Show; Mayberry, R.F.D.*), Charlotte Rae (*Car 54, Where Are You?; The Facts of Life*), Betty White (*The Mary Tyler Moore Show*), and Richard Kline (*Three's Company*). The most spectacular example of this strategy was the casting of *five* former members of the cast of *The Steve Allen Show*— Steve Allen, Jayne Meadows, Louis Nye, Bill Dana, and Tom Poston— as the parents of a variety of the residents. Though the stars in all of the above examples were now playing different characters, there were usually plenty of hidden references to the roles that made them famous. Don DeFore, for example, played a patient who reported that he was married to a woman "who keeps house and has beautiful hazel eyes." DeFore, of course, had starred in *Hazel*, a 1960s sitcom about a housekeeper. John Astin played the husband of doctor Paulette Kiem (France Nuyen), and, like his Gomez Addams character on *The Addams Family*, he was driven into erotic frenzies whenever his wife spoke French.

These three strategies would occasionally mix and get terribly confusing. In one episode, Warren Coolidge meets a character played by Timothy Van Patten in the hospital hallway. While Byron Stewart was still in his *White Shadow* role as Coolidge, Timothy Van Patten was no longer playing the role of Salami, one of Coolidge's *White Shadow* teammates. Needless to say, Coolidge is disappointed when Van Patten's character fails to remember him.

The in-jokes considerably lightened the tone of the series. *New York Daily News* TV critic David Bianculli, one of *St. Elsewhere*'s major boosters and the one who coined the term teleliteracy in his book of the same title, once said that "hunting for the in-jokes, hidden references, and bad puns within each episode of *St. Elsewhere* is one of the least known, but most enjoyable, spectator sports in America."[21] In a story in *People*, Howie Mandel called the series a "drama-game show."[22] Whereas shows like *Jeopardy!* required knowledge of traditional subjects like history and politics, scoring big on *St. Elsewhere* required one to be literate in the fields most of its viewers knew best: sports, movies, rock 'n' roll, and, most of all, television. To a great extent, *St. Elsewhere* was made by and for the segment of the baby boom generation that columnist Bob Greene dubbed the "yuppies," a group whose collective knowledge of these subjects was extraordinary.[23]

Intertextuality and self-reflexivity had, of course, been used in television before. As early as the 1950s, episodes of *The George Burns and Gracie Allen Show* would occasionally feature George retiring to his room to watch his personal TV set to see how the very episode we were watching would turn out. Years later, *Burns and Allen* alumni Al Simon and Paul Henning brought out *Green Acres*, an at-times surrealistic sitcom that often referred to its own sound track and production credits.[24] *Get Smart* was filled with allusions to everything from the writers' previous TV series credits to the name of the program's art director.[25] But it was MTM Enterprises that took these devices to a new level of sophistication.

The fun and games reached meltdown in the *St. Elsewhere* episode that aired on November 20, 1985.[26] A recurring character has been admitted yet again to St. Eligius's psychiatric ward because he has no memory of who he is. Referred to by the staff as "John Doe #6" (Oliver Clark), he makes valiant but unsuccessful attempts to work with the doctors who try to help him reestablish his identity. Unable to remember his own "reality," he eventually turns to television to adopt a new one. A confirmed couch potato, much of what comes out of John's mouth was originally written for TV. He strings together jingles from commercials, lines from classic series episodes, and trademark sign-offs of well-known news anchors. While most of the patients in the hospital are getting physical nourishment from an I.V. tube, John Doe #6 gets spiritual nourishment from a TV tube. Near the beginning of the episode, he watches the end of an installment of *The Mary Tyler Moore Show* and becomes convinced that he has finally discovered his true identity—he is Mary Richards.

From here on, the episode's intertextuality slowly achieves critical mass, as it becomes a seriocomic homage to the history of MTM Enterprises and of prime-time television itself. The interplay between different levels of fictional "reality" is staggering. Consider the following:

• Oliver Clark plays John Doe #6 playing Mary Tyler Moore playing Mary Richards.

• Also in the psych ward is Jack Riley playing Mr. Carlin, the same neurotic character he played in MTM's *The Bob Newhart Show,* but Clark/Doe/Moore/Richards instead recognizes him as Rhoda (Valerie Harper), Mary's best friend on *The Mary Tyler Moore Show* and the subject of her own spin-off series. So Jack Riley is playing Mr. Carlin who is being mistaken for Valerie Harper playing Rhoda Morgenstern.

• Betty White also has a role in this episode as a U.S. Navy doctor. John Doe #6, of course, recognizes her as "Happy Homemaker" Sue Ann Nivens, the character Betty White played in *The Mary Tyler Moore Show,* but she doesn't know what he's talking about, because she's now in a different role. Betty White's character is not, however, completely out of the TV loop. She refers to her boss at NASA as Commander Healy, whom we can assume was once NASA's Major Healy on *I Dream of Jeannie,* a character played by Bill Daly, who also starred in *The Bob Newhart Show* in which Mr. Carlin was a character but who John Doe #6 recognizes as a character from another MTM series, *Rhoda,* even though Jack Riley *is,* unlike Betty White, playing his original MTM role in this episode, complete with Mr. Carlin's old red cardigan sweater. The presence in the episode of Mr. Carlin and the mention by a sane character of Commander Healy imply that the world of *The Bob Newhart Show* and the world of *I Dream of Jeannie* are both part of *St. Elsewhere*'s "real" world, which would mean that Bill Daly exists simultaneously as both Commander Healy *and* Howard Borden from *The Bob Newhart Show*. Furthermore, if Healy exists as the boss of Betty White's character, that implies that Jeannie herself also exists. Another reference is made to *I Dream of Jeannie* in this episode when a born-again astronaut refuses to obey Commander Healy's orders, saying, "You can't serve two masters."

• Oliver Clark also appeared on *The Bob Newhart Show* as one of Dr. Bob Hartley's patients, the insecure salesperson Mr. Herd. Teleliterate viewers could, therefore, solve John Doe #6's identity problem, but Mr. Carlin doesn't recognize this fellow-group-therapy patient of Dr. Hartley's. To complicate matters further, Oliver Clark also played Dr. Charles Webner, one of the principal characters on *Operating Room,* the early prototype for *St. Elsewhere.*

• The wall of John Doe #6's room is covered with a jumble of letters of the alphabet. Compare this to the solid, single "M" that appeared in Mary Richard's apartment. Mary knew who she was and her "M" showed it; John Doe #6's only hope of getting the right personalized initial on his wall is to use the entire alphabet.

• As mentioned above, Warren Coolidge is an orderly at St. Eligius and wears a Carver High T-shirt. Though Coolidge's presence in *St. Elsewhere* implies that the world portrayed in *The White Shadow* was "real," not just a TV show, an episode of *The White Shadow* is viewed on a hospital TV set by John Doe #6 in this episode of *St. Elsewhere,* implying that the show and therefore Coolidge are fictional. As he watches *The White Shadow* with John, Mr. Carlin suggests that whoever came up with the program was "a real smoothy."

• Actual episodes of MTM shows play during this episode, with commentary by John Doe #6 and Mr. Carlin. We see the recognizable MTM kitty logo meow at the end of them. We'll also see it meow at the end of the episode we're watching.

• John Doe #6 throws a party in the psych ward and begins to quote dialogue directly from old *Mary Tyler Moore* episodes. At the end of the episode he tosses his Mary Richards-like hat into the air, just as Mary does at the end of the opening credits of her show, and, quoting from the *Mary Tyler Moore* theme song, he states that he's "gonna make it after all."

• John Doe #6 might remind the truly teleliterate of "Number 6," the only name ever given to Patrick McGoohan's character on *The Prisoner.*

• When commenting in this episode on names for babies, an ob/gyn doctor asks, "Whatever happened to good old-fashioned names like Bruce, John, Mark, or Tom." *St. Elsewhere*'s writer-producers are *Bruce* Paltrow, *Mark* and *John* Tinker, *John* Masius, and *Tom* Fontana.

• Dr. Auschlander sums up MTM's autobiographical approach (and a widely held theory of TV) by stating, "We look into the television and see ourselves."

On one level, *St. Elsewhere*'s intertextual in-jokes were just that: amusing little nods to the minutiae and effluvia of TV culture. But they were more than that. They announced that there *is* a television tradition and they helped position *St. Elsewhere* within that tradition. In high art forms, such a practice is admired by critics and scholars, but this has not been the case for more popular forms. When writing about mainstream movies, for example, Michael Wood claimed that:

> Movies rely on our experience of other movies, on a living tradition of the kind that literary critics always used to be mourning, because it died in the seventeenth century or fizzled out with D. H. Lawrence. The movie tradition, of course specializes in light comedy, well-made thrillers, frothy musicals, and weepy melodramas, rather than in such works as Donne's *Holy Sonnets* or George Eliot's *Middlemarch;* and we shouldn't listen too seriously to the siren voices of those critics who claim big things for Hollywood movies as art. But there *is* a tradition. We have in our heads as we sit in the cinema a sense of all the films we have seen, a range of common reference which is the Greek and Latin of the movies, our classical education. The classics here being the public's classics, rather than the critics'.[27]

As the readers of *Paradise Lost* understood that poem because they were intimately familiar with the Bible, we understood *St. Elsewhere* (or *Late Night with David Letterman* or *Saturday Night Live*) because we were familiar with television. *St. Elsewhere* didn't so much refer to the real world as it did to the mythological world made up from the entire history of TV. When Wood said "the movies *are* a world, a country of familiar faces, a mythology made up of a limited number of stories,"[28] he could have as easily been talking about television.

It is of course unlikely that a NASA astronaut from Cocoa Beach (Major Healy), a barber from Mayberry (Floyd), a cop from San Francisco (Mike Stone), and a failed basketball star from South L.A. (Warren Coolidge) would all end up in the same backwater ghetto hospital in South Boston. But this wasn't a show about the real world; it was a show about a created world, as the final episode would make clear. St. Eligius was a TV hospital, serving as a metaphoric dumping ground for canceled characters from television's world.

▪ ▪ ▪

The John Doe #6 episode also illustrates how densely packed *St. Elsewhere*'s episodes were. More than any other series in the history of

American television, *St. Elsewhere* rewarded the attentive viewer. The show's narrative consistency and attention to the tiniest of details was astonishing compared to other television programs before and even since, and it gave the series a literary value that extended beyond the mere playing of intertexual games. Examples of this are difficult to give without long and somewhat arduous descriptions like the two that follow.

In the pilot episode, victims of a explosion that went off in a bank are brought to St. Eligius. Over the next few episodes we get to know the ruthless terrorist (pre-*Player* Tim Robbins), who was himself injured when he set off the bomb, and the husband of one of the comatose victims, Mr. McAllister (Jack Bannon). Mild-mannered and excessively polite, McAllister faithfully stands vigil over his wife night and day. When she finally dies in the fourth episode, he goes to Dr. Westphall's office to make arrangements to have her body flown home to Minnesota. Mr. McAllister is examining a framed poster on the office wall that inspires him, as soon as Westphall arrives, to launch into a Proustian reverie about the day he fell in love with his now-dead wife:

MR. McALLISTER: Dr. Westphall. I was just noticing your native plant poster.

DR. WESTPHALL: My daughter Elizabeth gave me that. She thinks my office is too stark.

MR. McALLISTER: You garden?

DR. WESTPHALL: I try. Every year I try.

MR. McALLISTER (pointing to a plant on the poster): Viola tricolor.

DR. WESTPHALL: No, I think that's johnny jump-up, isn't it?

MR. McALLISTER (looking more carefully): Footsteps-of-spring, that's what it is.

DR. WESTPHALL: You got it.

MR. McALLISTER: My wife Catherine and I went to college in New Hampshire. There was a section of campus where we used to play touch football that was bordered by footsteps-of-spring. Hundreds of them. I remember this one Sunday we were playing—Catherine was the quarterback on the other team. And as she faded back, I came in from the right, from the blind side, and she didn't see me. She looked so hopeful—scanning the field, looking for someone to throw to. I almost didn't want to disturb her but it was a once-in-a-lifetime shot and I took it. Caught her just below the hip, and we both went flying into the footsteps-of-spring.

The metaphors of flowers, football, and spring were effective in fleshing out the relationship of two characters who have been given only a few minutes of screen time and one of whom was in a coma. Then the episode ends, quite shockingly, when the grief-stricken Mr. McAllister shoots and kills the terrorist as he's being moved to the prison ward.

That episode played on November 23, 1982, and it was the last we'd hear of Mr. McAllister for nearly three-and-a-half years. Then, in an episode aired in March of 1986, Dr. Jack Morrison (David Morse) is performing community service work in a local prison when he encounters McAllister doing time for the murder of the terrorist. McAllister has fallen in with a bad element, and during a prison uprising he helps hold Jack down while another prisoner rapes him. In the next episode we learn in a meeting of hospital administrators that Jack has gone to his hometown of Seattle to recover from the attack. In the very next scene, Dr. Phil Chandler (Denzel Washington) is buying flowers in the hospital gift shop as a peace offering to his once-girlfriend Dr. Roxanne Turner (Alfre Woodard). As he purchases them, he tells a fellow doctor: "Roxanne loves johnny jump-ups," to which the other doctor replies, "Too bad, those are footsteps-of-spring." In this one line we are asked to remember the gentle innocence of Mr. McAllister's monologue from three seasons back and to link it to his recent role in Jack's rape. Only the most zealous fans, of course, ever made the connection.

Whenever one did happen to catch one of these details—and they were quite common to the show—one would realize that this program was unlike any other. Never before had a television series maintained this level of intricacy and consciousness of its own history across seasonal lines. This sort of narrative consistency is unusual, partly because there is a great deal of turnover among the writing and producing staffs of most series from year to year. "I think it comes mostly from the fact that we were so inside the show," writer-producer Tom Fontana speculated. "It was so much a part of our reality that I knew as much about these characters' history as I did about my own."[29] For much of *St. Elsewhere*'s time on the air, every script, no matter who wrote it, took a final trip through the typewriters of Fontana and John Masius.[30] "It was important for us to do that in order to keep the consistency of the show," Fontana recalls. "We'd put something in a script in show number three that we knew would pay off in show number fifteen."[31]

A second example of *St. Elsewhere*'s attention to detail was so deeply embedded in the scripts that virtually nobody noticed. "I remember one of the things we did that I don't think anybody ever caught," Fontana said in 1993. "To this day nobody's ever told me if they did."

> In the fifth season, we were going through this story where Aushlander was having this mental breakdown—he was kind of getting senile over the course of the season. We wanted to end the season

with him in the hospital saying "Where are my toys?," as a baby again. What we did was—Aushlander was seventy-five, so we divided the twenty-three episodes of the season up into three or four year periods. So in episode number one he was talking about things that related to the year it aired—1986. The next week he would talk about things that related to 1983. The next week he would talk about things related to 1980. We'd try to write in such a way so you couldn't tell if he was just remembering it. By the final episode of that season, when he had been reduced to a baby again, if you'd been tracking it you could see him going bit by bit backward in time. We never even told Norman [Lloyd]. My point is that only Masius and I knew what we were doing. We never even told Bruce [Paltrow]."[32]

Sure enough, a very careful examination of that season's episodes reveals a number of little offhand remarks by Aushlander that don't quite make sense but that are so short that most viewers just let them go by. By episode 3 he mentions Jimmy Carter being at Camp David; in episode 5 he makes a very brief reference to Kent State; in episode 16 he lists a string of his favorite movies—*The Lady Vanishes* (1938), *Gone with the Wind* (1939), and *Goodbye, Mr. Chips* (1939); in episode 20 he remarks on Prohibition and bathtub gin; and by episode 23, he's sitting like an infant with his thumb in his mouth. To get this, of course, required more than just careful viewing; it required graduate level literary analysis.

▪ ▪ ▪

In spite of, or perhaps because of, its artistic sophistication, *St. Elsewhere*'s borderline ratings made it a seasonal candidate for cancellation. But the executives at MTM, not NBC, ultimately terminated the series after six seasons. In fact, *St. Elsewhere* was beginning to win its time slot in its final year, and it ended the season in forty-ninth place, its highest ranking ever. Executives at NBC were ready to schedule it for another year. With budgets skyrocketing, however, MTM insisted that they would produce another season of the show only if NBC would raise the license fee. The sixth season of *St. Elsewhere* would reportedly cost MTM 3.5 million dollars more than the network would pay them for it,[33] and the show was selling very poorly in the syndication market.[34] With 137 episodes already in the can, another season would not add much value to the show's syndication package, anyway. When NBC refused to come up with more money, MTM decided to call it quits.

By early 1988, the word was spreading that the end was near. A February episode of *Donahue* brought the entire cast together to reminisce about the show,[35] *People* magazine featured a six-page spread in May,[36] local news shows included feature stories about the final episode, and NBC took out a two-page ad in *TV Guide* to promote the grand finale. "*St. Elsewhere*," the ad proudly announced, "Where TV went to get better."[37]

Meanwhile, the faithful audience waited to see what final rabbit would be pulled out of the hat of the series that was always full of surprises. The writers flirted with a number of ideas. In one, Aushlander is in his office talking to Westphall when they see a nuclear flash and the film melts on the screen, in effect ending the series by ending the world. In another, Westphall confesses to Jack Morrison that he pulled the plug on JFK. In the end, however, the final episode owed more inspiration to *Dallas,* 1978–91, than to Dallas, 1963.

Written by coexecutive producers Bruce Paltrow and Mark Tinker, and directed by Tinker, the last episode fit perfectly into the classic *St. Elsewhere* formula. On the one hand, some restraints were exercised in the use of scatological humor. Other than a man with a hernia named Mr. Skank, a discussion by sentimental Wayne Fiscus on the possibility of saving his "last whiz at St. Eligius" in a bronze specimen cup, and some doctors' late arrival at a code blue emergency being blamed for having first barged into the wrong room in which a barium enema was being given ("We felt like a bunch of douches"), the episode pretty much laid off the potty talk.

Oblique in-jokes, on the other hand, ran rampant. In the very first scene, Fiscus treats an older gentleman. "So you see, General Sarnoff, it's quite a network," Fiscus says, "and optic nerves need their rest." Fiscus, whose residency at St. Eligius is over but who can't bring himself to go home, later laments to his colleagues that he doesn't want his last patient to be "someone who's spent his entire existence in front of the tube." The teleliterate viewer, of course, would know that General David Sarnoff was the founder and first president of NBC. Moments later, a man is heard talking on the telephone, delighted that he's going to get the "chance to do some television in New York." Many of the *St. Elsewhere* staff were at that moment gearing up for *Tattinger's,* a new MTM series that would appear on NBC in the fall and that would be shot entirely in New York. A few scenes later, a missing patient is identified as "an amputee, Dr. Kimball's patient . . . he's a fugitive." Dr. Kimball was the name of the principal character in ABC's 1960s adventure series, *The Fugitive.* He spent four seasons chasing a one-armed man who had killed Mrs. Kimball and pinned the blame on the doctor. In the final episode of *The Fugitive,* the one-armed man falls from a tower; in the final episode of *St. Elsewhere* the amputee is caught on the water tower on the hospital's roof.

And that's only the first act. After the first set of commercials, Warren Coolidge, wearing, as always, his Carver High T-shirt left over from *The White Shadow* days, runs through the hall in an emergency and shouts out to those in his way, "Move the gurney, Hal!" Hal Gurnee was the director of *Late Night with David Letterman*. Later in the same act, Dr. Carol Novino (Cindy Pickett) is speaking into a microphone as she prepares to do an autopsy: "Patient 4077. Blake, Henry. Cause of death thought to be injuries sustained in a helicopter crash." This, of course, was how Colonel Henry Blake of the 4077th Mobile Army Surgical Hospital was killed on *M*A*S*H*.

Things don't let up in act 3. A barber who looks an awful lot like (but isn't) Howard McNear, the actor who played Floyd, the Mayberry barber, on *The Andy Griffith Show*, is giving a haircut to one of the patients. Dr. Seth Griffin (Bruce Greenwood) tells the patient that "Floyd has been the barber at St. Eligius for years" and that he "may bury us all." A few scenes later, the hospital pager urgently announces, "Code blue, room 222," recalling the title of the series that played a crucial early role in MTM's history.

The most interesting of these jokes, however, were the ones that referred not to television history in general, but to *St. Elsewhere*'s own history in particular, including a direct quote from the final episode of the MTM series that launched the company. Most viewers would have remembered the classic last scene of *The Mary Tyler Moore Show*, in which the entire cast huddles up in a group hug and then is forced to move, en masse, in tiny little steps, to retrieve a box of tissues, whereupon they all sing "It's a Long Way to Tipperary." The same scene is dropped, with only a few minor adjustments, into the middle of this final episode of *St. Elsewhere*, a little narrative scrap tossed to the television generation. *Mary*'s final episode, incidentally, was titled "The Last Show"; *St. Elsewhere*'s was "The Last One."

The final episode brings many things around full circle. The hugging scene brought us back to *The Mary Tyler Moore Show* and the early days of MTM. And if the entire show started in Cleveland, where Joshua Brand and John Falsey had gone to do research at the Cleveland Clinic, it also ends there, at least for Dr. Craig. Just as he and his wife have reconciled, she gets a great job offer to be head of food services at Good Samaritan Hospital in Cleveland, and they decide to move to the city where the whole series was conceived. Dr. Westphall also returns after a half-season's absence to take over the hospital when Dr. Aushlander dies of a massive stroke.

The last patient to be admitted also pays homage to the early days of *St. Elsewhere*. Brand and Falsey had left the show at the end of the first season because they didn't like the lighter tone that the other producers were insisting upon. Insiders had nicknamed the pair "Dr. Death and Mr. Depression," apparently because they insisted upon indiscriminately killing off patients in the name of "realism."[38] In the final episode, a patient is brought into the hospital with severe chest pains. His assessment of the hospital reminds us of the way Falsey and Brand had originally created it: "Long corridors filled with sick people, the smells, angst hanging in the air." In one of the final scenes, a young new resident comes in to treat him, accidentally prescribing a dosage of medication ten times higher than it should be, enough to kill the patient. The resident's name, not surprisingly, is Brandon Falsey.

If the last episode belongs to anyone, it is Wayne Fiscus. For him, as for all of the remaining original residents from the first season, the time at St. Eligius is over. Fiscus just can't let go, however, continuing to treat a patient here and to save a life there. One of his patients is a fully costumed opera singer who has lost her voice hours before a big performance. The joke is set up in the beginning of the episode and the inevitable punch line comes near the end, when Fiscus's treatment has worked, the lady gets her voice back, and Wayne knows that it's finally time to go.

But even though the fat lady had sung, the show wasn't really over yet. The final scene was still to come, and it would change the meaning of the entire series. The last scene in the hospital shows Westphall and his son Tommy in the just-deceased Aushlander's office. Westphall is listening to opera music, as he and Aushlander had often done in the past. His son Tommy is staring out the window at the late spring snow. The connection to Tommy and the title character in the 1970s rock opera and movie (1975) featuring The Who is pretty clear here. Pinball wizard Tommy (Roger Daltrey) can't speak, see, or hear and looks into mirrors; Tommy Westphall (Chad Allen) is autistic and looks out windows. Both of them break a lot of glass.

The episode's final scene follows, but it takes place in a very different setting. Tommy is no longer gazing at snow through a window, but at a glass snowball toy of the variety that the title character dropped as he died in *Citizen Kane* (1941). Tommy sits on the floor of a grim urban apartment. Sitting on a stuffed chair reading the newspaper is Auschlander, no longer dead and certainly not a doctor. Westphall walks in wearing a hard hat, and we learn that he is a construction worker, that "Auschlander" is his blue-collar father, and that Tommy is his son. When "Auschlander" asks how work is going on the building, "Westphall" announces that they just "finished up on the twenty-second story." (*St. Elsewhere*'s final season, like most series, had twenty-two episodes.) Westphall then bends down to Tommy and says, "I don't understand this autism, Pop. I don't know if he can even hear me," a direct reference to the "Tommy, can you hear me?" lyric in The Who's opera. "He sits all day in his own world staring at that toy. What's he think about?" Westphall then takes Tommy to bed, sets the toy on the TV set, and the camera closes in to reveal that the toy encloses a building that looks just like St. Eligius. Tommy wasn't thinking about "rosebud" as he stared into the snowball all day; he was dreaming up 137 hours of Emmy-quality drama. All of *St. Elsewhere* is revealed as the autistic fantasy of the child, and, in the final image of the series, the inspiration for that fantasy is shown sitting *on TV*.

Tom Fontana, who helped come up with the idea for this ending, explained that St. Eligius had become such a real place for him that he felt the need to purge it from his mind. "We all needed to acknowledge that the show was fiction," Fontana told a reporter for the *Los Angeles Times*.[39] Bruce Paltrow agreed. The ending "was metaphorical for us," he said. "We created this life; we created it in our minds."[40] The staff had, in fact, flirted with another ending in which Tommy would set the snowball on the TV, which would already be holding seven or eight other balls. One snowball would contain the WJM newsroom from *The Mary Tyler Moore Show*, one would hold *The White Shadow*'s Carver High, in another would be Bob Newhart's psychiatric office from *The Bob Newhart Show*, and so on, implying that Tommy had not only imagined *St. Elsewhere* but the entire two-decade output of MTM Enterprises.

■　■　■

By the time *St. Elsewhere* ended, the MTM innovations as developed in 1970 had spread all over television. The workplace family was now commonplace in such hit shows as *Cheers* and *Night Court*, and it would continue in later shows like *Murphy Brown*. Furthermore, intertextuality and self-consciousness had devolved into downright cannibalism, most of it much less sophisticated than the earlier efforts. *Moonlighting* appeared in 1985 making references to its own commercials and ratings right in the show itself, and before long, even mainstream series like *Who's the Boss?* and *Growing Pains* were making painfully clever inside jokes about everything from their stars to their time slots. As far as "first rate people in a second-rate institution" were concerned, the MTM alumni were now all over the airwaves. Graduates like James Brooks, Jay Tarses, Ed. Weinberger, and Steven Bochco had really classed up the neighborhood, and big time film directors like Robert Altman, Steven Spielberg, and David Lynch had either already come to TV or were about to. MTM had started a new style that was innovative; now the style was a formula with widespread use. The John Doe episode of *St. Elsewhere* celebrated the company's glory days; the final episode eulogized them. After the end of *St. Elsewhere*, *Newhart* was the only MTM series left on the air, and months after the last episode of

*St. Elsewhere* aired, MTM would be sold and would become a very different kind of company.

▪ ▪ ▪

Needing a logo for the new company in 1970, having a company name that sounded a lot like their giant studio rival MGM, and having just sold a show that focused on the life of an independent woman, the founders of MTM Enterprises "feminized" the roaring MGM lion and introduced the MTM kitten. The kitten represented the Stradivarius of television brand names. Brandon Tartikoff once defined quality television as a show "that starts with low ratings and ends with a cat meowing."[41] Throughout the history of the company, the kitten would often take on details appropriate to the specific series onto which it was tacked. At the end of *The White Shadow* the cat bounced a basketball in its paw; for *Hill Street Blues* it wore a police cap; in *Remington Steele* it sported a Sherlock Holmes-style hat and pipe; in *Bay City Blues* it caught a fly ball in a bemitted paw; and in *Newhart* it meowed in the droll voice of Bob Newhart. In all other episodes of *St. Elsewhere*, the cat wore surgeon's greens, but in the final episode, the kitty is splayed out on a gurney, attached to an I.V. tube and an electrocardiograph machine. The machine beeps as the final theme and credits play, but as the music ends, the machine straight-lines and the beeping turns to a steady tone. The MTM kitty is dead, killed in the final episode of one of its own litter.

# The Second Golden Age of Television: *Cagney & Lacey, Moonlighting, L.A. Law, thirtysomething,* and *China Beach*

B etween 1980 and 1988, the percentage of households with VCRs grew from 1 to 58.[1] During that same period, the prime-time network schedules filled with programs that, by any fair aesthetic standards, were really worth recording. Thoughtful dramatic treatments of contemporary issues, striking visual styles, complex literary dialogue, and sophisticated comedy could be found in relative abundance in a medium not historically known for any of these qualities. During the 1986–87 season, for example, a viewer could find at least one quality program on five nights of the week. *Cagney & Lacey, Moonlighting, St. Elsewhere,* and *Hill Street Blues* were aired on Mondays through Thursdays, respectively, and the visually stylized *Miami Vice* and the verbally stylized *L.A. Law* played back-to-back on Fridays.

Although these shows were different in many ways, they also shared more in common than their high standards. Aggressively controversial story topics; behind-the-scenes battles between producers and networks over content, scheduling, and often imminent cancellations; and the general adoration of critics resulted in press coverage for these shows that was sometimes out of proportion to the size of the audience watching them. By the time the 1990s rolled around, the quality formula may have been growing a little stale, but for the better part of the 1980s that formula served as the means by which a lot of good television made it onto the air.

## CAGNEY & LACEY: CRUSADING FOR QUALITY

"I believe [that shows like ours] need extra nurturing," Barney Rosenzweig, executive producer of *Cagney & Lacey,* told *TV Guide* in 1983.[2]

To survive, quality TV usually needs some special dispensations. Sometimes network executives will give these willingly, as NBC's did to *Hill Street Blues* and *St. Elsewhere,* neither of which would ever have made it to a second season had certain programmers not been ready to bend a few rules and to play favorites. Other times they aren't so willing, as was the case with the CBS staff and *Cagney & Lacey.*

CBS debuted eight new series in the spring of 1982. Seven of them were canceled within two months. Some of these probably deserved to go; *Herbie the Love Bug,* for instance, quickly proved that the four already-released Herbie movies had pretty thoroughly explored the question of what would happen if a Volkswagen had a brain. Others probably deserved a little more of a chance; *Q.E.D.* featured classy actor Sam Waterston in a historical fantasy produced in England by John Hawkesworth, the same person who'd produced the critically acclaimed British series *Upstairs, Downstairs.* But CBS was in first place and therefore didn't need to be experimenting. The network had very few holes in its schedule, and if something didn't work, it was quickly replaced with something that might.

One of the other series CBS canceled that spring was *Cagney & Lacey,* a show that, like *Q.E.D.,* had done some bold and interesting things, but had not delivered the numbers and was destined for six-episode obscurity. But *Cagney & Lacey* wouldn't stay canceled. And though CBS, unlike third-place NBC, wasn't offering any special treatment to its good-but-low-rated shows in the early 1980s, the producer of *Cagney & Lacey* was going to demand it. The difficult history of the program demonstrated that network decisions are not intractable. CBS kept killing the show; the producer, the viewers, and special interest groups kept bringing it back to life. The maxim that a series lives and dies by its ratings—no arguments—was grudgingly set aside for *Cagney & Lacey.*

The long and contentious history of the show began seven years before it would first light up an American living room. In 1974, Barney Rosenzweig hired Barbara Corday to work on *Sons and Daughters,* a short-lived series he was producing at the time. Together the two of them, along with Corday's partner, Barbara Avedon, came up with the idea to do something that had never been done before: a "buddy" movie with women in the leading roles. Corday and Avedon had been writing partners for years and both were members of women's groups;[3] Rosenzweig was a self-proclaimed "product of the 1950s," who was "used to a woman whose primary function was managing the home and children."[4] But Rosenzweig, calling Corday "the first working woman, modern-day type I had ever spent time with"[5] and crediting her with raising his consciousness regarding women's issues, nurtured the project with the zeal of the newly converted.

Hyping the idea that would become *Cagney & Lacey* as "the first real hit feminist film,"[6] Rosenzweig pursuaded the head of Filmways to give him enough money to hire Corday and Avedon to write a screenplay. They came up with a story about two female officers working in the New York City Police Department. When no studio could be persuaded to produce the film, however, the script was shelved. It stayed on the shelf from 1974 through 1979, during which time Rosenzweig's consciousness hadn't been raised high enough to keep him from signing up as a producer of *Charlie's Angels*. Although hardly a show with the feminist seal of approval, *Charlie's Angels* gave Rosenzweig a feel for making a program that featured women working together both as friends and heroes. In spite of all that glamour and hair, and the contrived plots that required the "angels" to go undercover as hookers, college coeds, or members of any profession for which the uniform was sleepwear, evening wear, beachwear, or leotards, *Charlie's Angels* showed women pulling guns and chasing bad guys in ways that mostly only men had done on TV in the past. A man, the unseen Charlie, was still pulling all the strings, but we actually got to see women thinking and acting in ways that heretofore had been reserved for males in most American television programs. In some respects, *Charlie's Angels* had cleared the way for the show Corday and Avedon wanted to make.

By 1979, Rosenzweig had dusted off the five-year-old movie project and had been turned down twice by each of the three networks when he tried selling it as a TV series.[7] Having had the project rejected as both a movie and as a series, Rosenzweig was running out of ideas. As a last ditch effort, he returned to the networks with the suggestion that the project be produced as a made-for-TV movie. NBC and ABC both passed, but CBS, needing to fill a contractual commitment to *M*A*S*H*'s Loretta Swit, agreed to go along with the idea under the condition that Swit be cast in one of the leading roles.[8]

Before long, Rosenzweig was vehemently defining what his project *was* in terms of what *Charlie's Angels* was *not*. Arguing with CBS about their penchant for "sexy young actresses," Rosenzweig announced that "what separates this project from *Charlie's Angels* is that Cagney and Lacey are women; they're not girls, and they're certainly not objects."[9]

Corday and Avedon considerably reworked their original movie script to make it suitable for television, but both the content and the language remained more cinematic than most TV at the time. Tyne Daly was chosen to play Officer Mary Beth Lacey to Loretta Swit's Officer Chris Cagney. Though not as well known as Swit, Daly had credentials that were perfect for the part of a tough but modern woman cop. In 1976 and 1977, she had starred in three films as the tough cop able to hold her own as the partner of such macho stars as Clint Eastwood (*The Enforcer,* 1976), Joe Don Baker (*Speedtrap,* 1977), and Charles Bronson (*Telefon,* 1977). After that, she played strong female roles in a number of TV movies, including *The Women's Room,* an adaptation of Marilyn French's feminist novel, and *Intimate Strangers,* a story of a man who beat his wife, for which Daly was nominated for an Emmy as best supporting actress.

*Cagney & Lacey* was a hit when it finally aired on October 8, 1981. According to the Nielsen ratings, 42 percent of the televisions turned on that night were turned on to the show, a striking number even in the days before cable had made major inroads on the network audience. The people at CBS, who not long ago had rejected the idea as a series, had a sudden change of heart, and they asked Rosenzweig and his colleagues to gear up for a spring debut. Since Loretta Swit was still starring in *M\*A\*S\*H,* she was unavailable to reprise her role in the new series. The producers replaced her with the relatively unknown Meg Foster, a choice about which CBS executives were not happy. They believed that there had been some real contrast between Daly and Swit, not the least of which was the fact that one had blond hair and the other brunette. With Foster, they argued, both characters seemed too similarly blue collar.[10] But they let the producers have their way.

By the spring of 1982, six episodes were ready to go. After the first two aired in March and April, CBS programmer Harvey Shephard called Rosenzweig to tell him that the show had been canceled. Airing at 9:00 P.M., *Cagney & Lacey* had been losing a large percentage of the hit-sized audience of *Magnum, P.I.,* which aired at 8:00. Rather than accept the bad news, however, Rosenzweig started doing the network's job for it. He assessed the problem and decided that the 9:00 P.M. timeslot was too early for a show as gritty and real as *Cagney & Lacey.* He saw that the ratings among adults, both male and female, were quite respectable. It was the younger audience that was turning off in droves after *Magnum, P.I.,* was over. So he called Harvey Shephard with a suggestion. Rosenzweig recounted the story in *TV Guide:*

> Now this is late March, early April, and the program meetings, where they announce the fall schedule, are coming up. I said, "Harvey— you've got to put us on before the meetings. I know you've got two reruns at 10 o'clock on a Sunday and Monday in late April, a *Trapper John* [on CBS's strong Sunday night schedule] and a *Lou Grant* [with a *M\*A\*S\*H* lead-in]. Put us on. Give me those two spots and I'll spend $25,000 of my own money [actually, the production company's

money] and send Tyne and Meg across the country. We'll use the slogan, "Cagney and Lacey are back to back."[11]

Rosenzweig was, in effect, manipulating the network's programming strategy, planning and arranging financing for the promotional tour, and even coming up with the promotional slogan, all jobs that are usually done by the network. In an unusual move, Shephard backed off on the cancellation, agreeing to try the show out, as Rosenzweig had suggested, in *Trapper John, M.D.*'s Sunday night slot. He stopped short of also giving him the following Monday. Sunday night was CBS's strongest, with all five of the evening's series on Nielsen's top fifteen list. When *Cagney & Lacey* aired on April 25, it earned a thirty-four share and ranked seventh for the week, higher than *Trapper John* usually performed in that slot.

Rosenzweig's ploy had worked. CBS was pressed to announce the fall schedule at the spring program meetings, and though the April 25 rating for *Cagney & Lacey* might have been a lucky accident that could never be repeated, there was no time to wait for more data to come in. Enough doubt had been put into Harvey Shephard's mind to persuade him to argue with his colleagues to give the show another chance. CBS agreed to renew under the condition that Meg Foster be replaced. Rosenzweig capitulated, and the role of Cagney went to its third actor, Sharon Gless, a conventionally pretty TV series veteran and the person Corday and Avedon had had in mind for the role when they first wrote the TV movie.[12]

CBS ordered thirteen episodes for the 1982–83 season, and when they performed reasonably well, the season was completed with an order for nine more. In the fall, *Cagney & Lacey* had been good counter-programming against ABC's *Monday Night Football*, but when football was replaced with made-for-TV movies that competed for *Cagney & Lacey*'s targeted female audience, the ratings fell substantially. In what had become an annual rite of spring, Harvey Shephard called Rosenzweig on May 10 and canceled *Cagney and Lacey* for the second time.[13] This time it was the real thing. Rosenzweig called the cast and crew with the bad news. Five months later, Rosenzweig gave a post-mortem analysis:

> We had a shot at making television history. Harvey Shephard was responsible for putting us on, and he was responsible for canceling us. He was the best friend this show ever had. I'm sorry he lost faith. We'll never know if it would have been a success. That's the sad part . . . I believe that had we stayed on one more year we would have had that shot at television history. There are so few shows that are based on reality. But there's virtually no limit to how long a show can stay

on that's about real people. They are so rare, I believe they need extra nurturing. Now it's a question of definition. Maybe Harvey Shephard did give us extra nurturing—he gave us another year. We'll never know if I was right or not."[14]

But we would, and he was. Back in the spring, Rosenzweig had coordinated a major letter-writing campaign that resulted in thousands of letters in support of the show coming in to CBS from viewers across the country.[15] Then the summer reruns of the series consistently scored in the top ten, once landing in first place. Furthermore, the show was nominated for four Emmy Awards, and on September 25 Tyne Daly won for best actress in a dramatic series.

CBS waited a little while to change its mind this time, and the 1983–84 season went on without *Cagney & Lacey* on the schedule. Eventually, however, they reversed their decision again. A limited order for seven new episodes to be aired in the spring was made, and the far-flung cast and crew were reassembled in February. By this time the resilient show was becoming something of a legend. "Welcome Back, *Cagney & Lacey*," was blazoned across the cover of the March 17 issue of *TV Guide,* calling readers' attention to an inside article by novelist Erich Segal.[16] In the same issue, CBS took out a full two-page advertising spread announcing "YOU WANT THEM! YOU'VE GOT THEM! The award-winning favorite of viewers and reviewers returns by popular demand." No doubt helped by all the hype, the seven episodes that played that spring made *Cagney & Lacey* the tenth highest-rated series of the season.

It would never rank in the top twenty-five in the subsequent four seasons, and though it wasn't actually canceled again during that period, speculation was high each spring. But by then, cable penetration had made demographics the law of the jungle, and *Cagney & Lacey*'s demographics were good enough to keep it on through 1988. Besides, the show was providing CBS with status as well as headaches. It took the Emmy for Best Drama of the 1984–85 season, ending *Hill Street Blues*'s record-breaking four-year streak, and again for the 1985–86 season. Six out of the ten Best Dramatic Actress Emmy awards of the decade were given to either Daly (1983, 1984, 1985, and 1988) or Gless (1986, 1987). *Cagney & Lacey* had become one of the classiest feathers in CBS's cap, and after making such a big deal in the *TV Guide* ad to being responsive to "popular demand," the network wasn't about to abandon it casually.

Having beaten the odds and having defied network rules, the producers and writers went on to present a show that was consistently controversial. Some argued, in fact, that all the controversy is what finally hastened its third cancellation. By 1988, a *New York Times* TV critic opened his column on the show by asking, "Why does CBS keep conveying the distinct impression that, all things being equal, it would prefer not to have *Cagney & Lacey* on its schedule?"[17] Since the fall of 1982, when the show returned for its first full season, it had settled nicely into the Monday at 10:00 timeslot, following a string of top-rated sitcoms. In January of 1988, the show was moved to Tuesday at 8:00, and the end seemed near. Up against *Crime Story,* an artsy period piece by the producer of *Miami Vice,* and *thirtysomething,* a quality series that was targeted at the same audience as *Cagney & Lacey,* CBS essentially sacrificed the series.

However, by this time the show had been winding down anyway. Tyne Daly had asked Rosenzweig to get her out of what would have been the last year of her contract, and Rosenzweig had told CBS that he himself would be leaving at the end of the season.[18] In the meantime, Harvey Shephard, the show's long-time benefactor, had been replaced by Kim LeMasters, and LeMasters was eager to end the show a year early. After seven occasionally interrupted seasons, two cancellations and two resurrections, this time, it seemed, the show was gone for good.

But of course it wasn't. In the 1994–95 season, the series returned in its original form, the made-for-TV movie. *Cagney & Lacey: The Return* and *Cagney & Lacey: Together Again* earned high ratings and fueled speculations that a new series might not be far behind.

▪ ▪ ▪

*Cagney & Lacey* would have never been made in the first place, much less have survived for 125 episodes and four reunion movies, had it not been for the persistence and masterful lobbying efforts of Barney Rosenzweig. Under normal circumstances, an unusual series like this would have quickly been weeded out of the schedule by the established network programming processes. Rosenzweig and his staff, however, managed to subvert those processes over and over again. Rosenzweig simply wouldn't take no for an answer, in effect inventing another way to keep a show on the air when conventional network considerations were dictating that it be scrapped. Unlike the cases of *Hill Street Blues* and *St. Elsewhere,* which survived because the perceived needs of the network were in sync with what the producers were delivering, *Cagney & Lacey* was the result of a much more aggressive assault on standard network business practices.

One of the principal weapons in this assault was the mobilization of viewers and special interest groups, a task for which Barney Rosenzweig was uniquely qualified. A native of Los Angeles and a graduate of the

University of Southern California, Rosenzweig had parlayed a first job in the MGM mailroom into a position as a movie publicist, a job he claimed to hate but from which he would draw for the rest of his career.[19] His first assignment was to publicize the film *Ben-Hur* (1959), and his knack for attracting public attention became immediately evident when he organized a chariot race to take place in the L.A. Coliseum during a USC-UCLA game.[20] By 1967, Rosenzweig had become a producer for a string of movies and TV series, but his skills as a publicist would come in handy again when he began work on *Cagney & Lacey* in 1974.

Rosenzweig is known to many in the industry as a consummate promoter of his own projects, and right from the start, he put an intense lobbying plan in place for *Cagney & Lacey*. Presenting the original made-for-TV movie as an important step in the women's movement, he and his staff sent Gloria Steinem a copy of the script. She took the bait, appearing on *Donahue* with Loretta Swit to rave about the upcoming telefilm and dedicating the cover of October's *Ms.* magazine to a story about it. The story, written by feminist film critic Marjorie Rosen, concluded with a suggestion that *Cagney & Lacey* become a regular series and encouraged readers to write to the Filmways executive whose address appeared at the end of the article.[21] Steinem and other *Ms.* staffers also contacted CBS executives directly, and once the show became a series, they organized a reception for its cast and staff. Steinem even got involved in issues of scheduling, complaining in a speech at a Hollywood Radio and Television Society luncheon about *Cagney & Lacey*'s being aired against another "women's show," *9 To 5*,[22] and in the series' final season she wrote an article for *TV Guide* entitled "Why I Consider *Cagney & Lacey* the Best Show on TV."[23]

After Rosenzweig persuaded CBS's Harvey Shephard to withdraw his first cancellation and try *Cagney & Lacey* in a better time slot, he persuaded Filmways to pay for a week-long publicity tour during which Tyne Daly and Meg Foster appeared on radio and television talk shows across the country. He also got Filmways to foot the bill for a major publicity campaign aimed at working women. Upon the second cancellation of the series, Rosenzweig organized a major letter-writing campaign, this time with the help of the National Organization for Women.[24] He also arranged advance screenings of his most controversial episodes to enlist the support of special interest groups that would benefit from the episode and to stir up the ire of groups that would oppose it. In an episode about the bombing of an abortion clinic, for example, Rosenzweig began rallying forces against protests long before any such protests had materialized. Loudly acknowledging that the episode had a pro-choice message, Rosenzweig publicly stated that he expected complaints from pro-life groups. He got them, of course. After he arranged prebroadcast screenings for the National Abortion Rights Action League and the National Organization for Women, the National Right to Life Committee asked CBS not to broadcast the episode.[25] The controversy was reported in newspapers across the country, providing free publicity for the episode.

One of the most enduring results of Rosenszweig's promotional savvy is Viewers for Quality Television, a grass roots group that remains very visible and, many argue, powerful, to this day. Best known for a successful campaign to save *Designing Women* from cancellation in 1987, VQT is one of the few special interest groups that lobby to keep shows on the air, not to get them taken off. Each season the group releases a list of "endorsed shows," and occasionally coordinates letter-writing campaigns to protest the imminent cancellation of an endangered series.

The story of VQT began with Dorothy Swanson, a homemaker from Michigan, who liked *Cagney & Lacey*—a lot. Upon hearing of the show's second cancellation near the end of the 1982–83 season, she wrote to one of the writers expressing to him how much she enjoyed the show and asking if there was anything that could be done to save it. The writer, Steve Brown, suggested she contact CBS. She did, and she got a large group of friends and acquaintances to do so also.

It's difficult to tell whether her letters helped to save *Cagney & Lacey*, but her hard work and subsequent missives to the cast and staff of the show eventually won her an invitation from Rosenzweig himself to come to Los Angeles for a visit. In March 1984 she spent a week on the set as the last of the seven episodes that would air that spring was being filmed. No stranger to letter-writing campaigns, Rosenzweig saw in Swanson a perfect ally—someone from the outside who could rally the forces should it become necessary again. Letters from "real people," after all, would mean more to network executives than coordinated campaigns led by Rosenzweig.

While in L.A., Swanson mentioned that the group that had worked on saving *Cagney & Lacey* might stay together on a more permanent basis. Rosenzweig strategically mentioned this to a writer at a San Francisco newspaper, who wrote an article on Swanson and her group, which included the addresses of both Swanson and her partner, Donna Deen. The story was picked up by a national wire service, five hundred responses came in, and Viewers for Quality Television was born.[26] Rosenzweig gave the keynote address to the first national gathering of VQT, and he accepts credit for being the group's "founding father," but years later he and Swanson had what he describes as "a bit of a falling out" over comments Swanson made in the press about his series *The Trials of Rosie O'Neill.*[27]

•  •  •

At first glance, *Cagney & Lacey* appears to be the most traditional of the shows considered in this book. Like most quality series, it was part of a tried-and-true genre, but unlike the more radical reworkings of the cop/detective formula, *Cagney & Lacey* had neither the decentralized cast and narrative structure of *Hill Street Blues* nor the self-consciousness that would later be seen in *Moonlighting.* Most episodes were self-contained stories about two partners in crime solving, something we'd seen in a hundred series from *Dragnet* to *Starsky and Hutch.* David Friedman wrote in *Newsday* that he couldn't help comparing *Cagney & Lacey* to *St. Elsewhere:*

> While *St. Elsewhere* is a bona-fide "TV Show of the '80s"—that is, a program in which complicated characters respond in complicated ways to complicated situations—there are times when *Cagney & Lacey* seems a well-dressed imposter. That is, a '70s show (with one-directional plots and one-dimensional characters) that, in the name of "relevance," takes on '80s trappings once in a while.[28]

Unlike *Hill Street Blues,* which debuted nine months earlier, *Cagney & Lacey* stayed within the traditional cop show style: a small cast, self-contained stories that were given focus by the two principal characters, and a fairly unadulterated dramatic orientation. A few elements of the *Hill Street* style, including the crowded chaos of the police station as represented by people walking in front of the camera, had been adopted by *Cagney & Lacey,* but for the most part the look and sound of the show was fairly conventional. Tim Brooks and Earle Marsh pointed out in their encyclopedia of prime time that "with male leads [*Cagney & Lacey*] would have been a rather ordinary TV police series."[29]

The fact that it featured female leads, however, was at the center of what made the show unique. Female crime fighters were nothing new to prime time, but series like *Police Woman, Wonder Woman,* and *Get Christie Love!,* tended to show glamorous or comic book-style women working alone or with male colleagues. Female friendships had also been portrayed before, but pairs like Lucy and Ethyl and Laverne and Shirley appeared in slapstick comedies that didn't feature much serious talk. *Cagney & Lacey*'s most important roots could be traced to *The Mary Tyler Moore Show,* which, in spite of the fact that it was a sitcom, had often shown two working women, Mary and Rhoda, in a serious friendship. It is important to note, however, that *Cagney & Lacey* is one of the few series considered in this book that wasn't created at MTM or by its alumni, although one of its producers had written for MTM's *Lou Grant* and several of its writers had worked on MTM's *Hill Street Blues*.[30]

As *Hill Street Blues* renounced the mass audience in favor of a young, urban, and upscale demographic, *Cagney & Lacey* aimed chiefly at the specialized audience of working women. Like *Quincy* and *Lou Grant*, *Cagney & Lacey* depended heavily upon contemporary "issues" for its stories, but the emphasis here was usually on women's issues. Episodes featured Lacey as she dealt with her unemployed husband's loss of sexual interest, her own experience with breast cancer, and the birth of her third child. Cagney experienced a pregnancy scare, date rape, and a complex father-daughter relationship that contributed to her alcoholism. Other episodes explored pornography, battered children, battered women, abortion, sexual harassment in the workplace, and the problems experienced by both partners when they were assigned to protect a strident anti-ERA activist. The very premise of the series— two New York City police detectives, one married with children, the other happy to be single, both trying to balance their roles as women with their roles in an otherwise all-male workplace—provided a perfect setup within which these issues could be played out. Most important to the series was the intensely close but often pugnacious relationship between the two partners, who would verbally duke it out and make up in innumerable scenes in the ladies' room or en route to an assignment.

That many women's groups and female viewers responded very positively to the show owes a lot to the fact that there were women behind the cameras as well as in front of them. A quick look at the creator and producer credits of *Police Woman* and *Get Christie Love!*, two earlier TV treatments of female cops, reveals names like Paul, George, Peter, and David. *Cagney & Lacey*'s creative team, on the other hand, included women in most of the principal roles. The show was co-created by Barbara Corday and Barbara Avedon, and a number of the producers and writers were women, including Terry Louise Fisher, a former deputy district attorney who would go on to co-create *L.A. Law* with Steven Bochco. Of the 125 episodes in the series, women were credited as producer on all episodes, as writer or cowriter on seventy-five, and as director on twenty-nine.[31]

This, rather than the flashy stylistic games and innovations of later quality shows like *Moonlighting* and *Twin Peaks*, is what made the show unique and important. The presentation of a cop show from two women's points of view was not achieved, however, without some difficulty. As Julie D'Acci has described in detail in her book about the series, the creative team's efforts to portray contemporary professional women in a realistic fashion clashed frequently with the network's tendencies toward safer and more traditional territory.[32] An unidentified CBS programmer, in the most notorious example, explained why the network had insisted on replacing Meg Foster in the role of Cagney after the first six episodes by saying, "They [Cagney and Lacey] were too harshly women's lib. The American public approves of women getting the same pay for some jobs, but the public doesn't respond to the bra burners, the fighters, the women who insist on calling manhole covers people-hole covers. These women on *Cagney & Lacey* seemed more intent on fighting the system than doing police work. We perceived them as dykes."[33]

Nevertheless, *Cagney & Lacey* often succeeded in breaking many of the established traditions and stereotypes concerning female television characters. People on the production staff as well as at the studio and the network were aware that the show's primary audience was female. This was even more apparent when *Cagney & Lacey* became one of the anchors of CBS's "Ladies' Night" Monday, which included at various times from 1983 to 1988 such series as *Kate & Allie, Designing Women, Scarecrow and Mrs. King,* and *My Sister Sam.* As would be the case with all quality series, this target marketing strategy opened prime time to an alternative to traditional programming.

Some occasional male-factor jiggle could even be seen on *Cagney & Lacey.* Hunk-star Martin Kove, who played Detective Victor Isbecki, showed up shirtless in the opening theme credits of every episode, for example, and the hyper-hyped debut episode of the 1983–84 season included several scenes at a male strip club in a story about married women who go to the city once a month to patronize male prostitutes.

While anxious to attract an audience of working women, however, CBS executives were not completely willing to write off the rest of the mass audience. The replacement of Meg Foster was only the most drastic, if ill-reasoned, manifestation of this fact, but there were many others. Cagney and Lacey, as they eventually first appeared in the 1981 TV movie, were certainly not as young or glamorous as other women cops on TV, but their first assignment after being promoted to the rank of detective was "hooker detail." Although the premise was handled with more sensitivity than it had been on *Charlie's Angels,* the two women nevertheless spent several scenes dressed as prostitutes, and Lacey even wore her costume home in an effort to rouse her husband from his sexual hiatus. As we would see later in *China Beach,* there was still a sense that a portrayal of strong, professional women had to be balanced with a little skin.

## MOONLIGHTING: THE TROUBLE WITH QUALITY

In the spring of 1985, for the first time in ten years, NBC was no longer the lowest-rated network in the country. Its prime-time schedule had finally stabilized with a well-balanced combination of upscale dramas like *Hill Street Blues* and *St. Elsewhere,* mass-appeal series like *The A-Team* and *Highway to Heaven,* and mega-hits like *The Cosby Show* and *Family Ties.* ABC, on the other hand, had fallen into third place and posted its worst ratings in twenty-eight years.[34]

As already discussed, most of the credit for NBC's reversal of fortunes went to Grant Tinker, the president of the network, and Brandon Tartikoff, the head of NBC Entertainment and Tinker's chief programmer. As NBC moved swiftly from last to first place in the ratings race, critics and industry experts pointed to Tinker's often-stated programming philosophy as one of the principal reasons for the network's miraculous turnaround. Hire talented producers, Tinker had dictated to his staff, and don't interfere with them.

Tinker's time as head of NBC was drawing to a close, however. After guiding the network to its first number-one season in history, he departed in the fall of 1986. His successor, Robert Wright, was chosen by the management of General Electric, the company that had recently bought NBC. Unlike Tinker, Wright had no programming background and little sympathy for blue-chip shows like *Hill Street Blues* and *St. Elsewhere,* which he found "overly complex."[35] Furthermore, cutting costs seemed to be at the top of Wright's agenda.[36] Tinker's departure and NBC's status as the number one network made NBC a less likely place for innovation and quality during the last half of the 1980s.

Now in third place, however, ABC looked to the recent history of NBC for lessons on how to get out of it. By June 1985, ABC executives were announcing to the press that they would be adopting a new "hands-off" attitude toward their producers. Long known as a network that insisted on playing a major advisory role in the making of the programming they aired, this represented quite a change in the corporate culture. "It's too soon to tell," Morgan Gendel of the *Los Angeles Times* wrote after the announcement was made, "but ABC may have taken a big step toward a ratings recovery with its proclamation that it would no longer meddle with producers' creative efforts. In fact, third-ranked ABC could be positioning itself as the new NBC—the former last-place network that in recent years became a haven for visionary producers and the darling of the critics."[37] When ABC Entertainment President Lewis Erlicht told *Family Ties* producer Gary David Goldberg about the new policy, Goldberg reportedly responded, "You sound more like Grant Tinker than Grant Tinker."[38]

The policy turned out to be more than just hot air. Erlicht and his successor, Brandon Stoddard, in effect stole the quality title from NBC in the years to follow. Groundbreaking series like *thirtysomething, Roseanne, The Wonder Years, China Beach,* and *Twin Peaks* all aired on ABC, and quality producers like Steven Bochco, Mark Frost, Edward Zwick, and Marshall Herskovitz, all of whom had worked on NBC shows, jumped ship to the new "quality network."

Signs of a new deal at ABC had in fact already become evident when *Moonlighting* debuted in March 1985. Lewis Erlicht had been following the career of a relatively unknown writer-producer, whose work he found "weird." Weird was apparently good in 1985, because Erlicht approached the producer and asked him if he might come up with a show that was both "offbeat" and commercially viable. Erlicht made it clear that he wanted a detective show featuring a major star in a leading role, and that he wanted something that would appeal to an upscale audience. The producer, Glenn Gordon Caron, wanted to do a romantic comedy.[39]

Erlicht dealt with Caron according to the new noninterference dictum. Caron was given the go-ahead to create, write, and produce an upscale romantic detective show and given an enormous amount of freedom with which to do it.[40] The network approved Caron's decision to cast in the costarring role an unknown actor about whom they were more than a little wary,[41] for example, and when Caron asked for an immense budget to make some ambitious episodes, ABC gave it to him. All this for a producer who was only thirty years old and didn't have a hit to his name. After graduating from the State University of New York at Geneseo, Caron had written for *Taxi* and *Remington Steele* and produced and written for the short-lived series *Breaking Away* and the pilot *Concrete Beat*. In spite of his limited track record, ABC was giving him a lot of money and a lot of latitude.

Due to FCC regulations that greatly limited the practice, the networks seldom produced and owned their own prime-time series. The law did allow them to make a few hours of in-house programming per week, but by 1985 nearly all series production was farmed out to studios and independent production companies. Of all the prime-time shows airing that year, only CBS's *The Twilight Zone* and NBC's *Punky Brewster* were produced by the networks themselves. Caron's *Moonlighting* was to be ABC's experiment with in-house production. Under the network's subsidiary company, ABC Circle Films, which Erlicht would preside over when he stepped down as chief programmer several months later, the network itself would be the owners of Caron's show. This meant they would eventually reap the benefits of syndication deals that usually went to the outside program suppliers, but it also meant that they would have to absorb all budget overruns. With the promise of additional income from reruns, however, ABC was willing to pay more for the series than they did for shows they were simply "renting."[42]

For inspiration in the creation of *Moonlighting*, Caron depended heavily upon the romantic film comedies of the 1940s that featured couples whose rapid-fire sparring disguised a seething sexual subtext. The series premise concerned international fashion model Maddie Hayes (Cybill Shepherd), whose manager had absconded with her fortune and left her with nothing but a few tax shelters, including a floundering detective agency in Los Angeles. When she pays a visit to the agency in preparation for selling it, she meets wise-guy head detective David Addison (Bruce Willis), who persuades her to keep the agency and become her partner. Together the two go on to solve crimes while sublimating their desire for each other through high-voltage arguing and much slamming of doors.

Unlike most quality shows of the period, the cast was fairly small. At first the only other regular character was Agnes Dipesto (Allyce Beasley), the receptionist who answered the phone in doggerel. Curtis Armstrong and Jack Blessing joined the cast later as legmen-operatives vying for a crack at a decent case and the affections of Agnes. Relatives of the principals would be introduced as needed. Two golden age of television stars, Eva Marie Saint and *Your Show of Shows*'s Imogene Coca were cast as the mothers of Maddie and Agnes. Charles Rocket, who became notorious in 1980 for uttering the "f-word" on *Saturday Night Live*, showed up occasionally in the role of David's competitive brother.

The "will they or won't they?" feature of David and Maddie's relationship was part of a significant television trend that could be seen in both comedies and dramas of the 1980s. Sam and Diane had established the theme in the first season of *Cheers* and played out its variations for five years. *Who's the Boss*'s Tony and Angela began their repressed courtship in 1984 and stretched it out for almost a decade. In the detective genre, *Remington Steele* and *Scarecrow and Mrs. King* had both gotten a jump on *Moonlighting* as shows featuring couples reluctantly drifting toward the bedroom.

In this and other ways, *Moonlighting* was, in fact, a blatant rip-off of *Remington Steele.* The earlier series, a product from the quality masters at MTM Enterprises, also featured a love-hate relationship between two partners in a detective agency who had been thrown together under some unusual circumstances, and it also paid stylistic homage to old Hollywood movies. *Moonlighting*'s ties to MTM in general and *Remington Steele* in particular were significant. Glenn Gordon Caron himself had written multiple episodes for *Remington Steele,* and the director of *Moonlighting*'s pilot, Robert Butler, had been *Steele*'s co-creator. Butler had also directed the first five episodes of MTM's *Hill Street Blues.* Other former MTM employees that would join the *Moon-*

*lighting* production staff included Roger Director (*Hill Street Blues*), Charles Eglee (*St. Elsewhere*), and Karen Hall (*Hill Street Blues*).

But *Moonlighting* was a lot hipper than *Remington Steele*. And in many ways it outdid MTM at the quality game MTM had invented. Even more than *Hill Street Blues* and *St. Elsewhere*, for example, *Moonlighting* was a generic hybrid. The series star, Cybill Shepherd, had become famous for her dramatic roles in films like *The Last Picture Show* (1971), but in *Moonlighting* she could frequently be seen doing slapstick scenes involving cream pies and banana peels. For their annual awards, the Directors Guild of America nominated one *Moonlighting* episode in the category of best drama and another in the category of best comedy, both in the same season.[43] The Writers Guild of America gave the show the award for best episodic comedy in 1985, and then for best episodic drama in 1986. And the show was more than just a comedy and a drama. Stories concerning the developing relationship between David and Maddie played through the series like a nighttime soap opera, frequent song and dance numbers resembled a musical variety show, and one episode even used animated clay figures.

*Moonlighting* also took the inside joke to new levels. The self-reflexive humor that had been subtly punctuating quality series for years had now taken on a much more important role. It was not uncommon for the show to open with an introductory scene in which David and Maddie addressed the audience directly. They'd read letters from viewers or they'd discuss the show's slipping ratings, its high incidence of re-runs, or its poor showing at the Emmy Awards. Originally designed as padding for episodes that had come in a few minutes short, these introductions became one of the most talked about features of the series. Performed in character by David and Maddie, not Bruce and Cybill, these scenes established the fact that this was a series about two detectives who *knew* they were characters in a TV show.

These games would continue into the episode proper. Characters frequently referred to the writers, the commercial breaks, the generic conventions of the detective show, and even the cameras, behind which they had been known on occasion to step. An unrealistically quick end-of-episode deductive solution to a crime might be chalked up by one of the detectives to the fact that there were only five minutes left before the final credits. An overly used plot device might be derided in an aside delivered directly to the camera. One episode for which the writers couldn't figure out an ending simply finished up by following the actors out into the studio parking lots as they got into their cars to drive home. These ironic nods to TV's predictability announced the show as being somehow superior to the rest of television simply because it was aware of its own formulas. "[*Moonlighting* is] the fifty thousandth detective show," Caron proudly announced upon the series' debut, "but it knows it's the fifty thousandth detective show."[44]

The most memorable episodes of *Moonlighting* were those that were deliberately designed to break the expectations audiences had of a television series. Like *M*A*S*H*, which had presented a number of "experimental" episodes, including one which was shot entirely from the point of view of a wounded soldier and another that included no laugh track, *Moonlighting* specialized in episodes with a gimmick. One installment, for example, included a documentary about David and Maddie's (and Bruce and Cybill's) relationship narrated by Rona Barrett, and another was told in utero from the point of view of Maddie's unborn child. Plans were being made to make a 3-D episode when the series was canceled.

Two of these episodes, though, stand out above the rest. "The Dream Sequence Always Rings Twice," aired in the 1985–86 season, centered around an unsolved forty-year-old crime in which a woman and her lover were both executed for the murder of the woman's husband. Both of them went to the electric chair insisting that the other had been responsible for the crime. Once Maddie and David learned about the case, each appeared in a dream sequence playing out what they thought had really happened. Meticulously shot on black-and-white film in 1940s film noir style and introduced by 1940s film master Orson Welles (in his last public appearance), this episode perhaps best captured what *Moonlighting* was all about. It was atypical of commercial TV, it was fastidiously produced, and it cost a fortune. Other series, like *M*A*S*H* and *Fame,* had done episodes or portions of episodes in black-and-white before, but Caron and his staff were doing this one in the precise style of specific Hollywood studios. "The idea was to shoot one dream with a 1940s MGM look," Gerald Finnerman, the show's director of photography, explained, "and the other in the Warner Brothers style— more down and dirty."[45] Cybill Shepherd even got to sing two torch songs in a style typical of films of the era.

"Atomic Shakespeare" aired during the 1986–87 season and ranks among the most interesting examples of prime-time TV writing of the decade. Inspired by *The Taming of the Shrew,* the episode featured sixteenth-century sets and costumes, props ranging from joints of mutton to barrels of mead, and hundreds of extras. Written by Jeff Reno and Ron Osborn, the episode included long and manic stretches of hip, contemporary dialogue jammed into Elizabethan idioms and iambic pentameter. Even the show's characteristic double entendres were done in the style of Shakespeare. After a suggestive comment from David/Petruchio, for example, Maddie/Katerina replied "If you tryest to plow this acre, your blade may be broken off."

True to form, the critics came to love the show for what it was not—standard television fare—and they assigned to it the usual labels: "risky," "Russian roulette TV," "rule breaking," "willing to take chances," "an anomaly," "something truly different in the medium." The *Chicago Tribune*'s Steve Daley, describing the show as "an upwardly mobile paean to the screwball comedies of Howard Hawks and Preston Sturges," called it "the best written show on television."[46] By 1987, *Moonlighting* was the subject of a major event in the Museum of Television & Radio's TV festival, sharing a spot on the program with tributes to such respectable company as Lucille Ball, Woody Allen, Norman Lear, Sid Caesar, Ernie Kovaks, and Dick Van Dyke.

▪ ▪ ▪

The history of *Moonlighting* was not an uncommon one for quality shows of the 1980s. The series debuted as a spring replacement show to characteristically unimpressive ratings. The audience began to grow when the episodes were rerun in the summer, however, and by the next season, the show was a modest hit, ending the year in twenty-fourth place. As would be the case with *thirtysomething*, the attention from the press was even greater than that from the audience. The show made the cover of *Newsweek* in 1986 and before long, its stars were featured on the covers of *Rolling Stone, People, Us, McCall's, Esquire, GQ, TV Guide*, and many others. Only seventeen episodes were made for the 1985–86 season, but that was enough to make it a critical triumph. It led the pack that year with sixteen Emmy nominations, although it only won one.

By the 1986–87 season, the show had climbed to ninth place in the ratings. But production problems had already begun to plague the series. The ambitious goals of Caron resulted in a severe lag in the production schedule and episodes already advertised on the air and described in *TV Guide* were occasionally replaced at the last minute with reruns. A major narrative problem also began in this season. After two-and-a-half years of flirtation, viewers began to call out for the inevitable consummation of David and Maddie's romance. The producers finally caved in to the pressure, and the two main characters slept together for the first time in the final episode of the season.

But putting the two main characters to bed significantly altered the premise of the series that had been working so well. Once the question of "Will they or won't they?" had been answered, the main source of narrative tension in the series had been taken away. Caron and his staff had been faced with one of the greatest dilemmas inherent in telling stories in the series format. By delaying the climax indefinitely, viewers were sure to become impatient; by letting the story play itself out, the show ran the risk of losing its raison d'être.

By the end of the 1986–87 season, all the elements that would lead to the series downfall were in place. The sexual tension between the two leading characters had been temporarily relieved, actor Cybill Shepherd had announced that she was pregnant, and Bruce Willis was emerging as a movie star. Shepherd's pregnancy made it impossible for her to work a full schedule during the first half of the next season, forcing the writers to place her into plot twists that would not require her to be in every episode. Bruce Willis, in the meantime, began to resent the extra weight he was required to pull on the show, especially since he was now busy working on *Die Hard* (1988), a film for which he was paid an astounding five million dollars.[47] Before long, reports were appearing that Shepherd was feuding with both Willis and executive producer Caron.

The writers decided to use Shepherd's pregnancy in the series' story lines, ultimately with disastrous results. Among the many bizarre plot twists, the most upsetting to viewers was one that had Maddie, who claimed not to know the identity of the father of her unborn child, suddenly marry a stranger she met on a train (Dennis Dugan). Susan Faludi, in her influential book *Backlash*, claimed that Maddie's marriage "was only the latest development in a long-running campaign to cow this independent female figure." Commenting on a later scene in which Maddie grovels on her knees before David in an effort to win him back, Faludi claimed that:

> The shaming of Maddie Hays was no idle writing exercise. It mirrored the behind-the-scenes campaign, conducted by both executive producer Glenn Caron and actor Bruce Willis, to curb the single Shepherd's "aggressive" personality. They told the press they didn't like how she was always voicing her opinion when she disagreed with the show's direction. At Caron's behest, the network sent Shepherd a disciplinary letter. The memo ordered her, on penalty of suit or the show's cancellation, to follow the director's orders, submit to timed breaks, and ask for permission before leaving the set.[48]

All in all, the season, was peceived as "a huge head-on collision," according to creative consultant Roger Director.[49] The internal feuds helped to put an already lagging production schedule even further behind. By the end of the year, only fourteen new episodes had been made. The show managed an average seasonal rating that landed it in twelfth place, but by the spring the increasingly impatient audience was shrinking fast. Caron left at the end of the season to direct his first film, *Clean and Sober* (1988), starring Michael Keaton, and several sources reported that ABC had asked him to leave as a result of all the turmoil.

*Moonlighting*'s 1988–89 season opener didn't air until December 6. Jay Daniel had taken over as executive producer, and the relationship between Cybill Shepherd and Bruce Willis had considerably mellowed. In standard self-reflexive style, Agnes Dipesto answered the phone in the first moments of the first episode of the year with a rhyme that reflected the high hopes that things had returned to normal: "Good morning to you; it's a wonderful day. / Everything's great; I'm happy to say. / The sun's in the sky; the planets are spinning. / The universe is safe; it's a whole new beginning. / Our Miss Hayes is happy; Mr. Addison too. / We're back in full force; so what's up with you?" Maddie's sudden marriage having been conveniently annulled, the plan was to bring the show back in line with its original formula. "We've sinned," Jay Daniel said in a *Newsday* story about the producer's apologetic attitude toward the audience, "and now we're repenting."[50]

However, a return to the old formula wasn't the solution either. Like many shows that depend upon being different and surprising, the surprises themselves soon become commonplace when presented on a weekly basis. *Moonlighting* had gone in risky, innovative directions in the 1987–88 season and had alienated the audience by doing so. When the show went back to the old bickering David and Maddie in the next season, though, the whole thing seemed to be getting a little old. Jay Daniel seemed to know the end was near as soon as he took over. "An audience likes to feel comfortable with a show," he said at the start of the final season, "and along with the comfort sometimes comes predictability, and along with predictability ultimately comes boredom. So we've always taken surprise over comfort. But at times it's made our audience very uncomfortable."[51]

ABC's new policy of patience and noninterference had been exercised in good faith with respect to *Moonlighting*, but the deflated ratings of the 1988–89 season indicated that the series had lost a big chunk of its audience. *Moonlighting* and *Family Ties* both ended on the same night in May of 1989. In a final self-reflexive joke at the end of the episode, David and Maddie return to their office only to find a network executive supervising its dismantling. Still in character, they go to see a producer, who astutely tells them why they were canceled:

> Even I can't get people to tune in to watch what they don't want to watch anymore. Don't get me wrong—I love you two guys. But can you really blame the audience? A case of poison ivy is more fun than watching you two lately. . . . People don't want laughs, they want romance. And romance is a very fragile thing. Once it's over, it's over,

and I'm afraid for you two, it's over. . . . People fell in love with you two falling in love, but you couldn't keep falling forever. Sooner or later you had to land someplace.

The monologue said a lot about how developing relationships are a problem on series television, but the joke and the lesson were lost on most of the show's original fans. The episode drew a meager ten share of the viewing audience.

■ ■ ■

The inability to maintain the romantic tension between David and Maddie was not the principal reason for the ultimate collapse, however. When asked to explain how *Moonlighting* went from a top-ten show to cancellation in just two seasons, insiders summed it up by saying, "Cybill Shepherd got pregnant and Bruce Willis got rich."[52] Yet although internal strife between Willis and Shepherd and between Shepherd and Glenn Gordon Caron certainly contributed to the show's downfall, the root of the problem went much deeper. Personal and professional difficulties among the cast and staff that might otherwise have been resolved became insoluble given the manner in which the show was produced. More than anything else, it was Caron's quixotic quest for quality that ultimately did the series in. The standards he set for his program exceeded the industrial limitations of network television. Quality shows were often given some additional slack in the 1980s, but *Moonlighting* proved an impossible series to maintain on prime time.

Caron was widely known in the industry as a perfectionist. A look at any of the early episodes from the first three-and-a-half seasons of *Moonlighting* will reveal a strict attention to detail and production values far beyond those of most television series. Caron considered each episode to be an hour-long movie, and he did everything he could to make it look that way. In keeping with the style of 1940s Hollywood films, Caron prohibited the use of zoom lenses, an optical technology not yet available in the 1940s. Instead, the much more time-consuming process of moving cameras on tracks and constantly resetting the lights was employed. To give Cybill Shepherd that classic Hollywood softened look, she was shot through a special light-diffusing glass disk of the variety used on Joan Crawford forty years earlier.[53] The black-and-white episode could have been done much more cheaply by being shot in color and then decolorized, but Caron insisted on making it look more authentic by shooting it on black-and-white film, bringing the total cost of the episode to an unheard of two million dollars.[54] If a scene didn't look right when the film came back from processing, Caron was known to shoot it all over again.

In order to maintain his high quality standards, in fact, Caron was operating on what was reportedly the highest series budget in prime time. By the 1986–87 season, when most hour-long series were costing somewhere in the neighborhood of $900,000 to make, *Moonlighting* carried a price tag of almost twice that.[55] Caron justified the cost by saying that he was making a "quality show." Echoing the tag line his star Cybill Shepherd would make famous in her commercials for L'Oreal hair products—"It costs a little more, but I'm worth it"—Caron argued, "We're making a better product, so it costs more and takes more time."[56]

The reason for the expense had little to do with car chases, special effects, or exotic locations, none of which *Moonlighting* boasted very often. Besides some of the fancy production processes discussed above, most of the high costs could ultimately be traced to the excellent scripts. "The real star of the show," Joy Horowitz wrote in the *New York Times*, "is the written word."[57]

Although the script for an average episode of an hour-long series runs about sixty pages, *Moonlighting*'s scripts tended to be from 100 to 120 pages long.[58] The two principal characters talked twice as fast as most of their TV counterparts, and they often talked simultaneously. The scripts, therefore, took longer to write and were often late. On top of that Caron insisted on perfecting and rewriting them right up to the last minute, often as the episode was being shot. Caron not only wrote many scripts himself, he rewrote them all and even insisted on being called before a single line was changed during filming.[59] It was not uncommon for the crew to begin shooting an episode before Caron had figured out how that episode was going to end. Material was often written, rewritten, and filmed all on the same day.

Caron gives much of the credit for the show's unique character to this crazy method of production. "His particular brand of mania is to wait till the last minute to write, shoot and edit his show," Joy Horowitz wrote.

> He calls the process "stream-of-consciousness television," whereby the spontaneity and adrenaline generated offscreen seep onto the film. "A certain amount of madness," he explains, "is good for the exercise."[60]

Jay Daniel, the show's coexecutive producer and the one who would take charge in the final season, evoked memories of 1950s TV when he said "We're just about as close as you can get to being live without being live."[61]

Besides giving the show a manic, spontaneous feel, this last-minute approach helped in circumventing the network's standards and practices office. Like most quality shows of the 1980s, *Moonlighting* pushed at the boundaries set by the network "censors." Among other things, the show depended heavily on double- and triple-entendres that were quite suggestive for commercial television at the time. Standards and practices staff couldn't complain about a script that wasn't written, however, and by the time they saw much of the potentially objectionable material, it was already on film and way too late to change. Most episodes are delivered to the network three to four weeks before airing; it was not unusual for an installment of *Moonlighting* scheduled to air on Tuesday still to be shooting on Friday.[62] Completed episodes were sometimes delivered to the network just hours before air time.[63]

These late and ever-evolving scripts had their down side, however. Production crews and actors would be forced to wait around the set, sometimes being paid overtime and double overtime, for new pages to come in. Rewrites might call for new characters, often requiring actors to be auditioned, cast, and filmed all in the same day.[64] Once the pages were in and new parts filled, actors would quickly have to learn lines while the director was preparing the new material. The complex quality and the sheer quantity of the dialogue put additional pressures on the stars, of course. Not only did they have lots of difficult-to-deliver lines to perfect, but they had to work longer hours to get them all on film. Most TV series episodes are shot in a week; *Moonlighting*'s took two, requiring staff and cast to continue working late into the spring, long after most regular season series had wrapped.[65] The 1985–86 season began shooting in June, for example, and by March was still only on the sixteenth of twenty episodes.[66]

The grueling production calender exacerbated problems raised by Cybill Shepherd's pregnancy and Bruce Willis's stardom. Extended and often unpredictable work schedules made it difficult to accommodate the stars' need for time off and undoubtedly played a major role in raising the temperature of any interpersonal problems that were brewing. Furthermore, given this mode of production, Caron never managed to deliver a full season of twenty-two episodes.

ABC's new policy of noninterference had been employed to a fault on *Moonlighting*. Not only did the network allow Caron to do pretty much what he wanted, but they supported him with an enormous budget. *Moonlighting* was an experiment for the network, which was still new at both giving producers their way and at producing their own prime-time programming, and the system clearly still had a few bugs. Caron was young and inexperienced at producing a show that lasted more than a few episodes, and while the lack of interference and management from the network was good for art, giving us a few years of excellence, it was bad for the business of a long-term series. Of Caron's methods, Lewis Erlicht said, "In terms of operating a show, it's not the right way because there's no time to prepare and plan correctly. In terms of result, it's that extra attention to detail that gives the show its uniqueness."[67] In the end, there just wasn't room in series television for the degree of perfection that Caron was insisting upon.

Surprisingly, ABC did not abandon their noninterference policy as a result of the *Moonlighting* situation. The following season they would give free reign to the producers of *Twin Peaks* and once again the result would be an outstanding example of television art. But, like *Moonlighting, Twin Peaks* would prove to be both a critical and commercial flash in the pan.

## L.A. LAW: MAINSTREAMING QUALITY

Once *Hill Street Blues* established the quality formula in the form of a cop show, and once *St. Elsewhere* had replicated that formula using doctors, it was inevitable that the other standby dramatic TV genre would get the quality treatment sooner or later. While he was still serving as creator-executive producer of *Hill Street,* Steven Bochco had in fact already been planning to do a series about lawyers. He had assumed that he would produce the show at MTM, where he had been working since 1978, but company management fired him from *Hill Street Blues* in the spring of 1985, before the project was ever developed.[68]

With a commitment from NBC for a thirteen-episode series under his belt, Bochco was courted by several of Hollywood's major studios after his departure from MTM. He ultimately signed a lucrative deal with 20th Century-Fox and there began to put together what would become *L.A. Law.* The idea for a series about lawyers was reportedly resurrected by Grant Tinker, Bochco's one-time boss at MTM and at the time president of NBC. Just as Fred Silverman had gotten the ball rolling on *Hill Street Blues* by approaching Bochco with the desire to make a series inspired by a movie, *Fort Apache, The Bronx,* Tinker, Silverman's successor, got *L.A. Law* started by asking Bochco if he might develop something along the lines of another film, the legal drama *The Verdict* (1982).[69] By June, just weeks after his ties with *Hill Street* had been severed, Bochco was presenting a proposal to NBC executives.[70] Though Tinker would leave NBC just about the time *L.A. Law* premiered, it was under his watch that the show was ordered and scheduled.

By this time, the idea of a network series with modest overall ratings but great demographics was one with which network executives had grown quite comfortable. Months before the debut of *L.A. Law* in October of 1986, Bochco was talking publicly and casually about the fact that he didn't expect his upcoming series to be a blockbuster. "I'm making a show that I don't expect to be a monster hit," he was quoted as saying in the *Los Angeles Times* in April, "but given the network I'm making it for and its audience—which I also think is my audience—I know that there's a reasonably good bet to be made that a core group of people will watch it."[71] Bochco and NBC were clearly hoping to capture the upscale viewers that had been the base of *Hill Street*'s audience.

But they got more than they bargained for. While *L.A. Law* did indeed attract the desirable young, urban, and educated viewers it was designed for, it attracted a lot of other people as well. Overall the most consistently popular of the quality series of the 1980s, Bochco's quality formula had graduated to the mainstream. The average annual ratings of the show never dropped out of the top twenty-five through five full seasons, and never fell lower than thirty-ninth place during its final three years on the air.

The wide commercial success of *L.A. Law,* and the subsequent canonization of Steven Bochco, represented quality TV's zenith in the 1980s. Before *L.A. Law*'s debut, quality series like *St. Elsewhere* had for the most part been relegated to the lower-middle regions of the Nielsen landscape reserved for such upmarket offerings; a few years afterward the narrative sins of *Twin Peaks* would raise the threat of quality's ejection from television's garden entirely. But in 1986, *L.A. Law* stood as an example of the brief confluence of quality television and mass appeal.

Bochco's subsequent record-breaking deal with ABC is the best illustration of how network television had changed in the last two decades. In the fall of 1987, he signed an agreement with the network, effective July 1, 1988, that many claimed was the biggest ever made between a network and a producer. ABC agreed to buy ten series from Bochco, seven over the first six years of the deal and three more at an unspecified later date. Bochco would retain ownership of the shows, thereby keeping the profits they would make in syndication, and if ABC rejected any of his series ideas, he was free to take them to other distributors.[72]

The deal was especially interesting because it came right on the heels of ABC's dissolution of its eighteen-year-long exclusive agreement with producer Aaron Spelling. Spelling's "lowest-common-denominator" shows like *Charlie's Angels, The Love Boat, Fantasy Island, Dynasty,* and *Hotel,* seemed now to be symbols of the passing old order of network television. Bochco's quality product, on the other hand, was looking to many executives as the new way to commercial success.

Television reporter Diane Haithman saw the deal and its implications as part of what she called the "Bochco-ization of the networks." By that she essentially meant that the quality formula Bochco had come to represent was becoming part of insitutionalized programming strategy. "Both third-rated ABC and second-rated CBS seem to be struggling to adopt the 'quality television' policy that has made NBC the current Number 1 network," Haithman argued.[73] It is revealing to note that while ABC and CBS were scrambling to replicate the Bochco/ NBC/Quality formula, NBC itself had let Bochco slip through its hands. The network's first-place status left it little room for large-scale program development. NBC programming chief Brandon Tartikoff was unable to offer Bochco a deal like the one he got from ABC, he said, because NBC had "little room for new shows in its strong prime-time lineup."[74]

NBC had ordered *L.A. Law*, however, and the show's frequent appearances in the top-ten by 1987 undoubtedly made the network regret the loss of their golden goose to a rival. Part of the reason for *L.A. Law*'s success was its ability to adapt the quality formula to more commercial demands. Just as, years later, *ER* would dress up the premise and concept of *St. Elsewhere* enough to often earn nearly twice the earlier show's ratings, *L.A. Law* had tweaked the recipe of *Hill Street Blues* just enough to give it a wider appeal, but not enough to compromise its elevated artistic status. The cast was a little smaller, the lighting was a little brighter, and more than any of the other quality series of the period, this one injected a heavy dose of the romance, intrigue, and glamour of the nighttime soap opera. Office power plays and personal relationships among the show's main characters invited comparisons to the narrative devices used on recent hits like *Dallas* and *Falcon Crest*. In the type of story we expected to read about *Dynasty*, *Cosmopolitan* even featured an article that discussed *L.A. Law*'s forty-thousand-dollar per episode wardrobe budget.[75]

A fair amount of courtroom drama had been rehearsed on *Hill Street Blues*, but *L.A. Law* presented legal stories in a very different environment. The grimness of Hill Street station was gone, and in its place were clean, well-lighted offices filled with tasteful decor and ergonomically-correct furniture. Jerky hand-held camerawork gave way to smooth, fluid movements; phone tag replaced gun play; squad cars became Porsches; and psychic violence, not physical violence, was more likely to drive the stories. "*Hill Street* for me always was fundamentally a series about despair," Bochco said before *L.A. Law*'s debut, "an extended story about people doing everything in their power to keep despair at arm's length. This new show is not about despair," he went on. "This is an upscale show about by-and-large successful people who impact on the environment, often in a very positive way. They have some power, they have some money, they win battles, they lose battles."[76]

Whereas *L.A. Law* was more commercial and accessible, though, Bochco had not forsaken his quality roots. In fact he became quite bold in his role as the cultural *arriviste*, identifying what he did not as regular TV but as art:

> Traditionally television is not an art medium. It's not really an enter-tainment medium. It is really a commercial sales medium. It does not want to do anything to encourage controversy or distress. The ideal piece of programming for selling things, I suppose, lulls you into a pleasant sense of well-being, and that's what some of the most successful people in this business have done. There's nothing wrong with that, but they're entrepreneurs, not artists. That's not what I want to do.[77]

Bochco the artist was no doubt pleased when a special premier screening of *L.A. Law* was scheduled by a Manhattan museum. Paying guests at the Museum of Television & Radio saw the pilot months before it was broadcast.

The series received twenty Emmy nominations in its first season, just one shy of *Hill Street*'s record-breaking twenty-one, and nineteen in its second. It won the Emmy for best drama in four of its first five seasons, and collected an assortment of other awards, including Golden Globes, People's Choices, Television Critics Association Awards, and a Peabody. Although the praise was not unanimous, the by-now familiar kudos reserved for quality shows greeted *L.A. Law*'s debut. It was hailed as a "daring departure," "Serious Television," the "hot show of choice for couch potatoes with three-digit IQs," "provocative, sexy, classy, and smart," and "intelligent, stimulating, and precise."

Such praise was not just journalistic hyperbole, either. Unable to depend upon gunplay and heavy action sequences, *L.A. Law* was almost entirely dialogue-based, and its scripts were strikingly literate. Much of the credit for this was due to the fact that the writing staff boasted a lot more training in the law than in formula TV writing. Three of the five principal writers were lawyers, and two more legal experts were retained as consultants. The series was co-created by Terry Louise Fisher, a graduate of U.C.L.A. Law School, a former assistant district attorney for Los Angeles County, and a former writer and producer of *Cagney & Lacey*.[78] David Kelley, the most prolific writer on the series, had taken a leave of absence from his Boston firm to write for *L.A.*

*Law,* and William Finkelstein had come to the show after two-and-a-half years of practicing law in New York City.[79] Besides lawyers, the *L.A. Law* staff boasted, at various times during its eight-year run, writers and producers with solid backgrounds in quality TV series, including alumni from *Hill Street Blues, St. Elsewhere,* and *China Beach.*

The usual elements of the Bochco formula were in place on *L.A. Law.* Though the cast in the beginning wasn't as big as *Hill Street*'s, it still featured nine lawyers and a legal secretary. This crowd allowed for the characteristic multiple story lines that played in and across the episodes, and because the show had been set in an all-purpose law firm, the full spectrum of legal cases, from criminal actions to divorces, could be covered.

*L.A. Law* also displayed the usual disdain for television traditions that characterized the quality drama. This was no *Mr. District Attorney, Perry Mason,* or even *The Defenders.* Although the lawyers in the firm included the good (idealistic Michael Kuzak [Harry Hamlin]), the bad (divorce attorney Arnie Becker [Corbin Bernsen]), and the smarmy (partner Douglas Brackman, Jr. [Alan Rachins]), none of them were consistently likable. Bochco described lawyers as "mercenary warriors we civilized creatures employ to do battle for us"[80] and saw one of the principal themes of the show to be the eternal struggle within each character between ambition and integrity.[81] Paid to argue a case whether good or bad, the lawyers wouldn't always win, and when they did, the person they won for might turn out to be a bad guy.

In its presentation of sexual and downright bizarre material, and the attendant mixture of comedy and drama, *L.A. Law* followed right in the footsteps of *Hill Street Blues.* In fact, the show displayed more flagrancy in this regard. After all the critical praise Bochco received for *Hill Street,* he had become even more cocky in his defiance of network standards. Within the first minutes of the brand new series, for example, a disgruntled husband barges into divorce attorney Arnie Becker's office with a gun. "Dick, this is not smart," says the visibly rattled Becker. "Don't Dick me!" Dick replies, then follows one Bochcovian double entendre with another: "Not after that settlement you rammed down my throat." At times this kind of material provided some of the show's most amusing moments, as was the case with the "Venus Butterfly" story, in which Stuart Markowitz (Michael Tucker) employs a secret sexual technique he has learned from an eleven-timing bigamist. After sending his colleague/lover Ann Kelsey (Jill Eikenberry) into throes of ecstasy with the technique, the *L.A. Law* production offices were reportedly besieged with pleas to explain the procedure. At other times, however, the sexual material seemed more than a little sopho-

moric, although the fact that it broke TV rules kept many critics calling
for more.

The show's quirky comic relief devices also had their roots in *Hill
Street Blues*. In homage to the *Hill Street* episode that featured a man
who was living in a common-law relationship with a sheep, one case on
*L.A. Law* concerned a woman who was suing for divorce because she
claimed her husband was in love with a sow. The pig appeared in court
as a hostile witness. Another case concerned a dying man vying in
court for the right to have his corpse freeze-dried and displayed on
his front lawn.

In some ways, however, the show was quite different from *Hill Street*.
Major stories usually concerned cases that addressed complex contemporary legal issues, ranging from date rape and child abuse to capital
punishment and the euthanasia of AIDS patients. This kind of material
had been the province of Terry Louise Fisher when she was working
on *Cagney & Lacey*, and, as co-creator of *L.A. Law*, her influence was
clearly showing here. The fact that *L.A. Law* appealed to a much larger
female audience than *Hill Street* had was also undoubtedly attributable
to Fisher. Right from the beginning, the show was populated with
strong female characters, most notably lawyers Ann Kelsey and Grace
Van Owen (Susan Dey). The relationship between Kelsey and Stuart
Markowitz, for example, reversed gender roles in much the same way
as the relationship between Mary Beth Lacey and her husband Harve
had reversed them on *Cagney & Lacey*. Like Lacey, Kelsey was the ambitious, aggressive lawyer who often initiated the passion of the relationship; like Harvey, Markowitz was more passive and liked to cook. Just
after the show's premier, Fisher told a reporter that she had thought
*Hill Street Blues* had been "too male, too outer-directed" and that *Cagney
& Lacey* had been too female. With *L.A. Law*, she felt she had helped
create a show with a "synergistic . . . blending of the two."[82]

▪　▪　▪

As the highest-rated of the quality dramas, *L.A. Law* also stayed on the
air the longest, lasting for eight full seasons. During that time, the
series weathered a number of storms and experienced changes both
in front of and behind the cameras. Unlike most quality shows that
were introduced as desperate experiments by a floundering network,
*L.A. Law* had the advantage of airing on a first-place venue. NBC promoted it on all of its hit series, and to make sure the widest possible
audience saw the pilot, they aired it twice, once in prime time and
several days later in *Saturday Night Live*'s time slot. The series itself was
launched on Fridays after *Miami Vice*, but by the middle of its first
season, NBC showed its faith in the show by giving it the highly desirable Thursday at ten o'clock slot that *Hill Street Blues* had been occu-

pying for years. *Hill Street* limped through the rest of its final season on Tuesday nights, and Bochco had avenged the show from which he'd been fired.

After his legendary budget overruns on *Hill Street,* Bochco had come to *L.A. Law* with a little less profligacy. *L.A. Law* was designed as a show that would be a lot cheaper to produce than *Hill Street* had been. Nearly all the scenes took place in interior settings, and once the sets were built they could be used throughout the series. The smaller cast also helped contain costs, but by the second year, it had already begun to grow with the addition of two new staff members to the firm. Blair Underwood came on as Jonathan Rollins, a young, ambitious African-American attorney, and Larry Drake signed on as Benny Stulwicz, the new boy Friday who was mildly mentally challenged. In just a few seasons, the regular cast would be up to sixteen.

The biggest news of the second season involved a power play and a legal battle, but they were going on behind the scenes. Shortly after signing his production deal with ABC in the fall of 1987, Bochco announced that he would be leaving the day-to-day operations of *L.A. Law* at the end of the season. He named Terry Louise Fisher as his successor. Shortly thereafter, though, things soured between Bochco and Fisher, who had created both *L.A. Law* and *Hooperman* together. Misunderstandings and disagreements over the degree of power Fisher would have and the amount of money she would be paid for having it led to her being banished from the set in early December of 1987.[83] The fifty million dollar suit Fisher subsequently filed against Bochco and 20th Century-Fox would be settled out of court by February for an undisclosed amount, but part of the agreement included her leaving *L.A. Law* and *Hooperman.* Fisher went on to sign a development deal with Disney;[84] Bochco decided to remain at the helm of *L.A. Law* for another season.

By the show's fourth season, Bochco's first series in the ABC deal, *Doogie Howser, M.D.,* had debuted, and he stepped down as *L.A. Law*'s executive producer, assigning himself the much scaled-down role of "executive consultant." David Kelley and Rick Wallace were promoted to the role of executive producers and William Finkelstein moved up to supervising producer. For the next two years, they injected new energy into the series at a time when it was potentially vulnerable. Kelley had observed that as early as the third season "it was more hip to take shots at *L.A. Law* than it had been in previous seasons."[85] Actor Richard Dysart, who portrayed senior partner Leland McKenzie, aptly assessed the situation at the end of the third season. "[Hit] television series have a rather predictable history," he told the *Washington Post.* "There's the initial surge of energy and acceptance by the American public—ours came very fast and very strong—and then the years when the audience builds, and then somewhere around year four, problems can happen. I think it's the critical year."[86] This theory had been proved by *Moonlighting*, which had just left the air after never recovering from its "critical year."

One of the series most celebrated story arcs was introduced in the fourth season. Diana Muldaur was added to the cast in the role of Rosalind Shays, a fortysomething power monger whose rousing successes as a litigator won her an invitation from McKenzie, Brackman, Chayney, and Kuzak to join the firm and help bolster its billings. Before long, she had used her sinister devices to wrestle the senior partnership away from its patriarch, Leland McKenzie. She was eventually fired, to which she responded at the opening of the fifth season by suing the firm and winning over two million dollars in punitive damages. Later that season, in one of the show's most memorable episodes, Roz died after unwittingly stepping into an empty elevator shaft. The cast continued to swell in the fifth season with the introduction of three new lawyers, including C. J. Lamb (Amanda Donohoe) who aroused some controversy when, getting a few years' jump on *Roseanne*, she kissed her colleague Abby Perkins (Michelle Greene) after the two had gone out to dinner.

Season six proved to be a most problematic one. William Finkelstein had left the previous year to work with Bochco on *Cop Rock* and *Civil Wars*, and now Kelley was gone as well, off developing his own series. Kelley had been the heart of the writing staff and, along with Finkelstein, he had provided the show with his legal expertise. Patricia Green, an *L.A. Law* writer and producer and a former producer of *China Beach*, took Kelley's place in the sixth season. Green was not a lawyer, and the legal-oriented stories suffered. The ratings began to drop, Green was unfavorably compared to Kelley, and by midseason she had resigned. Adding to the show's problems, two of its stars, Jimmy Smits and Harry Hamlin, had also left at the end of the previous season, and Arnie Becker, the lecherous divorce attorney, had been put to pasture in a misguided plot line that had him in a monogamous relationship with his long-suffering secretary, Roxanne (Susan Ruttan). By early 1992, insiders were referring to the show as "*L.A. Lost*."[87] Bochco himself returned to clean up the mess by overseeing the scripts for the remaining eight episodes of the season, and his reputation got another boost when the ratings in fact climbed in the spring.

But Bochco left again at the end of the season, as did actor Susan Dey, and 1992–93 brought more trouble. John Tinker and John Masius, two of the principal writer-producers of *St. Elsewhere*, were hired to run the show this time around. The pair injected some of the playful *St. Elsewhere* intertextual style into the mix, including campy appearances by Homer Simpson and Erik Estrada from *CHiPs*, but the results were rejected by viewers and critics alike. As had been the case with Green, neither Masius nor Tinker were lawyers, and the general consensus was that the show's delicate balance between the elements of legal drama and soap opera had gone out of whack in favor of the latter. Tinker and Masius were gone by January, and William Finkelstein returned to set things right again. NBC print and on-air promotional advertisements for the Finkelstein episodes, which began airing in April, blatantly trashed the work Masius and Tinker had done. "Remember when *L.A. Law* was your favorite show?" a three-quarter-page ad in *TV Guide* asked. "Watch tonight—it will be again!"[88]

Yet another *St. Elsewhere* alumnus, Mark Tinker, John's brother, was brought in by Finkelstein for the eighth and final season in 1993. Some new characters were introduced as well, including two, played by Alan Rosenberg and Debi Mazar, who were brought over from Bochco and Finkelstein's recently canceled series about divorce attorneys, *Civil Wars*. New frontiers of moral dilemma were set up by Jane Halliday (Alexandra Powers), a highly competent graduate of Bob Jones University and Harvard Law School who brought her fundamentalist Christian values to her new job at the firm. Some argued that this sympathetic character was written in to appease some of the rancor against the series that had been publicly expressed by Christian leaders like the Reverend Donald Wildmon. By this time, though, neither Mark Tinker's refreshing directing nor Jane Halliday's prayers could save the show.

▪ ▪ ▪

Even before *L.A. Law*'s final season, however, a slow but steady backlash had been growing against quality television in general, and Bochco's brand of it in particular. The very fact that quality had become commercial was of great concern to some critics. Others began to turn away from the self-important hubris of Bochco himself, now a celebrity in his own right. Still others were simply tiring of what had clearly become a predictable formula. During the run of *L.A. Law*, the blush had begun to fade from the rose of quality TV.

Michael McWilliams got a jump on the others when he wrote a review of the *L.A. Law* pilot entitled "The Biggest Snow Job in Prime Time." Appearing in the *Village Voice*, the article aimed to expose Bochco's "genius" as a great big con, and *L.A. Law* as "a pampered child's vision of the grown-up world." He specifically challenged the idea that lies at the heart of the quality TV drama: the fact that quality is defined in terms of its being different from regular television. "The self-congratulatory reviews of *L.A. Law* reek of this videophobia—the show is being touted as this year's thinkfest for discriminating viewers, and it's being used as a club with which to beat TV itself."

> But any five minutes of *The Beverly Hillbillies* are funnier than *L.A. Law,* any episode of *The Avengers* more sophisticated, any stretch of *Route 66* more dramatically compelling. Bochco, who likes to refer to other TV producers as "entrepreneurs" and himself as an "artist," doesn't need to sell himself to TV critics, who are, with rare exception, committed to his brand of Babbitry.[89]

Three years later, Rick Marin of the *Washington Times* wrote in an article entitled "Television: The Party's Over," that the term "quality TV" had become a "meaningless buzzphrase." "First used to describe low-rated shows of some merit," he wrote, the phrase had now become "a self-conscious accolade awarded to pretentious series that aren't any good and that no one wants to watch." He included *L.A. Law* in a list of shows he denounced as exhibiting "style over substance."[90]

Although these early attacks on *L.A. Law* and its tradition were fairly uncommon, by the show's last two seasons critics who had raved about the series in the earlier years were bailing out in droves. Had *L.A. Law* left the air after five seasons, it would probably have gone down in history as one of the greatest dramatic series ever. As it was, it left with the collective footprint of a host of viewers and critics on the seat of its pants. Unlike most quality series, whose low ratings force them off the air before they begin their downward spiral, *L.A. Law,* like *Moonlighting,* may have been given one or two too many chances.

Steven Bochco seemed to have landed on his feet again with the commercial success of *Doogie Howser, M.D.* The next three series he did for ABC, *Cop Rock, Capitol Critters,* and *Civil Wars,* did not do nearly as well, however. *Cop Rock,* a sort of remake of *Hill Street Blues* in the style of a Broadway musical, proved to be too experimental even for ABC, the network that was making news by boldly going where no television had gone before. An underrated series, *Cop Rock* became one of the most notorious network failures since *Supertrain.*

Although it appeared that Bochco's star may have been setting, his biggest hit, *NYPD Blue,* was still to come. Back in 1992, Bochco had begun to talk with ABC about an "R-rated TV series" that would help the network compete with the offerings available on cable. ABC Entertainment President Robert Iger rejected the idea, but the network would soon reconsider.

## thirtysomething: WHINING AND NOTHINGNESS

Most of the backlash against *L.A. Law* didn't kick in until the show was in its final seasons. *thirtysomething,* on the other hand, was greeted with enmity and loathing right from the start. "The only thing worse than living in the middle of yuppies," Cifford Terry of the *Chicago Tribune* wrote in a review of the pilot, "is having to watch a program about them."[91] The *Washington Post*'s Tom Shales identified the major theme of the series as "yuppie angst," and predicted that the two leading characters could become "major irritants." In discussing the rabid tendency toward self-examination displayed by these liberally educated Everyboomers, Shales pointed out how "they are able to articulate, sometimes at length, every emotion and anxiety they feel. And they feel plenty. Not a thought goes unspoken in [their] house, and as a result, a certain nagging whininess sets in."[92] The charge that the show was nothing more than "a bunch of white guys sitting around whining" followed it throughout its four-year run. When one of the seven principal characters was killed in the fourth season, Jay Leno, who often used *The Tonight Show* as a forum to vent his distaste for *thirtysomething*, quipped, "one down, six to go."

As strongly as some people hated *thirtysomething*, however, many others loved it. The raves and attention it received in the media, often by writers who bore a distinct demographic resemblance to the show's characters, disguised the fact that it was ranked fiftysomething in the Nielsens for most of its run. A writer in the *New York Times* claimed that the show stretched the boundaries of prime-time TV even further than *Hill Street Blues*, *Moonlighting*, or *L.A. Law* had.[93] A story about *thirtysomething* in the British newspaper the *Independent* cited the series as evidence that the 1980s had indeed been a second "golden age" for American TV.[94] The program's collection of awards compared very favorably with the other quality dramas as well. It won a total of thirteen Emmys, including one for best dramatic program in its first season, and a Peabody, a Humanitas, a Directors Guild Award, and a Writers Guild Award. The writing on *thirtysomething* achieved a new apex of artistic legitimacy for prime-time TV when a collection of nine of the show's scripts appeared in book form in the spring of 1991.[95] The last time a mass-marketed anthology of network television scripts had been published was in the waning days of the anthology dramas back in the early 1960s.

Unlike the other shows considered in this book, *thirtysomething* was not based in a traditional television genre. Whereas the American family and its satellite acquaintances had long been the foundation of TV comedies, the drama—even the quality drama—has tended to be grounded in the franchises of medicine or the enforcement or practice of the law. There have been some exceptions, most notably *Family*, a critically acclaimed melodrama from the 1970s on which three of *thirtysomething*'s creative staff had worked, but most of them, like *Two Marriages* and *A Year in the Life*, were relatively short-lived.

Not one of the seven close Philadelphia friends whose lives were the focus of *thirtysomething* was a cop, a lawyer, a doctor, or a private eye. All seven characters were in their thirties, but each one was still in the process of growing up. Born in the 1950s, consciousness-raised in the 1960s, and dosed with irony and cynicism by the 1970s, each one was struggling to reconcile the idealism of their youth with their current desires for personal and material success. At the narrative center of the show were Hope and Michael (Mel Harris and Ken Olin), who, at the opening of the series, are still trying to reinvent themselves after the arrival of their infant daughter. Hope, a graduate of Princeton, has put her career in publishing on hold to rear her child; Michael, who really wants to be a novelist, has set up shop as an adman with his friend Elliot (Timothy Busfield). In contrast to the comparative bliss of Hope and Michael, Elliot's marriage to Nancy (Patricia Wettig) has produced two children and enough anomie to cause their eventual temporary separation from each other, if not from the group. Orbiting these two couples are three unmarried characters. Melissa (Melanie Mayron), is a photographer and Michael's cousin, appreciative of her independence but obsessed with her biological clock. Hope's childhood friend Ellyn (Polly Draper) has an important job at City Hall but a penchant for bad relationships, and Michael's best friend Gary (Peter Horton) is a professor of classics whose aversion to commitment and settling down has not only kept him single but eventually prevents him from getting tenure at the local college.

Like most 1980s quality television, the characters in *thirtysomething* were not typical of prime-time formulas. Their creators, Marshall Herskovitz and Edward Zwick, had set out to make a show that dealt with the problems of people that had not been treated in American television before. Zwick, a summa cum laude graduate in American History from Harvard, and Herskovitz, an English major from Brandeis, had met when both were attending the American Film Institute in 1975. Each went on to work on a number of projects, including *Family*, and Herskovitz wrote two episodes for MTM's *The White Shadow*. Their big break, however, came with *Special Bulletin*, a 1983 made-for-TV movie that they wrote and produced together and that Zwick directed. A mock newscast in the spirit of the 1938 radio adaptation of *The War of the Worlds, Special Bulletin* presented the chilling story of a terrorist group holding the city of Charleston, South Carolina, hostage with a nuclear bomb. The movie received an Emmy for best dramatic special and another for best writing in a special, and before long Herskovitz and Zwick were putting together their own series.

Traces of *The Big Chill* (1983), the domestic film comedies of Woody Allen, and Ingmar Bergman's Swedish TV masterpiece *Scenes from a*

*Marriage* could be found in *thirtysomething,* but Herskovitz and Zwick were both in their midthirties and fathers of young children when the show began, and they brought a good deal of autobiographical material to the story meetings. Herskovitz's father had died of cancer, for example, and so did Michael's in an episode for which Herskovitz won an Emmy. Like both Herskovitz and Zwick, Michael was a Jew married to a non-Jew, a fact that provided a source of occasional conflict between him and Hope. Zwick's wife, Liberty Godshall, who wrote for the series (as did Herskovitz's wife, Susan Shilliday) confessed that "Marshall and Susan and Edward and I have used these stories to talk about our marriages, what we fight about, and what we secretly cry over. Sometimes I even suspect we've found ways to articulate in public what we have never quite been able to put so well when looking into each other's eyes."[96]

This ability of the characters to articulate things even better than the people creating them was probably at the heart of why so many either loved or hated *thirtysomething.* These characters, more than any other in American television history, unrelentingly examined the minutiae of everyday life. For some viewers, this inspired a weekly epiphany; for others, it just made them sick. There were, of course, additional causes for complaint by critics and viewers. Susan Faludi, for example, accused the show of trotting out "a complete pantheon of backlash women . . . from blissful homebound mother to neurotic spinster to ball-busting single career woman,"[97] and others took issue with the fact that the ensemble was too upscale and too white. But it was the program's "whiny" nature, which essentially referred to the fact that the characters talked so much and so seriously about the tiniest of domestic details, that became both its most descried and its most celebrated feature.

Two seasons after the cancellation of *thirtysomething,* in an episode aired in September of 1992, the characters of *Seinfeld* started referring to their series as "a show about nothing." The subject matter *Seinfeld* had been presenting and continues to present, of course, wasn't really about nothing. Rather, it concerned the banal details of daily life that had seldom been featured as the stuff of television narrative. Indeed, stories about masturbation, waiting in line at a restaurant, losing a car in a parking garage, and being forced as an adult to move back in with one's parents were a lot more relevant to most viewers' lives than were stories about cops, detectives, and even doctors. *Seinfeld* was credited with inventing a new genre that took it to the top of the ratings.

But *thirtysomething* had developed the idea two years before *Seinfeld* first appeared. In describing the pilot script he wrote with Herskovitz, Zwick said, "It's sort of about nothing."[98] When a prospective writer for the series asked about its premise, Herskovitz told him that his goal was to "redefine drama, to search it out in the minute emotional lacunae that television . . . has never been interested in."[99] Susan Shilliday, a writer for the show, said that one of the things that the producers wanted to do was to "delve into the smallest, most intimate details, the most incredibly boring and utterly fascinating corners of a marriage."[100] When presented, as it was in *Seinfeld,* in the context of sarcasm and satire, talk about "nothing" was funny and was eventually embraced by the mass audience. When *thirtysomething* started serving up the raw details of domestic life without the benefit of a laugh track, however, it entered dangerous and uncharted territory. One episode, for example, followed a serious crisis in the relationship of Hope and Michael that stemmed mostly, we learned much later, from his inability to pick up around the house without being asked. Although a story like this could be pulled off as comedy on *Seinfeld,* as a drama it ran the risk of appearing to be making a big deal over a problem that was minor and inconsequential compared to the high stakes of most other TV drama. The American Psychological Association gave the show an award for promoting the idea of "inner thinking,"[101] but without the distancing provided by comedy, the line between enlightening self-analysis and petulant bellyaching was a fine one.

Whether you liked the show or not, *thirtysomething* did indeed examine the details of personal emotional life with a degree of subtlety heretofore unknown to commercial television, and it did so with some of the best writing the medium had ever seen. Zwick defended what he called the show's "mandate of smallness," which was committed to looking right under our noses for the material of great American drama.[102] His partner concurred, saying "I believe strongly that if you go into any home, office, gas station or factory in America and get close enough to those people, you will find that they are incredibly upset about incredibly minor issues. . . . The so-called petty issues become the major issues in people's lives."[103] The audience's ambiguous feelings toward the show may have stemmed from the fact that although it validated the quotidian aspects of their lives, it also confronted them with a sometimes dark and existential treatment of those lives.

If you identified at all with the characters, watching *thirtysomething* could be like a weekly trip to the psychiatrist. Herskovitz, who admitted to having always wanted to be a therapist, said that "the underpinnings of the show are completely based in psychoanalytic theory. We try to get across the insights of therapy using behavior in normal relationships."[104] Many reports surfaced during the run of the series, in fact, that told of how episodes were being used by therapists across the country as part of their regimen of treatment.[105]

▪ ▪ ▪

That ABC ever agreed to make a series with the not-ready-for-prime-time aim of searching out "the minute emotional lacunae" of its characters reveals a lot about the state of network television in the mid-1980s. Still in third place when *thirtysomething* was being developed, ABC seemed to be sticking to the strategy they'd adopted in 1985. Feeling the loss of viewers to cable and other programmimg sources more acutely than the other networks, ABC was hoping to compensate for their weak ratings with great demographics, just as NBC had done a few years before. *thirtysomething* provided a portrait of the very audience advertisers, and therefore networks, were eager to attract. Although it never ranked above forty-sixth place in the annual ratings list, it did deliver the audience it was designed for. Even in its final season, *thirtysomething* was ABC's top hour-long program among eighteen-to-thirty-four-year-olds, and among eighteen-to-thirty-four-year-old women, it was the second highest rated hour-long series of the year on any network.[106]

In dealing with *thirtysomething*, ABC had also remained true to its 1985 policy of noninterference. As the show was winding down in the spring of 1991, Edward Zwick said "we've enjoyed extraordinary freedom at ABC."[107] That this policy was still intact after several management shifts at the network was somewhat surprising. By this time, Robert Iger was the head of ABC Entertainment, having taken over the job from Brandon Stoddard, who had taken it over from Lewis Erlicht, the one who first introduced the policy. One of the biggest tests of the network's commitment to the autonomy of the producers had come in the middle of *thirtysomething*'s third season, and it concerned what would become the most controversial installment of the series. In November of 1989, an episode aired that featured two men, who appeared to have just had sex, talking in bed together. Although there was no kissing or even physical contact between the two characters, several sponsors pulled a total of more than one million dollars worth of advertising from the episode. The creative community congratulated ABC for allowing the episode to air in spite of this loss of revenue, but they were disappointed when the network elected not to rerun it the following summer. In an unusual move, however, Robert Iger apparently went to producers Zwick and Herskovitz before he made his decision. "I told them that if they felt it were important to run this episode, they would have my full support," Iger said, "but that if they did not consider it a particularly important issue, that I, based on the economic issue [the loss of another million], would not [re]run it. They came back to me and said that they did not find it important enough to fight for."[108]

Iger also made it clear that the producers were free to "explore new territory, even if the territory they explore creates economic hardship,"[109] and that they were free to include the two gay characters in future story lines. The characters did appear again the following season, this time exchanging a New Year's Eve peck on the cheek, and once again advertisers pulled out. One of the characters made his final appearance in April, having tested positive for the HIV virus.

*thirtysomething's* writers avoided the issue-oriented stories that had characterized *Cagney & Lacey* and *L.A. Law*,[110] but the subject matter they explored was certainly not typical of American television, and the show helped establish ABC's developing reputation as a risk-taking network. Zwick observed that *"thirtysomething* [disproved] every theory I would imagine the networks have about what people supposedly want from television."[111] Besides presenting controversial lifestyles and stories with no discernible "action," the series broke other rules as well. It had a very un-TV-like proclivity, for example, to be a real downer.

Take the subject of cancer. Long considered life-threatening not only to the patient that has it but to the TV series that dares to bring it into our living rooms, *thirtysomething* presented not one, but two major story lines dealing with the disease. Unlike shows such as *Melrose Place*, which several years later would give cancer to a principal character as a means of placing her into new sexual and professional power struggles before introducing a miraculous cure, *thirtysomething* presented the disease in a much more personal and frightening context. In the first season Michael's dad dies of cancer, and in the third Nancy is diagnosed with an ovarian malignancy. Extended over more than half-a-dozen episodes across two seasons, we watched as she underwent surgery, lost her hair to chemotherapy, and sweated through her follow-up examinations. Even *Cagney & Lacey* had contained their cancer story within a special two-part episode. The centrality of Nancy's narrative was revealed by the fact that the episode in which she gets her final prognosis from her doctor was the highest-rated of the series. Acclaimed for its sensitive writing and acting, this story was painful to watch in a way TV usually avoids. And though the story ultimately ended happily, in the same episode that Nancy's body is declared free of cancer we learn of the sudden, random death of another main character, Gary, in an automobile accident.

Stories about cancer and the death of a principal character were not the only nontraditional ones in the series, either. Hope had a miscarriage in one episode and was injured in a serious car accident in another. Ellyn had a long-term affair with a married man, Melissa had a long-term affair with a man ten years younger than she was, Gary had a child with a woman he never married, and the marriage of Nancy and Elliot self-destructed over an entire season. Serious issues of religion—like cancer, a taboo on TV—came up between Hope and Michael, especially during Christmastime, and Elliot had a crisis of faith during his wife's illness.

All of this was only surprising, however, when compared to television before the big changes that occurred in the industry in the 1980s. By the time *thirtysomething* premiered, the breaking of television rules had become a rule itself. ABC was committing large chunks of its schedule to shows by "iconoclastic" producers who they felt would lure cable viewers back to network TV by giving them something different from what had made them defect in the first place. By the late 1980s, ABC was enticing a crowd of "quality" producers to the network with fat exclusive contracts and guaranteed orders. By filling its stable with creators like Bochco, James Brooks (*The Simpsons*), and Neil Marlens and Carol Black (*The Wonder Years*), ABC was developing nontraditional television as the new tradition.

In April 1991, Herskovitz and Zwick themselves signed an agreement with ABC to supply three new series over the next five years. A month later, *thirtysomething* was canceled. The cancellation, like most of the run of the show, though, was without the scandal and ire that accompanied so many quality shows. ABC programming chief Iger announced the cancellation by saying, "The most difficult decision we had to make this year was not renewing *thirtysomething,* perhaps the highest quality drama ever on network TV."[112] The decision had been a mutual one. Zwick, on the heels of his directorial success with *Glory* (1989), was preparing to direct his third feature film, and Herskovitz was working on his first, *Jack the Bear* (1993). Both had planned to leave *thirtysomething* at the end of the fourth season anyway. Many critics mourned the show's passing, but congratulated it for bowing out before it, like *Moonlighting* and *L.A. Law,* had overstayed its welcome. Some critics were glad to see it go, but trashing the show had become much less fashionable than it had been four years earlier. Tom Shales represented the grudging respect even many of its detractors had developed for the program. "*thirtysomething,*" he said, "whined with style."[113] On *The Tonight Show,* though, Jay Leno announced that "a major breakthrough was made in helping to relieve headache pain. ABC canceled *thirtysomething.*"[114] Some last-minute talk of making thirteen final episodes for the fall went on into the summer, but they never materialized. Neither, so far, have occasional rumors of a *thirtysomething* movie or a reunion television show.

•  •  •

Unlike *Hill Street Blues* and some of the other quality series, *thirtysome-thing* had few direct imitators, unless you count *Seinfeld* and *Mad about You,* which translated the spirit of the show into a comic idiom. ABC filled the Tuesday night time slot vacated by *thirtysomething* with *Home-front,* a unique domestic drama set in a small Ohio town just after the end of World War II, but the show was much more like a hip *Peyton Place* than a reworking of *thirtysomething.* Other shows that had made nods to *thirtysomething, Almost Grown* and *Baby Boom,* were both gone in less than four months.

The strongest influence the show had, most agreed, was on language and commercials. The compound "thirtysomething" entered the na-tional vocabulary as quickly as the acronym-derived "yuppie" was leav-ing it. Before long "twentysomething" was being used as an alternative to "Generation X" to describe the vaguely defined demographic of the post-baby-boom adult population.

The greatest legacy of *thirtysomething,* however, was left to the tele-vision commercial. The show's relationship to the advertising industry was a complex and often ironic one. A classic case of target marketing itself, much of *thirtysomething* was set in an advertising agency where the strategy of targeting audiences was all part of a day's work. As heads of their own company, and later as part of a larger agency run by 1980s uber-boss Miles Drentell (David Clennon), Michael and Elliot's work as shameless hucksters was often used to balance and comment upon the lives they led at home.

Though advertisers had twice pulled their commercials from epi-sodes of *thirtysomething,* the industry at large had no problem ripping off its style. "I hate to say it," Marshall Herskovitz told an interviewer after the third season, "but the only definite influence I've seen our show have on television programming is in commercials."[115] Indeed, shortly after *thirtysomething* debuted dozens of TV ads showed wise-cracking-but-earnest people in their thirties sitting around talking about nothing, and how it related to peanut butter, trousers, soft drinks, or automobiles.

The writers did get a last laugh, however. In one of the final episodes of the series, Michael resigns his position at the advertising agency when Miles forces him to fire an actor who'd been working on a beer campaign. The patriotic sponsor, he told Michael, had been offended when the actor's participation in a rally protesting the Gulf War had been covered by a local TV news report. Reportedly based on a claim made by actor Woody Harrelson that he was taken off a Miller Lite commercial because of his publicly vocalized opinions against U.S. military involvement in the Persian Gulf,[116] the episode featured Drentell's insistence that the client's desires must be met at all costs.

For two years, Michael's relationship with Drentell had added an element of nighttime soap-opera intrigue to the usually domesticated series. The previous season had ended in a *Dallas*-like story of Michael and Elliot's almost-successful corporate takeover of the agency. Since then, Miles's Machiavellian pragmatism had come to represent both the antithesis of Michael's ideals and the key to his professional future. His resignation provided a climax to two seasons' worth of conflict. Assessing Michael's moral outrage over the mandate that the actor-activist be fired, Miles, with thunder clapping in the background, launched into an eloquent if manic expose and damnation of how the advertising business works in the real world:

> He [the actor in question] expressed an unpopular opinion. No one wants to be unpopular. That's why we're here. That's the dance of advertising. We help people become popular. Through popularity comes acceptance. Acceptance leads to assimilation. Assimilation leads to bliss. We calm and reassure. We embrace people with the message that we're all in it together. That our leaders are infallible and that there is nothing—absolutely nothing—wrong. That is what we do. It's what we've always done, and under your gifted stewardship, what we will continue to do onward toward the millennium. In return for our humanitarian service, we are made rich. I'm sorry if you misunderstood the nature of this covenant, but you've done so well up till now—I thought you knew.[117]

The author of the episode, Joseph Dougherty, acknowledged that the monologue was Zwick and Herskovitz's way of "getting even a little" with the advertisers who bailed out on the episodes featuring the two gay characters. "Ed even used the phrase, 'We're biting the hand that feeds us,'" Dougherty reported.[118]

■　■　■

Herskovitz and Zwick began to fulfill their three-series deal two years later. The pilot of *My So-Called Life* was ready by April of 1993, but conditions at ABC had changed by then. Now punctuating the end of their programs with the promotional boast, "Watched by more people than any other network," ABC apparently had no appropriate time slot for the series and it would not finally be scheduled until August of 1994. Whereas it pretty much did to teenage life what *thirtysomething* had done to people in their thirties, critics were nearly unanimous in their praise for *My So-Called Life*. But the ratings were considerably lower than even *thirtysomething*'s had been.

After sixteen months of trying, ABC might have come up with a better position for the show. Scheduled on Thursday nights at eight o'clock, *My So-Called Life* was up against NBC's hit sitcoms *Mad about You* and *Friends,* both of which appealed to the same audience it was hoping to attract. Not only was the competition devastating, but the producers also felt that the show was being aired too early. They'd been delighted with the time slot of *thirtysomething,* which followed some of ABC's highest-rated comedies, and felt that the "intense drama" of *My So-Called Life* needed to be aired later. "Even people who are sympathetic to this kind of programming are not prepared to sit down and watch this kind of drama at 8 o'clock in the evening," said Scott Winant, one of the show's executive producers.[119]

Indeed, the one time the show aired at ten o'clock on a Tuesday, its ratings climbed dramatically. But Tuesday at ten was the regular time slot of *NYPD Blue,* a massive hit no one at ABC was ready to move, and the ten o'clock slots on Wednesdays, Thursdays, and Fridays were devoted to inexpensive and profitable newsmagazines. Winant acknowledged that he was aware that because of ABC's success "there's not a tremendous motivation to move shows around to try and make hits."[120]

Just as ABC had followed NBC's pursuit of quality for ratings, it was now experiencing, as NBC had, the inflexibility brought on by success. After only nineteen episodes, *My So-Called Life* was canceled.

## CHINA BEACH: HISTORIC QUALITY

In the years between the downfall of the Western in the early 1960s and its reappearance in the early 1990s, TV set in the historical past didn't play much of a role in prime time series television. With the exception of the pop nostalgia of *Happy Days* and *Laverne & Shirley* and the occasional family fare of *The Waltons* and *Little House on the Prairie,* audiences seemed to prefer taking their history lessons in the more limited dosages offered by blockbuster miniseries like *Roots, Shogun,* and *The Winds of War.* The only regular series with a historical setting to hit the top twenty-five in the last decade were *The Wonder Years, In the Heat of the Night,* and *Dr. Quinn, Medicine Woman.* Amazingly enough, even war, a mainstay of the cinema, has not played very frequently or successfully on series TV, and not surprisingly, the comedies have done better than the dramas. *Hogan's Heroes, McHale's Navy,* and *M\*A\*S\*H* played to bigger audiences and are easier to find in syndication than *Combat, Rat Patrol,* or *12 O'Clock High.* Television is often turned to for escape and relaxation, and perhaps war is only relaxing when it's funny.

*Holocaust,* for instance, worked because it lasted only four evenings as part of NBC's *Big Event.* When designed for weekly viewing over six consecutive years, however, life in a Nazi prisoner camp was reduced to the madcap shenanigans of Colonels Hogan, Klink, and their wacky troops.

The Vietnam War, especially, was ignored by network series television for years. *M*A*S*H* may have managed the only prime-time critique of the war while it was still being fought in 1972, but only by leavening its message with a laugh track and by disguising itself in the setting of 1950s Korea. It wasn't until sixteen years after the debut of *M*A*S*H* and thirteen years after the last American choppers had left Saigon, that commercial series TV was finally ready to treat the Vietnam War directly in a dramatic context. Then, within seven months of each other, two network programs premiered that were set in Vietnam during the 1960s. *Tour of Duty* and *China Beach* were part of a delayed genre syndrome that was also evident off the networks. Between 1986 and 1988 *Platoon* (1986); *Hanoi Hilton* (1987); *Full Metal Jacket* (1987); and *Good Morning, Vietnam* (1987) were released in theaters, and the fact-based series *Dear America: Letters Home from Vietnam* and *Vietnam War Story* debuted on cable.

*Tour of Duty* got the jump on *China Beach* by half a season when it began airing in September 1987. It was a valiant if ultimately hopeless attempt to bring the grim realities of *Platoon* to television on a weekly basis. Most of the action took place right on the battlefield, and the body count started to mount within the first three minutes of the pilot episode. Bloody corpses, muddy soldiers, rat-infested foxholes, and inexperienced officers announced that this was no *Gomer Pyle, U.S.M.C.,* a 1960s armed forces sitcom that took place during this same period but that avoided any mention of the war. Traditional TV rules were broken regularly on *Tour of Duty.* Two principal characters were killed in action in the first season, and another became a drug addict in the second. All this combined with its large ensemble cast (headed up by *St. Elsewhere's* Terence Knox), its liberal politics, its classy writing and acting, and its low ratings placed it right in the tradition of quality TV.

As good as it was, however, the show ultimately succeeded best in proving that there were some things that movies just did better than television. Set amid a large group of men going regularly into battle, the language alone was by necessity too sanitized to ring true. Whereas the script of *Platoon* was able to turn the profanity-laced vernacular of the American soldier into a kind of macabre poetry, *Tour of Duty's* vocabulary was gagged by network standards and television traditions. During one mission, an angry private lashes out by calling a fellow soldier "dumb and ugly," words that were grossly overpowered by the images on the screen. For that matter, the images themselves, though more graphic than most we'd seen in previous TV series, could never approach the brutality of what was possible in movies. Even had network standards allowed such brutality, it is likely that many viewers would have found it far too depressing to watch week after week. Strangely enough, CBS exacerbated the problem by scheduling the series at eight o'clock for two of its three seasons, a time slot that usually accommodates the fact that younger viewers are still awake and watching. *Tour of Duty's* ratings started low and fell throughout its three-season run.

Although it lasted only a half a season longer than *Tour of Duty*, *China Beach* was something else entirely. Its story is a compelling example of the struggle between art and commerce in a mass-distributed commercial medium. In its original Wednesday night berth at least, when the show was for a while consistently winning its time slot, a workable balance between the two elements seemed to have been struck. Like *Cagney & Lacey*, *China Beach* played by enough of television's rules to allow it to break a few.

Most critics raved about the innovation and quality of the show, but it still bowed to a lot of the old-fashioned demands of prime-time TV. For all its groundbreaking features, *China Beach* had a lot in common with *Charlie's Angels*. The series concerned the activities at a combination recreation area, EVAC hospital, and USO Club on China Beach near Da Nang, South Vietnam. The very first scene of the very first episode featured a young woman, the series' leading character Nurse Colleen McMurphy (Dana Delany), in a bathing suit on a beach. Before the episode was over we'd see her undressing, taking a shower, and sporting a tight, shiny minidress while dancing with a group of go-go-booted women singers who figured prominently thoughout the story. One of the show's other principal characters was a prostitute (Marg Helgenberger) who was introduced every week in the opening credits in a slow, caressing camera shot that started at her feet and slowly slid up her long, naked legs.

Though the female characters on *China Beach* were offered up as sexual objects for the voyeuristic male gaze,[121] ABC was also eager, and thus so were the producers, to achieve the difficult task of making a war series also attractive to a female audience. Toward this end, the show selected as its primary focus the unsung women heroes who served in Vietnam. Besides Nurse McMurphy and prostitute K. C., the major cast included Red Cross volunteer Cherry White (Nan Woods), entertainer Laurette Barber (Chloe Webb), journalist Wayloo Marie Holmes (Megan Gallagher), and Major Lila Garreau (Concetta Tomei). "I think [ABC] liked the idea of women [as leads]," series co-creator

William Broyles, Jr., told a reporter for *Electronic Media,* "because they felt they could perhaps build a female audience."[122] On another occasion, Broyles said that he sold the show to ABC as "a women's steambath inside a big men's locker room, a show about how women have to deal with men far away from home, and form friendships with each other."[123] Romance, an element many network executives have traditionally thought of as de rigueur in any show aimed at women viewers, also played a major role in the series.

Broyles believed that telling a Vietnam story about women allowed him and co-creator John Sacret Young to eschew the battlefield for more personal manifestations of the war. "Because we're about women, we're removed from traditional storytelling," he explained, "and we're liberated from traditional combat shows. We can explore what war does to people."[124] Indeed, except for the sounds of explosions in the background, some of the tent talk on *China Beach* sounded a little familiar. "If *Tour of Duty* is the war genre's *L.A. Law,*" a story in *Time* suggested, "*China Beach* is its *thirtysomething:* narratively loose-jointed, laced with ironic dialogue and moral introspection."[125]

By featuring women as both sexual objects and narrative centers of identification, *China Beach* was clearly attempting to cater to the heterogeneous demographic needs of network TV. In doing so it succeeded in reaching a considerably larger audience than the more conventional *Tour of Duty* had. In a final season attempt to save itself, in fact, *Tour of Duty,* which included not a single woman on the screen when it started, introduced two female characters and the attendant romantic story lines. Although most veterans didn't experience Vietnam the way it was presented on *China Beach,* Broyles and Young managed to bring a sincere treatment of the war to prime time by presenting it in a context that wasn't completely unfamiliar and alienating to most viewers. Furthermore, for all its marketing savvy, *China Beach* did manage to inform viewers that women had, in fact, served in Vietnam.

The romance and coed status of *China Beach* by no means captured the true essence of the war, of course. Much of what was portrayed on the show could have really happened, and some of it probably did, but a distinct emphasis was placed on the made-for-TV qualities of the American experience in Vietnam. One of the stories in the pilot episode, for example, concerned an aspiring singer who had flown in on a volunteer mission to perform in a show at China Beach. In a plot more reminiscent of *A Chorus Line* (1985) than of *Platoon,* the singer realizes her future hangs upon the performance when she learns that an important talent agent will be in the audience.

In fairness to the show's producers, however, it should be pointed out that these R & R facilities really existed and a good deal of effort was made to present them with accuracy. Co-creator Broyles, a marine lieutenant during the war, had himself spent a few days at China Beach. Dozens of women veterans of the war were interviewed during the development of the show, some of whom were featured talking about their experiences in an episode that won a Peabody Award. Furthermore, a former evacuation hospital nurse had been employed as the series' technical adviser, and two of the show's stars, Dana Delany and Jeff Kober, visited Vietnam in 1988 as part of an attempt to strengthen the realism of their characters.

▪ ▪ ▪

The history of *China Beach* was fairly typical for a quality drama in the 1980s. A contemporary of *thirtysomething* and another beneficiary of ABC's last-place-inspired experimental mood, the show was developed in an environment of comparative creative freedom.

John Sacret Young had been writing in network television for over a decade before he became half of the creative team that developed *China Beach*. He had worked on an unsold pilot, a short-lived series, and a few made-for-TV movies before he would find a project that would stake out important new narrative territory for him. When CBS decided to bring Philip Caputo's novel *A Rumor of War* to television as a two-part, four-hour miniseries in 1980, Young was hired to write the screenplay. Based on Caputo's own experiences leading up to, during, and following his service in Vietnam, this was the first TV movie to treat the war as a major theme. A writer for the *Washington Post* said Young's script had "caught the cadences of men in combat about as well as anyone has done it on film."[126] From there, Young left network TV to work in the higher-brow media of the novel and PBS. *The Weather Tomorrow*, his short book about two down-and-out buddies failing to grow up in California, was published by Random House in 1982, and his sceenplay for *Testament*, a film about the effect on one family of the outbreak of nuclear war, was produced as a 1983 installment of *American Playhouse*.

The other half of the *China Beach* team was William Broyles, Jr., who, like many of the staff of 1980s quality shows, came to the project with little experience in television. A graduate of Rice and Oxford universities, Broyles had worked as an editor of *California* magazine, the founder and editor of *Texas Monthly*, and editor-in-chief of *Newsweek*. An ex-marine and a Vietnam vet, Broyles wrote of his return to Vietnam in 1984 in a memoir entitled *Brothers in Arms*.[127] Young encountered the book while doing research for a miniseries he was working on, and the two were soon discussing doing a project together.[128]

The comparison between what Young and Broyles eventually came up with and *M*A*S*H* was inevitable. In fact, Broyles had originally conceived of *China Beach* as a sitcom about Vietnam nurses.[129] Both shows examined the war through the eyes of medical staff trying to heal the wounded, both favored interpersonal exchanges over battle-field action, and both were critical of war and the bureaucratic powers that waged it. Both series even ended their runs with extended mov-ielike final episodes—*M*A*S*H*'s "Good-bye, Farewell, and Amen" and *China Beach*'s "Hello, Goodbye" each showed the characters responding to the ambiguous end of an ambiguous war.

*M*A*S*H* had been a comedy seasoned with a little drama, however, and *China Beach* was a drama occasionally lightened by comedy. But the most significant difference between the two shows was that *M*A*S*H* was essentially about men, and *China Beach* was essentially about women. The only female in the regular cast of *M*A*S*H* was Major Margaret Houlihan (Loretta Swit). Though her character devel-oped and strengthened considerably over the years, and her nickname "Hot Lips" was dropped, Major Houlihan's presence in the early sea-sons was used mostly as a foil for the male leads. Other women charac-ters came and went as they were needed, and actors were used interchangably for these nearly anonymous parts. *M*A*S*H*'s cast ros-ter lists ten women playing multiple roles as "various nurses."[130] On *China Beach*, the equation was flipped. The show did feature male leads in significant roles, but the central narrative focus was nearly always on the women. Women played a major role in the production of the series as well, writing and/or directing over half the scripts. The story editors were all women, as were many of its producers, including Lydia Wood-ward, a former writer on MTM's *St. Elsewhere*.

Women's issues were not addressed on *China Beach* to the extent that they were on *Cagney & Lacey*, but they were certainly an important part of the narrative mix. Both McMurphy's alcoholism and K. C.'s drug problem, for example, were reminiscent of the problems Chris Cagney had gone through a few seasons back. One of the most famous episodes of the series, though, concerned the botched abortion of Holly, a "do-nut dolly" volunteer played by Ricki Lake. Told backward in time,[131] beginning at the end of the story and ending at the beginning, the episode was, for television, daring in both form and content. Hoping not to enrage large blocs of an already small audience, the writer re-frained from making this either a pro-choice or a pro-life episode. On the one hand, a clear message in support of legalized abortion was implicit in the presentation of the life-threatening horror that results from Holly's back-alley job; on the other hand, McMurphy, the show's moral center, comes out dead set against the procedure in any context. Balanced treatment or not, having a main character choose to have an abortion was a big risk on network television. The response by several advertisers was the same as it had been a few months ago toward the *thirtysomething* episode that showed two men in bed together: many of them pulled their commercials from the show.[132]

Occasional ad defections, though, had become one of the defining characteristics of a quality drama. And network executives, who traditionally took the blame for artistic timidity, could now point to advertisers as the bad guys—spineless pitchmen too scared to stick with the exciting experiments going on at the network. "It's a sorry state of affairs," ABC programming head Robert Iger said of the *thirtysomething* and *China Beach* sponsor pull-outs, "when advertisers are acting as skittish as they are. . . . The networks seem to get a lot of grief for it; the sponsors are the ones that should really get the pressure in some cases."

The occasional upset advertiser was not the only thing about *China Beach* that placed the show within the quality tradition either. The series employed the characteristic large ensemble cast, and it borrowed from a wide variety of generic conventions. Part medical show, part domestic drama, and part occasional comedy, *China Beach* even used its setting in a recreational facility as an excuse to become a musical every now and again. And the killing off of a major character that, because it wasn't expected of traditional TV, had also become a quality must, was done by *China Beach* in the first full season of the series. In an episode entitled "Tet '68" (the same title used in an installment of PBS's 1983 documentary series *Vietnam: A Television History*), Red Cross worker Cherry White is killed while comforting a soldier at a nearby fire base.

*China Beach*'s rise and fall also followed the quality perscription. Critics called it a "masterpiece" and "TV art," saying "even TV this good is rarely this good."[133] It won a Golden Globe for best drama, a Peabody, and two Writers Guild Awards, and if it only won two Emmy Awards, it was due to the fact that the quality field was getting pretty crowded by this time.

Introduced late in the 1987–88 season with six episodes, *China Beach*'s ratings ranged between sixtieth and seventieth place for the next two seasons, but it often won its Wednesday time slot for ABC, and it became part of one of the network's most successful evening lineups. Originally designated for cancellation near the end of the 1989–90 season, the show was revived at the last minute but exiled to a new and less desirable part of the schedule. This move represented what would become a fairly typical strategy that all three networks would develop toward some of their lower-rated quality series. Committed enough to air the shows for their prestige and premium demographics, network executives often weren't committed enough to give them good time slots or to leave them in slots where they thought other programs might do better. *Hill Street Blues, Cagney & Lacey, L.A. Law,* and *Twin Peaks* would all eventually be moved from their established places on the network schedule. *China Beach* was first moved to Mondays in the spring of 1990, then banished at the start of the 1990–91 season to Saturdays, the worst-rated night of the week. There it went up against NBC's hit sitcoms *The Golden Girls* and *Empty Nest.*

Perhaps network executives thought that the upscale audience for quality shows was so smart that surely it would be able to follow the schedule changes and set its VCR timers if the new time periods were inconvenient. Or perhaps they were simply putting these shows out to pasture. Whatever the case, none of the series mentioned above survived the move for more than a few months. *China Beach*'s ratings went down 42 percent when it moved to Saturdays,[134] and by December it left the air on indefinite hiatus. *Twin Peaks* had also been moved to Saturdays that fall, but its producers persuaded ABC to return it to its original Thursday night period in March. John Sacret Young rallied for the same treatment for *China Beach* to no avail. The final seven episodes, including the two-hour finale set at the Vietnam War Memorial, weren't aired until the dog days of June and July, in yet another time slot. By that time the fall schedule was set and *China Beach* wasn't on it.

Young lamented that ABC had "shot the life out of *China Beach*"[135] and that the schedule changes had "slowly maimed" the show.[136] But some argued that the Saturday time slot was not the only thing that caused *China Beach*'s ratings to plummet in its final season. Although the Gulf War wouldn't begin until the show was already on hiatus, by January 1991, when the future of the series was hanging in the balance, overt antiwar sentiments like those expressed on *China Beach* suddenly became a lot less fashionable. Young, of course, said the war was a good reason to bring *China Beach* back and that its message was needed now more than ever.[137] Robert Picardo, who wasn't a doctor but played one on *China Beach*, went so far as to say that "if *China Beach* got the ratings *L.A. Law* got, we would not be in the Persian Gulf right now. There's a very strong and solid antiwar message in *China Beach* toward the policy that had us engage in that conflict. That would be a lesson we all deserve to examine in light of our present conflict."[138]

Also contributing to the final season ratings slide may have been the innovative but confusing narrative experiment the show had launched that year. Episodes began to flash back to when McMurphy first arrived at China Beach and flash forward to when she'd returned home again. The season opened with a scene set in 1985, then shifted to 1967. In an attempt to examine the effects of the war on its participants, the writers showed them in stories that were spread over two continents and a twenty-year period. 1969, 1970, 1972, 1988: a casual viewer might not know where or when they were in any given episode. An artistic triumph, the strategy stretched the narrative structure of television more than any TV drama to that date. As with other quality series, however, the brave new style was probably made possible by the fact that the producers felt they had nothing to lose. "The visual grammar that *China Beach* has mastered in its last season, so reflective of the war experience and yet so foreign to the medium, probably could have only happened when the end of the story was in sight," Gail Caldwell wrote in the *Boston Globe*. "This is one of the black-hearted ironies of TV drama—that it rises above the constraints of its form only when threatened with the kiss of death. You can't bring home a bunch of war-damaged vets, facing rehab centers and second marriages, with the intent of dragging them all through it again for yet another season."[139]

Whatever the reasons for *China Beach*'s downfall, the 1990–91 season marked a major change in ABC's programming philosophy. The relegation of *China Beach* and *Twin Peaks* to an evening that had been a ratings graveyard for ABC for a decade, and the subsequent cancellation of both series as well as *thirtysomething* seemed to indicate that Robert Iger had lost faith in the commitment to quality that he and his two predecessors had been following since 1985. Some evidence of this was apparent as early as the summer of 1990. Although, as we have seen, Iger had publicly stated that he would have rerun the controversial episode of *thirtysomething* featuring a gay couple had the producers insisted, the sincerity of that statement was called into question when he also decided not to rerun the episode of *China Beach* that dealt with Holly's abortion. Carol Flint, a producer of the show who had written the episode, aggressively requested that the rerun be rescheduled. It wasn't.[140]

■   ■   ■

Cable TV not only frightened the networks into launching the second golden age of television, it also provided a place for the shows to go once the networks were finished with them. All five of the series considered in this chapter were rerun on Lifetime.

# 7

## Quality Goes Quirky:
### *Twin Peaks, Northern Exposure, and Picket Fences*

F or the makers and distributors of quality television, the 1980s was a tough act to follow. During that decade, after over thirty years of safe, conventional programming, television had finally caught up with other artistic media in a massive aesthetic updating project. In a few short years, *Hill Street Blues* and *St. Elsewhere* had replaced *T. J. Hooker* and *Trapper John, M.D.,* as the standards in their respective genres, and shows like *thirtysomething* had established new narrative approaches to televised dramaturgy. Commercial television could no longer be fairly accused of being nothing but a cultural junkyard.

But the revolutionary shows of the early- and mid-1980s had become the prototypes for what was fast becoming yet another set of predictable formulas. "Realistic" cop shows where the bad guys sometimes win, "realistic" sitcoms where the family dinner is often poured from a jar, "realistic" medical dramas where the patients don't always get well— these brave, new ideas now had imitators all over the network schedules. Since it had worked so well in the 1980s, many producers and program executives continued to hold onto the idea that constant innovation and surprise would be the best way to deal with the shrinking audiences and expanding competition that faced them in the new decade. ABC, and to a lesser extent CBS, embraced the notion that continuing to push the envelope would be the most effective way to overtake the increasingly vulnerable first-place NBC and to curb the flow of the audience from network to cable programming.

But somewhere along the way, this strategy got a little out of control. Providing programs that were *different* seemed to become a higher priority than providing programs that were *good.* Shocking iconoclasm for its own sake became more associated with "quality" than solid stories told in more traditional ways. *Quirky,* the word many viewers and critics enlisted to describe these shows, "became not just an adjective but an objective, a goal that producers sought when writing and designing (and most especially pitching) new shows," according to Jeff MacGregor in the *New York Times.*[1] Once television began trying to keep ahead of the cutting edge, its discovery of the truly bizarre couldn't be far behind. Perhaps one of the comforting things about television programming before 1981 was that it evolved and changed so slowly. Now, as each quality drama vied to be more revolutionary than the last, the quality revolution itself was about to blow its fuse. The journey from the quiet beginnings of *Hill Street Blues* to the loud crash that ended *Twin Peaks* took ten years, but the latter was the inevitable outcome of the former. The hubris displayed when the makers and buyers of *Hill Street Blues* defied conventions in an effort to make money by making art, was probably destined to lead, eventually, to a series that made no sense.

## *TWIN PEAKS:* FROM ART HOUSE TO OUR HOUSE

The new artistic possibilites introduced by quality TV had begun to attract the notice of successful film directors by the mid-1980s. Throughout its history, of course, TV had always been considered the gross aesthetic inferior of the cinema. Many aspiring directors would slum around in television only until their big chance came, at which point they'd quickly beat it for the more legitimate world of film. During the 1980s, however, the old TV neighborhood began to look a lot classier. TV's audience was potentially more mature than the teen-skewing audience of most movies; the ongoing series offered narrative possibilities not available in a two-hour film; and both the networks and cable outlets were demonstrating an occasional willingness to let television makers experiment.

Michael Mann was one of the first to repatriate his old stomping grounds. Having cut his directorial teeth on trash shows like *Starsky and Hutch* and *Vega$,* Mann went on to direct oblique and artsy films like *Thief* (1981) and *The Keep* (1983). After he left television, however, the medium came a long way; *Hill Street Blues* was a far cry from *Starsky and Hutch.* In 1984, Mann paired up with a former *Hill Street* writer, Anthony Yerkovich, and brought his cinematic sensibilities back to TV with *Miami Vice.*

A year later, Steven Spielberg, the most commercially successful director in history, followed Mann back into television. Spielberg began his TV career while still in his twenties when he directed a segment of the pilot for the NBC series *The Night Gallery* in 1969. As an itinerant laborer at Universal, Spielberg directed episodes of *Columbo, The Psychiatrist,* and *Owen Marshall: Counselor at Law,* as well as three made-for-TV movies.[2] One of the movies, *Duel,* established his reputation when it garnered awards and critical praise after being released theatrically in Europe. From there, Spielberg began a breathtaking decade of box office record-breaking as the director of *Jaws* (1975), *Close Encounters of the Third Kind* (1977), *Raiders of the Lost Ark* (1981), *E.T. The Extra-Terrestrial* (1982), and *Indiana Jones and the Temple of Doom* (1984). Anxious to get this now legendary personality back into the fold, NBC offered him a deal that was both unprecedented and very lucrative. Before seeing a pilot or a rating point, they agreed to buy two entire seasons—forty-four episodes—of any series he saw fit to deliver. They also agreed to leave him alone to do it his way,[3] and they gave him $650,000 per episode with which to do it.[4] That was the highest fee given by any network to a half-hour series in 1985 and double what many sitcom producers were getting. In return, Spielberg gave them *Amazing Stories,* an anthology of supernatural tales inspired by *Night Gallery.* He directed a couple of episodes himself, and other established film auteurs, figuring what was good enough for this *wunderkind* was good enough for them, gladly agreed to have a go at making nineteen-inch pictures. Before the series was over, heavy hitters like Martin Scorsese, Clint Eastwood, Robert Zemeckis, Joe Dante, and Paul Bartel had each directed an amazing story.

Robert Altman was the next film *artiste* to return to television. Before directing such critically acclaimed movies as *MASH* (1970), *McCabe and Mrs. Miller* (1971), *Nashville* (1975), and *A Wedding* (1978), Altman had made a living directing segments of 1950s and 1960s TV series like *The Whirlybirds, Route 66, Maverick, The Millionaire, Alfred Hitchcock Presents,* and *Combat.* Twenty years later, he was back to do a few chic and quiet one-shots for TV—*The Laundromat* for HBO in 1985, a restaging of Harold Pinter's *The Dumbwaiter* for ABC in 1987, and a TV movie based on Herman Wouk's play *The Caine Mutiny Court-Martial* for CBS in 1988. Seeing the expanding creative freedoms offered by cable, Altman then teamed up with Garry Trudeau, the comic artist who wrote and drew *Doonesbury,* to create his first series, *Tanner '88.* An extraordinary program coproduced and occasionally directed by Altman for HBO, *Tanner '88* did to a presidential primary campaign what Garry Shandling's *The Larry Sanders Show* would later do to the talk show.

By 1990, it had become positively fashionable for big directors to create for the little screen. In April alone, two of them introduced new series to network television. One was John Sayles, a versatile director, writer, and actor who'd created a number of respected films including *The Return of the Secaucus 7* (1980), *Matewan* (1987), and *Eight Men Out* (1988). His series, *Shannon's Deal,* was about a Philadelphia lawyer who opened up his own practice after nearly destroying his life by gambling. The other was David Lynch, a master of the cult film whose most commercial project to date was *The Elephant Man* (1980). His series, *Twin Peaks,* was about a corpse wrapped in plastic, a woman who talked to a log, and a dancing dwarf who spoke backwards. A little more than a year later, *Shannon's Deal* was off the air. *Twin Peaks* didn't last much longer, but it changed the face of television.

That an artsy director like David Lynch would want to work in TV may have seemed a little surprising; that TV was interested in having him was downright bewildering. While Spielberg had a long track record of commercial bonanzas, Lynch, if he was known to the public at all, was known for odd and difficult films. With the exception of *The Elephant Man,* Lynch tended to make movies that were often incomprehensible by traditional Hollywood standards. In *Eraserhead* (1978), *Dune* (1984), and *Blue Velvet* (1986), images seemed to spill onto the screen from Lynch's id without benefit of translation. Film critic Richard Corliss called Lynch's body of work "fifteen years of the strangest characters and most hallucinogenic images an American filmmaker has ever committed to celluloid."[5] Though embraced by critics and serious cinéastes, Lynch's visions seemed highly unlikely candidates for television, even quality television.

But that was just the point. Quality television had helped networks like NBC and ABC fend off the onslaught of cable competition by giving the audience something different and unexpected. When the quality formula began to lose its novelty, ABC executives decided simply to look for something *more* different and *more* unexpected. So when David Lynch arrived at their door in 1989, they were ready to listen. If Michael Mann, a director of weird but visually stunning films, had been able to deliver a hit like *Miami Vice* to NBC, they reasoned, just think what Lynch, a director of even weirder and more visually stunning films, might be able to deliver to them. It didn't hurt that Lynch, like Mann, had joined forces with an ex-*Hill Street* employee, in this case Mark Frost. So a series that under normal circumstances would have been considered an absurd choice for network television actually seemed at the time like a great idea.

■　■　■

The *New York Times* reported that *Twin Peaks* was "the last important link in ABC's five-year plan for rebuilding the network."[6] As discussed in the previous chapter, the execution of that plan had commenced in

1985 when ABC Entertainment President Lewis Erlicht announced that the hands-on approach to programming that had characterized ABC since the Fred Silverman days was being abandoned. Brandon Stoddard replaced Erlicht shortly after this announcement, and most of the job of remaking ABC's corporate image fell to him. He operated under the assumption that if he could establish ABC as a haven for creative producers and innovative programming, profits would follow automatically.[7]

This "first be best, then be first"[8] approach that Grant Tinker had used to bring NBC to the top of the ratings had proven fairly effective for Stoddard as well. Series like *Moonlighting, thirtysomething, Max Headroom,* and *The Wonder Years* had succeeded in establishing ABC's reputation as the network of innovation, and this reputation had, among other things, helped Stoddard to lure quality king Steven Bochco away from NBC. "While fat, first-place NBC counts its profits," Howard Rosenberg reported in the *Los Angeles Times* in 1990, "and creaky, third-place CBS counts its aches and pains, viewers should be counting their blessings as second-place ABC continues to move crisply forward with some of the boldest programs to be found on American TV."[9]

That competition should be met with innovation[10] was another one of the Tinkerisms that Stoddard and his staff adopted. Innovative programming meant programming that was different—different from the kind of TV ABC had been insisting upon from producers in the years before 1985. The network was actively looking for shows that would defy the very rules that they had so stubbornly adhered to throughout most of the medium's history. The traditional, old-fashioned programming was now being used as the definition of what they *didn't* want. This desire for uniqueness was, of course, at the heart of the quality revolution. It meant that the network and the critics were looking for the same thing, if for contrasting reasons. The networks were trying to bring back some of their shrinking audience by giving them something completely different; the critics, who as a rule disdain regular TV, saw anything different as better than the same old thing. As the quest for the unusual continued to escalate, ABC was about to let Lynch take prime-time television to a whole new place.

Dino DeLaurentiis's studio, for which David Lynch had made *Dune* and *Blue Velvet,* went bankrupt just before Lynch was to begin shooting his next feature, *One Saliva Bubble,* with Steve Martin and Martin Short. Mark Frost, his friend and the cowriter of *One Saliva Bubble,* shared an agent with Lynch, and while their current projects were tied up with DeLaurentiis, the agent suggested that they do some television together. They came up with a proposal for a show about aliens called *The Lamurians* and took it to NBC, the network that at the time still had the reputation for doing the most daring projects. Riding high, however, NBC had few spots to fill and was playing it safe. So the two producers went to ABC with their next project, where the response was much more enthusiastic.[11]

Lynch and Frost were signed up by one of Stoddard's deputies, vice president of drama series Chad Hoffman. "We had a strategy to turn the network around by taking shots and being patient [which is] basically what NBC had done to pull itself up in the early eighties," Hoffman said, a good company man repeating the Stoddard philosophy.[12] Hoffman saw the script for the pilot of *Twin Peaks*. He saw the bewildering proliferation of characters, the subtle nuances, the obscure inside references and allusions. He knew what he was getting into, and that was exactly what he wanted. Not only did Lynch not have to fight for his quirky ideas, as Steven Bochco had so often had to do in the early days of quality TV, but he was being encouraged to indulge them to his heart's content.[13] Both Stoddard and Hoffman left the programming department in the spring of 1989, before *Twin Peaks* was given a place on the ABC schedule, but Stoddard strongly recommended to his successor, Robert Iger, that the show be given a chance.[14]

Since Lynch's television experience was limited to a few commercials, Frost's participation in the package probably helped clinch the deal for Iger. As a former writer-producer for *Hill Street*, Frost knew how to write for television and he'd be supervising the production of the new series. ABC executives were pinning a lot of hope on Lynch's ability to deliver a unique product, but they seemed to believe that they couldn't build a marketing strategy around someone most viewers had never heard of. Although they would sell *Cop Rock* the following season by celebrating its creator, Bochco, who had a history of appearing in person in on-air promotional ads,[15] ABC placed a three-page advertisement for the debut of *Twin Peaks* in *TV Guide* that didn't even mention Lynch's name.

The TV critics, on the other hand, made Lynch the center of their attentions. An art-house film director working in television seemed a godsend to these college-educated journalists who were professionally overdosed on traditional TV. They gushed on about the show, finding it different from regular TV and therefore excellent, and they became fascinated by the quirky oddness of its creator. Lynch spoke and behaved like an Artist was supposed to, and most critics lovingly reported the romantic idiosyncracies of this mysterious genius who had come along and given them something else to write about besides sitcoms and cop shows. For months, Lynch's face could be found on the covers of publications from *Time* to the *New York Times* magazine. Personal details about everything from his diet (heavily sugared coffee and milk shakes from Bob's Big Boy gave him inspiration) to how he wore his shirts (top button closed because he was afraid of exposing his neck) appeared over and over again in stories throughout the popular press. Working in a medium known for its anonymity, Lynch had become a bona fide auteur. "*Hill Street Blues* will probably have a far bigger effect on the history of television than *Twin Peaks* will," one critic said, "but nobody cares what Steven Bochco has for lunch."[16]

▪ ▪ ▪

The entire series portrayed thirty-two days in the life of the surrealistic small town of Twin Peaks, Washington. Filled with intricate details, baffling non sequitors, and nonlinear narratives, the series began when the dead body of seventeen-year-old homecoming queen Laura Palmer (Sheryl Lee) was found wrapped in plastic. Boyish F.B.I. agent Dale Cooper (Kyle MacLachlan, star of *Dune* and *Blue Velvet*) comes to town to investigate the murder and, together with the local sheriff, Harry S. Truman (Michael Ontkean), he encounters the strangest goings-on ever portrayed on American entertainment television.

Agent Cooper and Sheriff Truman were surrounded by a perplexingly huge ensemble cast of thirty additional regular characters, each bearing a passel of bizarre eccentricities ranging from an obsession with draperies to an ability to knot a cherry stem using nothing but tongue. Some of the characters, including a giant and a dwarf, seemed to exist only in the mystically rich psyche of Agent Cooper himself. At the heart of all this strangeness, it was slowly and ambiguously revealed, was BOB, a killer-spirit who could inhabit the bodies of others. By series end, BOB seems to have taken up residence in our hero, Agent Cooper himself.

Beautifully written, shot, and performed, there is no doubt that the thirty episodes of *Twin Peaks* are among television's most interesting and compelling aesthetic achievements. Not only did Lynch himself direct five episodes, but he enlisted other film auteurs to take on episode assignments as well, including Graeme Clifford (*Frances*, 1982), Caleb Deschanel (*The Escape Artist*, 1979), Uli Edel (*Last Exit to Brooklyn*, 1989), James Foley (*Glengarry Glen Ross*, 1992), Tim Hunter (*River's Edge*, 1986), Diane Keaton (*Heaven*, 1987), and Tina Rathborne (*Zelly and Me*, 1988).[17] ABC had certainly reached its goal of breaking the rules, and, in the beginning at least, the critics raised hosannahs. *Time* called it "the most hauntingly original work ever done for American TV,"[18] and a writer in *Connoisseur* magazine, echoing hundreds of similar sentiments being printed in magazines and newspapers across the country, called *Twin Peaks* "the series that will change TV forever."[19]

Undoubtedly prompted by all the hype in the press, viewers responded just as positively. The two-hour pilot, aired on April 8, 1990, was the highest-rated TV movie of the season. Before long, magazine covers, fan books, and merchandising tie-ins were announcing that this might just be the blockbuster series for which network TV had been waiting. Lynch, Frost, and a coauthor came out with an "Access Guide" to the town of Twin Peaks; Lynch's daughter Jennifer wrote a novel, *The Secret Diary of Laura Palmer;* and series writer Scott Frost whipped up *The Autobiography of F.B.I. Special Agent Dale Cooper.*[20] An audiotape featuring the memos Agent Cooper dictated on the show to his never-seen secretary Diane could be found in bookstores; a CD of selections from the sound track could be found in record stores; and "Who killed Laura Palmer?" became the biggest TV–inspired question since "Who Shot J.R.?"

One of the most interesting things about *Twin Peaks* was the care and dedication with which many viewers watched it. David Bianculli wrote in his book *Teleliteracy* that "never before, in the history of television, had a program inspired so many millions of people to debate and analyze it so deeply and excitedly for so prolonged a period."[21] Searching the intricately dense episodes for clues to Laura's murder, for example, inspired thousands of fans to subject the show to deep scholarly analyses.

*Los Angeles Times* critic Howard Rosenberg specialized in one particular type of clue and dedicated a series of columns to the identification of the intertextual allusions in *Twin Peaks* to old films and TV shows.[22] Before long, Rosenberg was getting letters by viewers from across the state who had noticed things he hadn't. Most of these clues were being used as a means to prove the speculation that Madeleine Ferguson (Sheryl Lee), Laura Palmer's lookalike cousin who had arrived in Twin Peaks after Laura's murder, was in fact Laura herself. The hypothesis held that Laura, about to be exposed for her scandalous activities involving sex and drugs, had killed her innocent cousin and assumed her identity. Among the supporting evidence turned up by the textual sleuthing of Rosenberg, his colleagues, and his readers were the following:

• The 1944 Otto Preminger film, tellingly titled *Laura,* told the story of an apparent murder victim who turns out to be still alive. The man who stalked Laura in the film was named Waldo Lydecker; the veterinarian and the myna bird in *Twin Peaks* were named Lydecker and Waldo, respectively.
• The insurance man in another 1944 film, Billy Wilder's *Double Indemnity,* was named Walter Neff. The insurance man in *Twin Peaks*

was also named Mr. Neff. The 1981 film *Body Heat* was inspired by *Double Indemnity* and featured a woman—named Maddie!—who faked her own death by assuming the identity of a lookalike friend she arranged to have killed.

• In Alfred Hitchcock's *Vertigo* (1958), a police detective named *Ferguson* falls in love with a girl named *Madeleine.* The girl, who had blond hair (like Laura Palmer), later is believed to have committed suicide, but she reappears in a new identity with dark hair (like Madeleine Ferguson).

And this was just the tip of the iceberg. Others found hundreds of similarly "meaningful" connections to everything from Tennessee Williams' *The Glass Menagerie* to the 1960s TV series *The Fugitive.* One critic even saw importance in the fact that a mysterious letter "J" found in Laura's diary, and an "R" cut from a newspaper found under the fingernail of her corpse might allude to *Dallas*'s J. R. Ewing, Laura's partner in TV cliffhanging.

■    ■    ■

In spite of all the hype, the magazine covers, the tie-ins, and the careful viewings, however, *Twin Peaks* fizzled fast. Many of the viewers who had tuned in to see this strange new sight, soon got their fill. While interest in the series remained strong in the press for the eight episodes that played in the spring of 1990, millions of people had already returned to their old viewing habits once the second episode had settled into its regular Thursday night slot against NBC's hit sitcom *Cheers.* In spite of the falling numbers, and perhaps because Lynch and Frost had left the identity of Laura Palmer's killer unsolved, Iger renewed the show. But he banished it, along with *China Beach,* to the scheduling gulag of Saturday night. That fall, the show got off to a slow start. By the time it got around to solving (sort of) the Laura Palmer mystery, the heat was already off. With no adequate stories to replace Laura's, the show seemed to lose its way. When it returned after a long holiday hiatus, much of its already small audience didn't return with it. After the February 16 episode ranked eighty-eighth out of ninety-four shows aired that week, the series was pulled from the schedule, and its future seemed uncertain.[23] The last six episodes played sporadically between April and June. The visually striking and narratively surprising two-hour Lynch-directed finale ranked third in its time slot, losing to reruns of *Designing Women, Murphy Brown,* and *Northern Exposure* on CBS and to a rerun of a TV movie on NBC.[24]

Richard Corliss had said that with *Twin Peaks* Lynch had "proved that an eccentric artist can toil in American TV without compromising his vision,"[25] but the fourteen-month rise and fall of the program may also have proven that he can't do it over the long haul of series television. For as much as Lynch said he loved the series form for its ability to draw things out, he ultimately failed at drawing them out indefinitely. He delivered what ABC wanted: something unlike anything else in the medium. But series television is incapable of sustaining constant innovation. Lynch could no more have continued to deliver the original concept of *Twin Peaks* season after season than James Joyce could have continued to write additional chapters of *Ulysses,* ad infinitum. *Twin Peaks* introduced an exciting new style and a bizarre new world to network TV, but it couldn't stay bizarre and exciting forever. At the foundation of the show's "difference" and its "art" was its rejection of television norms, including those of the ongoing series.

Traditional ways of judging creativity in a medium like television, according to Marc Dolan, an English professor who, like many other academics, have carefully studied *Twin Peaks,* stack the deck against the series form:

> If one is going to try to be an artist within the television medium, one must either: (a) create a work of intentionally finite length, like *The Day After, Scenes from a Marriage, The Civil War,* or a *Masterpiece Theatre* or *Mystery* adaptation of an already published novel; or (b) play with the medium itself, like Ernie Kovaks, Steve Allen, or their heir David Letterman. In neither mode is one permitted to sincerely create a good, ongoing series, since that would imply both implicit approval of the aesthetic of mass production and a certain respect for the medium itself. In other words, if a television series is going to be "art," it must go against the grain of the medium.[26]

*Twin Peaks,* in defying the series orientation of traditional television by focusing on the finite story of Laura Palmer's murder, was forced to redefine itself once that murder had been solved. The first season had played like a miniseries, and neither critics nor many regular viewers were comfortable when the second season began to resemble a more conventional series. Just coming up with new story lines for the characters wasn't enough either. Once the town and its denizens became familiar, the very strangeness that had been at the center of the show's appeal became normalized.

In spite of its quick demise, Iger and his colleagues at ABC were delighted with *Twin Peaks.* While still deciding whether or not to renew the series in the spring of 1990, Iger was crediting it with playing an "immeasurable" role in establishing ABC as the most adventurous network. Even then, though, he seemed to sense the show's limited life expectancy. "This experience, whether it ends up being long-term in nature, in terms of *Twin Peaks*'s life on ABC, or whether it is in fact short-term, will still be very, very positive for us," he was quoted as saying in a cover story in *Us*.[27]

．　．　．

In the long run, the most pervasive message of *Twin Peaks* may have been the way it made fun of the very types of interpretive urges described earlier. Indeed, each episode of the series was like catnip to well-educated, amateur semioticians who weren't used to TV that gave them so much to work with. Anyone who'd learned in college how to explicate a text could find a bonanza of raw material here. *Twin Peaks* sure looked like art. It even had subtitles in a few episodes. And all those symbols! The coffee, the cherry pie, the doughnuts, the chocolate bunnies, the Douglas firs, the ceiling fans, the owls, the long lingering shots of a changing stoplight—surely they all stood for something profound, because they didn't make much sense by themselves.

Trying to understand the show, and pretending to your friends and colleagues that you did, was great fun while it lasted, but one can't help but think that Lynch was having a good laugh at the expense of professors, critics, and viewers who were just learning to take the medium of television seriously. All the allusions ultimately added up to no coherent comment on filmic or televisual traditions. The many signs, symbols, and metaphors remained for the most part indecipherable. Like a Rorschach test, viewers found all kinds of meaning in *Twin Peaks*, but in the end it turned out to be just a blotch of ink—postmodern bluster, ultimately signifying nothing.

That, in fact, might be the show's greatest genius. David Lynch once said, "I don't know why people expect art to make sense,"[28] but the whole point is *they don't*. They expect *TV* to make sense and when it doesn't, then maybe it must be art. *Twin Peaks* in its odd way provided a critique of the quality TV genre of which it was the most extreme manifestation. By pretending not to be TV, it garnered the glory and respect that most would never have given to a conventional series. The definition of quality had come to say more about what a show was not than what it was. Appropriately enough, reruns of *Twin Peaks* played on Bravo, the exclusive art-house cable channel, with the promotional tag, "TV too good for TV."

．　．　．

For a select few, the careful study of the show is continuing years after its cancellation. A *Twin Peaks* newsgroup on the Internet recorded over six hundred postings per month in 1994, and *Wrapped in Plastic,* a bimonthly fan magazine dedicated exclusively to stories about the series, has been in publication since October 1992.[29] Even academics jumped and stayed on the bandwagon. Earnest critiques of the show began appearing in scholarly journals shortly after its debut, and in 1995 Wayne State University Press published a book of thirteen essays by twelve Ph.D.s entitled *Full of Secrets: Critical Approaches to "Twin Peaks."*[30]

The show's influence on prime time was also very strong, at least at first. After the explosive launch of the series, the other networks were all anxious to imitate it. In May 1990, Bill Carter reported in the *New York Times*, "Brandon Tartikoff, president of NBC Entertainment, and Jeff Sagansky, president of CBS Entertainment, have said that a main goal for the coming season is to create original programs with new formats. Their statements, made when they announced their program development plans to advertisers, have widely been interpreted in the industry as allusions to the creative originality of *Twin Peaks*."[31]

The most blatant knockoff, Oliver Stone's *Wild Palms*, was also aired on ABC. The hot film director, the reminiscent title, the hypersymbolism, the meandering antinarrative—they were all here. The surrealistic scene of a horse in a living room that had inexplicably appeared in *Twin Peaks*, for example, gave way in *Wild Palms* to an equally surrealistic scene of a rhino in an empty swimming pool. But by now this kind of thing was as passé as one of Sonny Crockett's pastel T-shirts. By the time *Wild Palms* came out, it had been two years since *Twin Peaks* had left the air with only its most dedicated fans left to mourn its passing, and the 1992 *Peaks* movie prequel, *Fire Walk with Me*, had been booed by audiences at Cannes and ignored by audiences in America.

The failure of *Wild Palms* put a quick end to direct imitations of *Twin Peaks* (until CBS brought out *American Gothic* in 1995), and the quick cancellations at all the networks of new series by film directors like Tim Burton, Robert Townsend, and Penny Marshall demonstrated that the importation of cinema artists was not necessarily a guarantee of successful television. Still, the spirit of *Twin Peaks* lived on in other shows. The celebrity Lynch had achieved with his artsy style was not lost on serious television makers, for whom a little respect went a long way. New standards for the quality drama had been set, and, for a while at least, they were fairly specific ones that called for a small town setting, idiosyncratic characters, bizarre story lines, and "deep" symbolism. All these elements had been part of what made *Twin Peaks* work, and many of them would find their way into the next generation of quality dramas.

## NORTHERN EXPOSURE: A KINDER KIND OF QUIRKY

In July 1990, CBS offered up something for all those viewers who were spending the summer wondering who killed Laura Palmer. Though

*Northern Exposure* was set in the fictional town of Cicely, Alaska, it was filmed in Roslyn, Washington, just down the road a piece from Snoqualmie, the town that stood in for Twin Peaks. The similarities between the two shows didn't stop with the scenery either. *Northern Exposure* had its own rural quirkiness, surreal story lines, and ensemble of off-centered characters. It wasn't just an imitation, however. *Northern Exposure* had already been conceived and developed before *Twin Peaks* premiered. The striking similarities between these two independently created series suggests that quality TV was following a distinct evolutionary path. The artistic mandate for innovation that had engendered *Twin Peaks* had apparently been yielding similar results elsewhere as well. Still, the writers of *Northern Exposure* began reacting to *Twin Peaks* early in their first season. *Exposure*'s fifth episode even featured a scene shot at Snoqualmie, in which the characters gaze at the waterfall as *Peaks*esque music plays in the background and mentions are made of coffee and cherry pie.

The media blitz that had surrounded the April and May episodes of *Twin Peaks* and that had inspired a large percentage of the television audience to sample the show at least once probably helped to create a friendly environment for the debut of *Northern Exposure*. *Twin Peaks* had taught millions of people how to watch TV in a way they never had before. Those skills would come in handy when those same viewers encountered *Northern Exposure*. At the same time, *Twin Peaks* had beaten *Northern Exposure* to the punch. Had it not been for the former, the latter would have probably been hailed as one of the most groundbreaking series to come along in many seasons.

Instead, *Northern Exposure* was called *"Twin Peaks* for beginners." But this was usually meant as a compliment. Tom Shales, who reviewed *Northern Exposure* in April 1991, suggested, "Former fans of *Twin Peaks* who feel that show has become too ridiculous to bear may find the snowy terrain of *Northern Exposure* a pleasing substitute. The series seems to have struck a happy balance: just ridiculous enough."[32] Although many critics agreed that *Twin Peaks* had gone too far, many still seemed to feel that a little "ridiculousness" was now a prerequisite for good TV. *Picket Fences* would continue in this tradition starting in the fall of 1992.

*Northern Exposure* was indeed more accessible than its predecessor. The fir-lined rural setting was still intact, but gone were the darkness and evil that colored every frame of *Twin Peaks*. Gone also were some of the astonishing cinematic high jinks and the totally over-the-edge characters of the earlier show, but in their place came a more domesticated oddness that was gentle enough to sustain a series through more than a hundred episodes.

The basic premise of *Northern Exposure* was pretty conventional. An urbane young doctor, born, reared, and educated in New York City, is forced to serve as the only physician in an isolated Alaskan town in order to fulfill the conditions of his medical school scholarship. Appended to this city mouse/country mice theme was the ongoing relationship between Dr. Joel (Rob Morrow) and local bush pilot Maggie (Janine Turner), which fell right into the tradition of Sam and Diane, David and Maddie, Tony and Angela, and a dozen other reluctant couples that had slowly slouched, season by season, toward the primetime bedrooms of the 1980s.

This is not to say that *Northern Exposure* didn't trot out its own collection of idiosyncracies. But while *Twin Peaks* had placed weird characters and stories within a weird premise, *Northern Exposure* anchored its weirdness in a premise with which any sitcom viewer would be comfortable. In fact, *Northern Exposure* owed as much to *Green Acres* as it did to *Twin Peaks*. Joshua Brand and John Falsey, the creators of the series, often explained in interviews that *Northern Exposure* was "a fish-out-of-water show."[33] Falsey went so far as to say that "the idea of urban versus rural is where it started."[34] In *Green Acres,* Oliver Wendall Douglas was an Ivy League (Harvard)-educated professional (lawyer) from the big city (New York) who came to the sticks to work the land. Joel Fleischman was an Ivy League (Columbia)-educated professional (doctor) from the big city (New York) who came to the sticks to heal its people. The only difference is that Oliver (Eddie Albert), moved by a 1960s-inspired Transcendentalist fever, went voluntarily; Joel, who wants no more to do with the wilderness than he gets taking a cab through Central Park, thinks he's been banished to an American Siberia. In both cases, the homegrown wisdom of the natives, though it may seem bizarre to the superiorly educated newcomers, turns out to be the best way of getting by.[35]

■ ■ ■

One of the inspirations for *Northern Exposure* was Lance Luria, Joshua Brand's former college roommate. A decade earlier, Luria's medical residency at the Cleveland Clinic had given Brand the idea for *St. Elsewhere.* When Luria opened his practice in a small upstate New York town surrounded by rural countryside, he provided Brand with the model for *Northern Exposure.*[36]

Brand and Falsey had left *St. Elsewhere* after its first season because they felt the show was giving up its dark and realistic edge in favor of a more comic approach. After a stint producing *Amazing Stories* and *A Year in the Life,* however, the pair returned to the doctor genre in a distinctly mellower mood. "We think of it, first and foremost, as a comedy with dramatic overtones," Falsey said of *Northern Exposure,* "as opposed to a drama with comedic overtones."[37]

With the appearance of *Northern Exposure,* it looked as if CBS was preparing to assume the throne of quality. The network had fallen into third place, and at the end of the 1990–91 season ABC had shed most of its experimental series from its schedule. Falsey and Brand were aware of the creative possiblities of working with a struggling network. "We were fortunate that when we first did [*St. Elsewhere*] NBC was the last-place network so they were willing to stick with the show a little longer," Brand observed just before *Exposure's* debut. "In this case, we're with CBS, and again, they're the last-place network, so hopefully, if the show is good, they will stick with it."[38] The new direction of CBS became even more apparent when the network introduced *Picket Fences* in 1992 and then signed Steven Bochco to a multiseries deal in 1995.

Like *Hill Street Blues, Cagney & Lacey, Moonlighting, China Beach,* and *Twin Peaks, Northern Exposure* did not premiere in the fall with most of the other new series. This was probably not a coincidence. Innovative programs like these needed all the help they could get, and second-season series had a potential competitive edge because they were airing alongside fewer new series and their promotional announcements weren't diluted and buried by the promo blitzkrieg that was launched by all the networks in the fall. These other quality dramas had begun in the spring, but *Northern Exposure* didn't make its first appearance until the middle of the summer, when overall viewership is way down. Though shows introduced in the summer have a dismal survival record, in the case of *Northern Exposure* the strategy may have been its salvation. It was scheduled against mostly reruns on the other networks, and it attracted a fairly large number of viewers who were wandering around the dial looking for something new.

CBS introduced more new series than usual in the summer of 1990, but a tight budget situation forced all five of them to be done on the cheap. One series, *Wish You Were Here,* was shot almost entirely with hand-held video cameras, and another, *Prime Time Pets,* depended heavily upon home videos sent in by viewers. The eight episodes of *Northern Exposure* that aired that summer were made on a shorter-than-average shooting schedule and with a budget of only two-thirds of what most other prime-time dramas received.

In searching for new ways to finance their ambitious summer schedule, CBS also came up with a deal for *Northern Exposure* that harked back to the golden age of the 1950s. Procter & Gamble, the veteran television advertiser that had put the soap in soap operas, agreed to pay for part of the production of the show and to buy half of its commercial slots in exchange for partial ownership.[39] This was consistent with Grant Tinker's frequently offered suggestion that the future of quality might lie in corporate sponsored programming.[40]

After the surprisingly strong performance of the eight episodes in July and August of 1990, CBS ordered seven more that would be ready for airing in April and May of 1991. In its first full season, 1991–92, *Northern Exposure* was a hit, ranking sixteenth in the annual ratings list and one week climbing as high as third. Showing its confidence in the series, CBS renewed it for two full seasons in March 1992.[41] Though Falsey and Brand left the day-to-day operations of the show shortly thereafter to develop *Going to Extremes,* a series about American students at a medical school in the Caribbean, the ratings of *Northern Exposure* climbed to eleventh place that year and held on to sixteenth place the following season.

As had been the case with *Twin Peaks,* merchandise based on the show began to flood the retail outlets. Believing that the type of person who watched *Northern Exposure* was also likely to read books about it, publishers came out with a veritable library of volumes celebrating the series, including a cookbook inspired by the show's obsession with food, feasts, and other culinary matters.[42]

Not surprisingly, the critical response to the show was also very enthusiastic. By 1992, *Northern Exposure* had won, as best dramatic series, an Emmy, two Golden Globes, and an *Electronic Media* Critics Poll Award. The Television Critics Association had named it their "Program of the Year," and it won the Peabody two years in a row. Most critics effervesced about the show for all the usual reasons. One of them showered it with praise by saying, "Watching *Northern Exposure* is a lot like reading a good book."[43]

Sometimes *Northern Exposure* wasn't just *like* reading a good book, it actually presented people reading good books. Throughout one entire episode, for example, new age ex-con-cum-disc-jockey Chris Stevens (John Corbett) reads passages from *War and Peace.* In the meantime, according to the producers' plot synopsis, the residents of Cicely "experience Tolstoyesque nightmares and Dostoyevskian passions."[44] Chris, an intellectual dilettante who seemed to be taking all of his on-air rambling patter from a college syllabus, went a long way in giving the show its cerebral if somewhat self-important veneer. At one time or another during the course of the series, Chris made references to works by Hegel, Kierkegaard, Kant, Nietzsche, de Tocqueville, Jefferson, Whitman, Baudelaire, Melville, Shakespeare, Jung, Jack London, Edna St. Vincent Millay, and many other authors. No nerd, Chris was just as fluent with Raymond Chandler or Def Leppard, but it was his perpetual name-dropping and passage citing from the Great Books that seemed to announce, as Falsey and Brand had often boasted, that *Northern Exposure* wasn't written for the "mass audience."[45]

Sly allusions to and inside jokes about television, on the other hand, were less important in *Northern Exposure* than they had been in some of the earlier quality dramas. The pilot did include a quick reference to Falsey and Brand's *St. Elsewhere*, and, in a second-season episode, Joel breaks character, *Moonlighting* style, during a scene in which ex-astronaut and town tycoon Maurice Minnifield (Barry Corbin) and a visiting Russian are about to engage in an old-fashioned duel. In the latter example, actor Rob Morrow, no longer playing "Joel," complains that the television audience will never accept the way the story is going, and all the actors agree to move on to the next scene.

But *Northern Exposure* came to depend less and less upon "inside" jokes for its hipness. "Outside" was more what this show was all about. Shot mostly near Seattle, the show's physical distance from Hollywood was reflected in its style and attitude. The scenery was different from most TV, and so were the clothes that occasionally reflected the Pacific Northwest grunge that was about to go mainstream. Most representative of *Northern Exposure*'s "alternative" status was its use of music. While familiar songs by familiar artists might be among the mix of the twelve or so recordings that would be used in each episode,[46] it was just as likely that the music would be that of an unknown regional group, a garage band, or a Hawaiian slack key guitar duo. Rather than making fun of popular culture, which *St. Elsewhere* had done so adeptly, *Northern Exposure* seemed more concerned with ignoring it in favor of the culture that flits about the fringes of popularity. Eclecticism took the place of irony in *Northern Exposure* as the principal source of hip.

■    ■    ■

By the 1994–95 season, *Northern Exposure* had begun to succumb to the disease that eventually afflicts all television series, especially those that depend upon their own uniqueness. The unusual people and activities of Cicely weren't so unusual anymore after five years. When Paul Provenza replaced Rob Morrow as the show's leading medical man midway through the season, it appeared that maybe some fresh themes might be introduced. Provenza's character, Dr. Phillip Capra, had come willingly to Cicely with his journalist wife Michelle (Teri Polo) to escape the bustle of the big city, and the way he related to the locals was very different from the way Joel had.

The new chemistry of the show never had time to establish itself, however, before CBS executives moved the series from its cushy Monday berth to make room for David Kelley's *Chicago Hope*. Like *Hill Street Blues*, *Cagney & Lacey*, *L.A. Law*, and *China Beach*, *Northern Exposure* didn't survive the switch to a second-class time slot. It ended its final season in fiftieth place.

Five years on the air, however, is nothing to scoff at. *Northern Exposure* had managed what *Twin Peaks* had not: a respectably long run that would assure it of a decent syndication package. It had done this, for the most part, by tempering the freaky outlandishness of *Twin Peaks* with the careful psychic exploration of *thirtysomething*. As was decidedly not the case with *Twin Peaks,* there was something in each of *Northern Exposure's* eccentric characters with which viewers could identify. Chris Steven's desire to create the ultimate conceptual art performance by flinging a live cow across the tundra with a catapult, for example, was a story line that would have felt right at home on *Twin Peaks.* The crazy premise, however, was used as a launching pad for some serious dramatic exploration of the nature of creativity, inspiration, and moral compromise.

Like *thirtysomething, Northern Exposure* often employed dream and fantasy sequences as a means of getting inside the heads of its characters. An ongoing series story concerned Maggie's "curse," which results in the anomalous death of any boyfriends she sleeps with. To wit, Harry was poisoned by bad potato salad; Bruce went while fishing; Glenn accidentally drove his car onto a live missile testing site; Dave froze to death on a glacier; and Rick was hit with an errant communications satellite and had to be buried in a coffin with holes out of which two antennae could stick. For all this kookiness, though, Maggie's curse was often used as an effective means by which she explored her inability to maintain a stable relationship. In one episode, she goes off camping by herself as a way to deal with a major personal crisis brought on by her thirtieth birthday. In a series of fever-induced hallucinations she meets with and talks to all of her late former boyfriends. Their frank discussions about what went wrong in each relationship are as narratively probing and as psychologically relevant as anything that had played on *thirtysomething.*

▪  ▪  ▪

The real cornerstone of *Northern Exposure,* the glue that kept it all together in a way *Twin Peaks* never managed, was its spirituality. Represented most prominently by deejay Chris, a mail-order minister who preached a creolized blend of every major world faith and them some, and the community of Native American townsfolk and visitors, the spiritual life played a crucial role in the daily operations of Cicely. From the Pilgrims' crossing of the Atlantic to the Mormons' trek to Utah, the quest for religious and individual fulfillment in the American experience has often involved an urge to go West. Alaska, the nation's "last frontier," then, was a perfect setting for a new age Western of the 1990s. The state represented, according to Brand, "something very fundamental in everyone's imagination—and the place where everything that wasn't nailed down in society could end up."[47]

And quite an assortment of characters ended up in Cicely. The town was founded as an artists' colony by two women lovers back in 1909, as revealed in a third-season, fully costumed flashback episode. One of the women, Cicely, had converted the settlement's motley collection of cowboys, trappers, and miners into a community of tea-sipping aesthetes using nothing more than her hauntingly beautiful interpretive dance honoring the earth goddess. The tiny town had been a haven of tolerance ever since, offering its citizens the "freedom to be who they want to be," and ultimately offering Joel more examples of multiculturalism and political correctness than had Manhattan. It was a town where a man could marry another man and a sixty-two-year-old outdoorsman could shack up with an eighteen-year-old former beauty queen and they could all still get along with the other 837 residents.

Although a variety of organized religions were explored in the series, especially Joel's reluctant brand of Judaism, the entire populace was guided by a natural religion that the awesome scenery, mighty climate, and diurnal irregularities seemed almost to force upon them. Special days were marked less by the doctrinal calendar than by the dictates of Gaia. In an episode entitled "Spring Break," the townspeople go sexually and/or mentally mad as they wait for the annual melting of the ice that marks the start of spring; in "Aurora Borealis," the imminent appearance of the Northern Lights sends mysterious companions to both Chris and Joel; in "Midnight Sun," Joel experiences uncharacteristically strong physical and libidinal energy as a result of his exposure to Alaska's twenty-four-hour sunlight.

An inclusion of the spiritual and the sacred was very unusual for a prime-time series at the time, but it wouldn't be for long. Shortly after the debut of *Northern Exposure*, David Kelley would make religion and ethics a prime focus of his new series, *Picket Fences*.

## PICKET FENCES: BORN AGAIN QUIRKINESS

Shortly after becoming a lawyer, David E. Kelley began spending his spare time writing a screenplay about one.[48] A graduate of Princeton University and Boston University Law School, he'd had no formal training in creative writing, but an interested producer bought his script in 1986. Around the same time, Steven Bochco was casting about for writers with legal experience to work on his upcoming series, *L.A. Law.* Bochco saw Kelley's script, interviewed him over the course of a week, and hired him as writer and story editor for the series.[49]

The movie, *From the Hip*, was released in 1987 and quickly forgotten. The stint at *L.A. Law*, on the other hand, would last for five years and establish Kelley as one of Hollywood's hottest new arrivals. As previously discussed, he quickly ascended the ranks at the series, and after three years Bochco left the show and chose Kelley as his successor. An unusually fast and prolific creator, Kelley either wrote or cowrote nearly two-thirds of *L.A. Law*'s first five seasons. He collected a batch of Emmy Awards, including two for writing, and when he left at the end of the 1990–91 season, it was reported by many critics that the superior quality of the show had left with him. "The difference between good and bad *L.A. Law*, future doctoral dissertations on American culture in the late 20th century will argue, was David E. Kelley," according to *Newsday*'s Marvin Kitman.[50]

When it came time to search for a buyer for his own show, a series about a sheriff, his doctor wife, and their family, colleagues, and fellow citizens in a small town in Wisconsin, Kelley shopped around at all of the networks. At first he thought CBS would be unwilling to consider a show that seemed so closely related to *Northern Exposure*, but the now quality-conscious network was anxious to sign him up. CBS Entertainment President Jeff Sagansky, who had been an executive at NBC during its quality heyday in the early 1980s, gave Kelley a three-series deal,[51] and senior vice-president Peter Tortoreci said that "of all the people doing one-hour drama, we think he is the next real superstar."[52]

CBS followed in the footsteps of NBC and ABC by giving their quality producer a great deal of creative latitude. Kelley conceived *Picket Fences* and fine-tuned it according to his own dictates, not those of the network. "[CBS has] been great about artistic freedom," he told the *New York Times* during the series' second season. "They've stayed completely out of content."[53] This was pretty clear, given the fact that *Picket Fences* regularly treads on dangerous ground. Only once had the network insisted upon a major change in an episode when they asked that a scene depicting the sheriff's daughter experimenting with kissing another girl be made a little less explicit.[54]

CBS also gave the show preferred treatment when it came to renewals and promotion. After sticking with the series for an entire season only to see it ranked in the lower half of the Nielsens, the network nevertheless ordered an entire season of twenty-two episodes when renewal time rolled around. Sagansky justified the decision by comparing the show to *St. Elsewhere, Cagney & Lacey,* and *Hill Street Blues.* "The legends of television are all those shows that took a long time to be found and become hits," he observed. "I think *Picket Fences* is going to be one of them."[55] The second-season debut was heavily promoted across the schedule and especially during CBS's highly rated World Series broadcasts. The episode lost its time period to *20/20* and a rerun of a *Perry Mason* movie, but by the end of the year, the overall ratings had picked up about 10 percent and the series finished in sixty-first place out of 118 regularly scheduled series. CBS continued to support the show. In the summer of 1994, reruns of *Picket Fences* were aired twice a week in prime time in the hopes of introducing the program to as many new viewers as possible. Even when ratings failed to climb the following season, CBS still renewed it for a fourth year.

The motivations behind CBS's largesse toward the show were familiar ones. *Picket Fences* was delivering desirable demographics and prestige to a network badly in need of a little of both. The ratings of the show, as might have been expected, were respectable among younger, urban viewers, and the series had won the Emmy for best drama in both of its first two seasons. Having snagged David Letterman from NBC in 1993, CBS was looking to follow in that network's quality tradition as well.

Kelley's only gripe with the folks at CBS was that they had scheduled his show on Fridays, a night of traditionally low viewership, especially for his target audience, and one unconducive to next-day word-of-mouth promotion in the workplace. But CBS had reason to believe *Picket Fences* could thrive on Fridays. Ten years ago, after all, *Dallas,* a CBS Friday night series, was sitting at the top of the ratings list. And NBC had managed to keep hip young viewers at home on Fridays for a few years with *Miami Vice. Picket Fences* was, in fact, part of a careful plan crafted by CBS executives to make Fridays as successful as Mondays had been for the network. Since Mondays had worked with four sitcoms (*Evening Shade, Major Dad, Murphy Brown,* and *Designing Women*) followed by a quality drama-comedy (*Northern Exposure*), CBS decided to try a similar strategy on Fridays. *Golden Palace,* a retooled version of the hit *Golden Girls,* opened the night, followed by the transplanted *Major Dad* and *Designing Women,* Bob Newhart's latest comedy, *Bob,* and the quality comedy-drama *Picket Fences.* The plan didn't work as well as expected, but to date, short of a few experiments, CBS has refrained from moving *Picket Fences* to another time slot.

▪ ▪ ▪

Kelley not only created and executive-produced *Picket Fences,* but he wrote or cowrote nearly every episode in its first three seasons. An output almost unheard of in series television, where the show's creator usually only writes three or four episodes per year, *Picket Fences* truly revealed the stamp of a single artist. "In Hitchcock movies, the hand of the master is seen in every picture," Steve Bell, the head of Twentieth Television's network production department, said, "and this series is about as close as you can come in this collaborative medium to one guy's vision."[56]

That vision included the most extreme case of generic hybridization we'd seen since *Hill Street Blues* had started the practice a dozen years ago. *Picket Fences* was a cop show, following the law enforcement duties of Sheriff Jimmy Brock (Tom Skerritt) and his officers, Maxine Stewart (Lauren Holly) and Kenny Lacos (Costas Mandylor). It was also a medical show whenever it told a story about Jimmy's wife Jill (Kathy Baker), one of the town's doctors. Frequent courtroom scenes featuring Judge Henry Bone (Ray Walston), defense attorney Douglas Wambaugh (Fyvush Finkel), and, starting in the second season, district attorney Jonathan Littleton (Don Cheadle) could have come right out of *L.A. Law*. The family-oriented stories about the Brock children, Kimberly (Holly Marie Combs), Matthew (Justin Shenkarow), and Zachary (Adam Wylie) had roots in domestic dramas like *Family*. The series even became a musical every now and again, mostly when presenting pageants and performances at the local school. And within each episode—indeed within individual scenes—*Picket Fences* would oscillate between high tragedy and low comedy.

■  ■  ■

Though the ingredients of the program included nearly all the traditional television genres, however, their combination turned out to be anything but traditional. The preternatural proceedings of Rome, Wisconsin, invited immediate and apt comparisons to those of Twin Peaks, Washington. A review of the episodes in the first two seasons alone clearly reveals *Peaks*'s influence. A woman is killed by being stuffed into a dishwasher and sent through the rinse cycle with her favorite collector plates; a young girl brings a severed human hand to school for show-and-tell; a point-of-view shot from an elephant's rectum punctuates a story about a man and his constipated pachyderm; nuns perform mercy killings while humming "Killing Me Softly"; a "serial bather" is obsessed with using the tubs of strangers without permission; a woman kills her husband with a steamroller and blames it on symptoms brought on by menopause; an overweight woman kills her husband by sitting on his head; an elementary school teacher turns out to be a transsexual; the town priest is discovered to have a shoe fetish: the mayor dies by spontaneous combustion . . . the list goes on and on. Most of the regular characters were a little more normal than they had been in *Twin Peaks,* but there were exceptions. Town coroner Carter

Pike (Kelly Connell), for example, is Quincy with a genital fixation. He always finds an excuse to do a thorough examination of the private parts of any dead body that comes his way. If that weren't strange enough, he usually finds some important clue there, and then gets away with talking about it, in Bochcovian style, on prime-time TV because, in his clinical jargon, it doesn't sound so dirty.

But even as it was being compared to *Twin Peaks*, *Picket Fences* was benefiting from the *Twin Peaks* overdose from which many critics had suffered. By praising *Fences*, critics could get one more dig at *Peaks* without appearing to have thrown the baby out with the bathwater. While admitting that *Picket Fences* reminded him of *Twin Peaks*, one critic qualified his comparison by saying that it was "not as weird and ultimately stupid."[57]

Unlike *Twin Peaks*, which in the end was really a show about little more than its own strangeness, *Picket Fences* used its strange elements in the service of solid linear narratives about serious issues. "Often we try to seduce the audience at the beginning that this is going to be fun, a romp or a ride," Kelley explained, "and then once the ride had begun to reveal some serious subject matter for them to think about."[58] The serious subject matter usually was of a particular variety. The legal-minded Kelley specialized in stories that presented a difficult ethical issue that could ultimately be argued at length in court and summarized in an impassioned closing speech by Judge Bone.

One of its writer-producers, Ann Donahue, called *Picket Fences* "a First Amendment show":

> What you'll find time and time again is that the episodes deal with everybody's right to their space, their religion, their death, their life. Everybody's always saying, "I want to do this," which is what we do in America. Everybody says, "Well, that's fine until it's in my back yard or against my beliefs or . . ."—fill in the blank. . . . That's where the drama and humor come from.[59]

In the context of all of those bizarre story lines, the characters had complex discussions about the issues surrounding abortion, fetal tissue transplants, birth control, date rape, euthanasia, prejudice of many stripes, guns and drugs in school, religious freedom, sexual freedom, and many other contemporary ethical topics.

The way it treated these moral and ethical issues made *Picket Fences* stand out as prime time's first post-politically correct television series. Consider its take on the issue of sexual harassment, for example. In one episode, sixteen-year-old Kimberly is infuriated by the fact that her boyfriend, who has graduated with honors from the high school's "seminar on sexual correctness," has eliminated all the spontaniety and romance from their relationship by his constant requests for permission whenever he wants to kiss or touch her. This swipe at post-Anita Hill sexual paranoia was far from politically correct, but it wasn't just an example of backlash either. The episode carefully examined the issue of harassment from several angles. Ann Donahue pointed out, "[Kelley] always goes down the middle, and he's able to show each side. So the first act you root for one side. The second act of the episode you root for the other side because you finally understand them." The issues are presented in a way that is ambiguous, not preachy. "It's always gray," Donahue claimed.[60]

One of the ways this grayness was maintained, said Kelley, was by confronting bigotries and prejudices in the show's likable characters. "We like to see our own people fall into the traps of paranoia, to find story lines that raise moral or ethical questions without easy answers."[61] The usually liberal-minded and tolerant Brock parents, for example, are not so tolerant when they suspect that their own daughter may be exhibiting signs of lesbianism, and Jimmy Brock has a fit when he learns that his wife, respecting doctor-patient privilege, has kept secret the fact that their kids' dentist is HIV-positive.

In spite of all this quirkiness and relevance, *Picket Fences* remains strikingly sincere and without irony. Characters listen to reason in the show, and most of the people in the town seem to be struggling to do the right thing.

Not surprisingly, viewers and critics soon began to point out that a disproportionately large number of strange and challenging things happened in this town of only thirty-thousand residents. Characters within the show itself began to make fun of this fact on several occasions. When a legal case seems cut-and-dried in the third act of one episode, defense attorney Douglas Wambaugh announces to the judge: "Things are never so simple. Not in Rome, Wisconsin." Later that season, Wambaugh auditions for the town musical with songs that celebrate a long list of macabre events of episodes past.

Indeed, when the series is looked at as a whole, it is hard to believe that so much could happen in one small town over the course of just a few years. But if each episode is examined individually, it becomes clear that Kelley was using Rome as a crucible, a model community that he would expose each week to a new dramatic dilemma. With doctors, lawyers, cops, and nuclear families at his disposal, Kelley could tell about any story he wanted to, just as the anthology series of the 1950s could. Unlike the anthologies, however, viewers were able to see these dilemmas played out by continuing characters they had come to know over a long period of time. *Picket Fences* melded the continuing serial form and the anthology form to make a hybrid that was potentially more versatile than either form was by itself. Each week, audiences got to see characters they knew well react to profound problems that made more sense if they suspended their memories of the many other profound problems that these same characters had already confronted. For anyone who'd ever seen *Murder, She Wrote,* of course, this wasn't much of a stretch. Watching Jessica Fletcher solve a crime in any given episode makes perfect sense; thinking back to how many murders she's coincidentally stumbled upon doesn't.[62]

•  •  •

An extended discussion of a third-season episode that aired in December 1994 will illustrate many of the artistic strategies of *Picket Fences.* The episode begins in *Twin Peaks* fashion when Jimmy and his officers stumble upon a high-tech farm outside Rome where cows are being used as surrogate mothers for human embryos. As the cops burst into the barn to arrest the proprietors, a bouncing baby boy is being delivered from the womb of a prostrate bovine. This outrageous scene is spiked with irreverent humor. When a suspect asks why she is being arrested, Sheriff Brock incredulously responds, "You've got human babies coming out of cows here!" Coroner Pike, who broke the case by characteristically examining the genitalia of a dead cow that had been surreptitiously buried, muses that "the breast-feeding possibilities are endless."

The humor quickly tranforms into an ethical dilemma, however. For the first half of the episode, we side with the sheriff, the town minister, and the district attorney, all of whom find this a violation of all that is right and natural. When a prankster puts the Baby Jesus underneath the cow in the creche that sits in the town square, it is clear that viewers are being asked to side with the notion that making babies in cattle is sick, sick, sick.

But in the second half of the episode, things get more complicated. The judge has ordered that no more embryos be placed into cows, but it turns out that six pregnant animals are already carrying the children of six infertile couples. District Attorney Littleton, believing that technology has gone too far, wants the pregnancies terminated, but the minister, now that abortion is the issue, has switched sides, and the couples for whom this is a miraculous chance of becoming parents want the cows left to complete the cycle of gestation and delivery. Rachel Harris, whose boy was born to her cow Wanda in the first act, explains that she is unable to carry a child herself and that she didn't want to risk the possibility that a human surrogate would decide to keep a child for whom she had supplied the egg. And Littleton himself, it turns out, has a daughter whom he loves dearly but who exists only because of an in vitro fertilization.

An episode that began with a comically grotesque and absurd premise, then, turned into a serious debate of the kind that might have played on *Nightline* about the degree to which technology and science should be allowed to interfere with the process of human pregnancy.

And it didn't stop there. Kimberly Brock, a good Congregationalist, has a major crisis of faith as a result of the whole cow controversy. She rejects the existence of God based on the claim that He is being factored out of the equation of life by science. Her mother tries to convince her that perhaps God meant for humans to use science to create miracles, and a theological discussion, heavy for television but all in a day's work on *Picket Fences,* ensues.

Judge Bone ultimately orders that the six enceinte cows are not protected by Roe v. Wade and therefore the state's interest in the lives of the unborn children is uncontested. The story that touched upon virgin birth (the already fertilized embryos were artificially placed into cows Coroner Pike had determined were maidens), abortion, animal rights, and the clash of science and religion ends with the happy promise that Rome will soon have six more citizens. As children sing "Away in a Manger" around the town creche, the cows are led back to the barn, Rachel Harris's beautiful baby coos, and the viewer is left with the odd feeling that even after two-and-a-half years, this show was still not easy to predict.

■　■　■

As the above episode indicated, by the second season, *Picket Fences* had become, in many ways, not so much about crime solving or life saving as it was about God. Like *Northern Exposure,* the show started out with a propensity toward exploring spiritual issues, but soon religion had become one of *Picket Fences*'s principal franchises. *St. Elsewhere,* as its title implied, had flirted with religious subject matter in a number of moving and ambiguous stories. And if *St. Elsewhere* had introduced God to prime time, *Twin Peaks,* by showing BOB as the Evil that lurks not only in the woods but in the hearts and minds of us all, had introduced the Devil. *Northern Exposure* lightened up the palate considerably. The woods contained beauty rather than evil; the town was populated by gentle eccentrics with odd habits rather than dangerous psychotics with deadly secrets; and God showed Her/His benevolent self in the form of Native American spirits or a New Age nondenominational presence whose gospel was preached by the morning deejay.

But *Picket Fences* didn't present the vague "natural" religion of *Northern Exposure;* it told stories about organized religion itself. Catholics,

Protestants, Jews, Mormons, Christian Scientists—all these and more came under the scrutiny of the series. It featured not only cops, lawyers, doctors, and kids but *clergy* as regular characters, and, as was the case with its ancient namesake, Rome, Wisconsin, was a hotbed of religious discussion. Surprisingly, the scripts managed pretty adeptly to treat religious issues without taking sides, while at the same time not tossing all existing organized faiths into Chris-in-the-morning's theistic melting pot. The show also managed to acknowledge acts of divinity without falling into the maudlin "I can walk again!" melodramatics of *Highway to Heaven.*

Although quality TV has historically leaned to the left, and organized religion has increasingly come to be associated with the right, the union of religion and quality TV was probably inevitable. As the creators of these shows continued to strive for something new and original, something that hadn't been done before, religion remained as one of the last frontiers. Though televangelists discussed God on the fringes of television, this was fresh territory for prime time, which, since Bishop Fulton Sheen's *Life Is Worth Living,* had pretty much ignored the subject in all but the occasional Christmas episode. Always on the make for something out of the ordinary, quality TV finally turned to God.[63]

Religion was a perfect fit in other ways as well. The subject had great potential to appeal to a mass audience, for instance. Concerns about the existence of a deity, the nature of the afterlife, and the role of God in an increasingly scientific and secular world are central to the tradition of Western art and found among people of all demographic identities. Furthermore, questions about religion are perceived as "deep," perfect fodder for the quality TV mill, which, for all its mixing of comedy and drama, usually strives to grind out material that has a serious aura to it. Finally, the subject was easily integrated into traditional genres, like cop shows and doctor shows. In the face of all the inexplicable death and sadness that doctors and police officers encounter, it seemed perfectly natural that they would occasionally wonder about the mystery of God's purpose. Some pretty heavy religious discussions could be seamlessly injected into the dialogue between car chases or emergency room heroics.

Starting in the second season, hardly an episode of *Picket Fences* went by without some mention of God, and frequently religion was at the center of the story. In the second-season Christmas episode, for instance, a comatose woman pulled from a car accident is found (by Carter Pike, of course) to be both a virgin and pregnant. Father Barrett (Roy Dotrice), minister Novotny (Dabbs Greer), and clerics who descend upon the town are eager to find a logical explanation for this apparent immaculate conception. They all worry about what a mess the coming of an actual Messiah would make of church politics and structure. In the third-season opener, nine-year-old Zach brings charges against the Rome school board for allowing his teacher to include creationism in the curriculum, catalyzing long, earnest discussions among the Brock family about what features of their Protestant faith they actually believe. Later that season Zach exhibits the signs of the stigmata, prompting even more specific debates over the basic tenets of Christianity. In several episodes, Douglas Wambaugh finds he must defend his colorful brand of Judaism against both the predominantly Christian townsfolk and the traditional Jewish establishment.

▪   ▪   ▪

Innovations and Emmy awards notwithstanding, *Picket Fences* didn't meet with the unanimous critical approval that had been bestowed upon *Hill Street Blues* and the other early quality dramas. Since the turn of the decade, a small but vocal group had been challenging the automatic reverence that was so often given to these kinds of shows. As the quality formula became more established, some began to reject it.

Though Kelley had begun to move away from *Twin Peaks*-inspired craziness in the first season of *Picket Fences*, deciding to "exalt the drama over the eccentricities,"[64] a few critics still insisted upon seeing the show as part of a phase of television history that was just about washed up. Most critics extolled *Picket Fences*, but some, like the *New York Times*'s Jeff MacGregor, expressed a view that was becoming more common in the post-*Peaks* days.

Identifying that "quirkiness" had, since the mid-1980s, become a formulaic prerequisite for quality on television, MacGregor pointed out in 1995 that both *Picket Fences* and *Northern Exposure*, two of the holdout quality shows in the early 1990s, had become painfully predictable. Once shows like these get "hip to [their] own cute eccentricities," MacGregor pointed out, they "[tire and devolve] pretty rapidly into cloying self-parody. Characters start to do the unexpected only because it's expected of them."[65]

Although his assessment of these shows is perhaps unfairly harsh, MacGregor provided an interesting description of the state of quality television in the early years of the 1990s:

> [The word "quirky"] quickly became the shorthand darling of the critics, who, when bestowing their stingy benedictions on a favored series, wanted a more convenient way of saying, "it's a smarter-than-average show that demands the fullest attention of its audience because it proceeds in a nonlinear manner, and it wouldn't hurt if you've attended an accredited university, either, come to think of it, since

they make use of a lot of gratuitous literary references that don't make any contextual sense really, but they sound good, and that in and of itself implies a certain sort of excellence, doesn't it? Or at least ambition, or maybe it's just the self-congratulatory kind of cynicism that passes for true intelligence in Hollywood, I'm not sure anymore, but it's better than nothing, isn't it, that they're speaking to one another instead of just getting kicked in the groin or blown up or talking to their car, even if they aren't like any real people you've ever met anywhere in your life or even seen in the 'proactive personal empowerment' section of a small college bookstore and, fine, so a little bit of Taoism goes a long way at 9 o'clock after a tough day at the office, there might be an angry midget in it, too, someplace; at least it's not 'Barnaby Jones' again, O.K.?"[66]

# 8

# The Future of Quality

Although it inspired a little subgenre of "quirky quality" series like *Northern Exposure* and *Picket Fences, Twin Peaks* had an overall negative effect on the quality drama. By so strikingly taking the quality formula to its extreme only to alienate most of its once dedicated audience by the middle of its second season, *Twin Peaks* sent a message to network programmers that boundless experimentalism alone couldn't sustain a series over the long haul.

ABC, the network that had been so eager to program shows that were "different" and that had encouraged David Lynch to ignore the conventions of traditional TV, seemed to be virtually getting out of the quality business at the end of the 1990–91 season. In one fell swoop, ABC executives dumped not only *Twin Peaks,* but also *China Beach, thirtysomething,* and *Equal Justice,*[1] a series that had mixed the gritty realism of *Hill Street Blues* with the legal drama of *L.A. Law.* Midway through that season, they had canceled *Cop Rock,* Steven Bochco's almost universally maligned experimental musical police show, after only three months on the air. NBC seemed to have the same idea. Having already rid their schedule of *Hill Street Blues* and *St. Elsewhere* a few seasons back, they canceled *Shannon's Deal* and *Midnight Caller,* two of the critics' favorites, while ABC was undergoing its own quality purge.

In the summer of 1991, just as the last seven episodes of his lame duck *China Beach* were about to air, John Sacret Young lamented in *USA Today* that we had come to "the end of a cycle that started with *Hill Street Blues* and *St. Elsewhere* and continued through *Moonlighting* and *thirtysomething.* It was a renaissance of the hour drama," he said. "This was the best group ever and they're gone."[2] Barney Rosenzweig, producer of the already-departed *Cagney & Lacey,* agreed, declaring that 1991 was "the beginning of the end of network television and the one-hour drama."[3]

Still, contract obligations and wishful thinking had a few new quality dramas already waiting in the wings. NBC brought in the quality melodrama *Sisters* as a summer replacement and that fall introduced *I'll Fly Away*, a late-1950s Southern period piece created by Joshua Brand and John Falsey, the team that had come up with *St. Elsewhere* and *Northern Exposure*. ABC debuted Steven Bochco's *Civil Wars*, a specialized variation of *L.A. Law* that concentrated exclusively on divorce cases, and *Homefront*, a classy ensemble drama that was set in a small Ohio town at the end of World War II. CBS brought back *Northern Exposure* for its first full season that fall and debuted *Brooklyn Bridge*, one of the best of the "dramedy" genre. Within two years, however, *Sisters* and *Northern Exposure* would be the only two of these series still on the network schedules. Over the next two seasons, several other shows in the quality mold would come and go without much ceremony. Brand and Falsey's *Going to Extremes*, Bruce Paltrow's *The Road Home*, and Bochco's *The Byrds of Paradise* all lasted less than a full season, proving that even the quality all-stars were susceptible to the slump hour-long dramas were experiencing.

In the 1993–94 season, *Murder, She Wrote*, a good old-fashioned formula mystery, completed its tenth year on the air. It was the only hour-long drama in the Nielsen top fifteen, helped into ninth place by its desirable time slot, right after *60 Minutes*. In fact, *Murder, She Wrote* was the only drama to reach the annual top ten since 1987. Out of the 118 regular series that aired on the four networks during the 1993–94 season, only thirty-two were hour-long dramas, seventeen of which ended the year in the bottom half of the ratings and only seventeen of which were back on the schedule the following fall.

By the 1993–94 season, critics, insiders, and prognosticators all across the country had declared the death not only of the quality drama but of the hour-long drama in general. When commenting on a report that an *L.A. Law* star had complained that *Homicide: Life on the Street* had temporarily taken *L.A. Law*'s time slot, *Homicide*'s executive producer Tom Fontana said, "I want *every* drama to succeed. . . . We should be circling the wagons shooting at sitcoms."[4]

There were several good reasons for the impending disappearance of drama programming. The most obvious was the fact that hour-long shows don't do nearly as well in the syndicated rerun market as half-hour comedies do. Since production companies in fact lose money on their series during their network runs, the value of those series in syndication is of paramount importance. Unable to deliver a guaranteed financial bonanza in reruns, dramas were seen as a much riskier programming form for these companies. Quality shows in particular are especially hard to syndicate. Often serialized, they have to be both aired and watched in the proper sequence in order to be fully enjoyed. Since most shows are syndicated five days a week, most viewers don't catch them every single day. As is usually not the case with a sitcom, it's hard to drop into a serialized drama an episode at a time, and when you do, you're committed for the entire hour. Furthermore, quality dramas have a tendency to deal with serious and timely issues. Viewers looking for a rerun to watch right after dinner are often unprepared for the emotionally draining and thought-provoking subjects explored in these dramas, and the timeliness that had made the shows relevant when they first aired often renders them dated the second time around. For these reasons, the more traditional hour-long series like *Magnum, P.I.*, have done reasonably well in syndication, while a quality show like *St. Elsewhere*, as noted earlier, remains unavailable in many markets. As early as 1987, in fact, Brandon Tartikoff, then president of NBC Entertainment, speculated that MTM "might not have made *Hill Street Blues* knowing what they know now" about how it would perform in syndication.[5]

Furthermore, although cable opened up more venues on which reruns could be played, the boom in first-run syndicated programming ended up taking a lot of the best time slots. Many stations wishing to program hour-long shows could do much better with original syndicated series like *Baywatch* and *Star Trek: The Next Generation* than they could with warmed over quality network reruns.[6]

The network drama also suffered because it was so costly to make. Production costs for individual programs were skyrocketing at the very time when the audiences for those programs were getting smaller. Once again, the quality dramas were most vulnerable. With their high production values and large casts, the genre was simply becoming too expensive. Most drama series cost production companies more to produce than they received from the networks, and by the end of the series' runs these companies were usually millions of dollars in debt and had no guarantee that the money would be made back in syndication in the near future. Grant Tinker predicted in 1994, "Programming will get worse. The financial pressures on the networks will continue to put a premium on low-risk, low-cost programming."

> Don't hold your breath waiting for the next *Hill Street Blues*. . . . That kind of program was risky and hard to find even when network license fees covered most of the production cost, and the syndication market was still good. Today, no production company in its right mind will accept the prospect of a weekly deficit of hundreds of

thousands of dollars with little prospect of ultimately making some money on the back end. Networks have always been "department stores," offering an array of programming of all shapes and sizes, from which we selected merchandise we liked. The assortment is already more limited, and the quality line is nearly out of stock.[7]

By 1993–94, the newsmagazine was promising to take over the hour-long format. While these were even more timely and had virtually no future in the rerun market, they were very cheap to make and as a result very profitable. There were nine such shows on the air during the season, and the following year NBC would give its newsmagazine, *Dateline, three* weekly hour-long slots in prime time.

Furthermore, sitcoms had to some extent taken back the quality mantle from the drama. Self-conscious generic critiques once done so expertly by *St. Elsewhere* and *Moonlighting*, for example, were now the province of *The Larry Sanders Show* and *The Simpsons*. The treatment of the minutiae of middle-class daily life that *thirtysomething* innovated was now being done better by *Seinfeld* and *Mad about You* than by any contemporary dramatic series. *Seinfeld*, in fact, merged many of the elements of the quality drama with the user-friendly and eminently syndicatable form of the sitcom. More than any sitcom before it, *Seinfeld* was about the quotidian, the daily, the unspectacular. Such subject matter had for some time been the exclusive territory of stand-up comics, who began a massive migration to television at around this time and brought their material with them.[8]

*Mad about You* did for married couples what *Seinfeld* did for single people. Based almost entirely on the idea of presenting familiar, instantly recognizable details of domestic married life in a comic context, *Mad about You* had been sold to NBC as "*thirtysomething*, only shorter and funnier."[9] An entire theory of commercial television is suggested in this description. Given where, when, and how it is watched, perhaps TV needs to be short and funny. *Mad about You*, after all, will last longer and plays to a much wider audience than *thirtysomething*, and it's a good bet it will enjoy a more visible life in syndicated reruns. Seven of the eight highest-rated shows of the 1993–94 season, and eleven of the top fifteen, were sitcoms.

Finally, it may also not be a total coincidence that the quality drama hit its lowest point in over a decade just as the Ronald Reagan-George Bush era was drawing to a close in 1992 and as a Democratic president was returning to power. For all of its progressive and experimental content, in fact, quality television drama had flourished during the Republican regimes of Reagan and Bush. The return of the Democrats to the office in 1993, on the other hand, put new pressures on the creators of quality dramas.

The Reagan-Bush years not only included no significant threats of possible new content regulations that would affect prime time,[10] but they also promised the dismantling of many economic regulations already in place. As ironic as it may seem, the healthy development of quality dramas in the 1980s was consistent with the deregulatory spirit that Mark Fowler and Dennis Patrick, both FCC chairmen appointed by Reagan, stood for. While *Hill Street Blues* was already being filmed before Reagan won the election, it premiered and developed in an environment where its creators could work unencumbered by a content-conscious FCC. Furthermore, the free-market philosophies inherent in deregulation fostered the growth of cable services that ultimately pushed the networks toward quality. Fowler looked at modern television not as a service to the public but as a business like any other. "Television is just another appliance," he said in 1984. "It's a toaster with pictures."[11] Seen as just another business, network TV was given tacit leave by the FCC to do whatever it took to compete in the marketplace. Since that marketplace now included cable, part of what it took to compete was the sexual subject matter, the adult language, and the occasional violence that cable was offering and that the quality drama depended so heavily upon.

It may be significant to note that quality television drama flowered during two periods that were dominated by firmly established conservative Republican presidential regimes. Most of the first golden age came and went with the Eisenhower administration, and another began, with the debut of *Hill Street Blues*, five days after the inauguration of Reagan. The great anthology dramas of the 1950s (*Playhouse 90*) soon gave way to the rural comedies of the 1960s (*The Beverly Hillbillies*) when Kennedy moved into the White House, and the gritty realism that characterized Steven Bochco's 1980s TV series (*Hill Street Blues*) was held up to a great deal more scrutiny when Bochco went for an encore (*NYPD Blue*) during Bill Clinton's first fall season as president. Dan Quayle and Robert Dole's attacks on Hollywood notwithstanding, conservative Republican presidential administrations seem to have been very good for good television. Some of the most daring, revolutionary, and, indeed, *liberal* shows—*Rowan and Martin's Laugh-In, All in the Family, M\*A\*S\*H, Hill Street Blues*—all debuted and prospered while a Republican was president.

This is not to say that Republicans haven't historically had plenty of nasty things to say about prime-time TV. Attacks on television content by officials of the federal government have, of course, been a bipartisan pastime throughout the medium's history. On the Republicans' side, for example, Quayle and Dole are just the latest in a long list of media bashers that also includes Senator Joseph McCarthy, Vice President Spiro Agnew, President Richard Nixon, and Senator Jesse Helms. Those who have zealously taken on TV for the Democrats include Senator Estes Kefauver, FCC chair Newton Minow, Senator Thomas Dodd, Attorney General Janet Reno, and Senator Paul Simon.

But the Democrats have often been more inclined to add substantive threats to all their bluster. So far, the federal government's control over TV program content via the FCC has been for the most part limited to the equal time law, the fairness doctrine, and restrictions on indecency and profanity. Implied warnings that this could change, however, have on occasion had a profound impact on programming. The effect of Minow's "vast wasteland" speech (see chapter 1) is the most well-known example, but more recently Paul Simon's recommendations resulted in both the networks and the cable industry engaging outside agencies to monitor violent content in their programming,[12] and Democratic Senator Ernest F. Hollings has sponsored a bill that could result in legal restrictions being placed upon violent shows.[13]

The case of Law & Order is the best example of how directly these issues can affect quality television. In the fall of 1993, Janet Reno loudly began to announce her commitment to reducing violence on television, suggesting that government legislation might be necessary if the industry was unable to shape up on its own. Michael Moriarty, one of the stars of Law & Order, was among a group of representatives from the television community that met with Reno in November. Outraged at what he saw as Reno's blatant attempt at government censorship, Moriarty launched what some thought was a rather impolite public attack on the attorney general. Before the smoke had cleared, Moriarty had resigned from Law & Order. While the series' executive producer, Dick Wolf, took issue with the tone of Moriarty's campaign, he agreed with him in principle. "Today I couldn't do the first six episodes of Law & Order that I did five years ago," Wolf said in February 1994, citing the new subject taboos.[14]

Needless to say, significant changes in television content are influenced not only by the reigning president and his FCC appointees, but by Congress, the courts, and an assortment of other political and cultural powers. By the early 1990s, for example, highly organized pressure groups threatening advertiser boycotts had resulted in the networks pulling back from much of the controversial material that filled their programs in the 1980s. By August 1992, Bochco was complaining in a Los Angeles Times op-ed piece that the networks had "become increasingly skittish about any program content that is perceived by pressure groups as objectionable."[15]

▪ ▪ ▪

Bad ratings, bad syndication deals, inflated production costs, the lure of more lucrative forms like sitcoms and newsmagazines, and a changing political climate were all clearly announcing that the golden age of television drama that had started with *Hill Street Blues* was going to end soon. But, all of the above notwithstanding, that's not what happened. Reports of the demise of drama (and the G.O.P.) soon turned out to be greatly exaggerated. During the very season in which everyone was eulogizing the form, *NYPD Blue* was becoming one of the highest-rated new shows of the year, earning an average rating that ranked it in nineteenth place. A year after Bochco's *Los Angeles Times* article railed that "Networks don't want controversy . . . , bad language . . . , [or] sex,"[16] his *NYPD Blue* characters began regularly taking their clothes off and uttering *bons mots* like *douche bag, asshole,* and *dickhead.* That spring, the show was nominated for a record-breaking twenty-six Emmy Awards.

Seeing that there were still dollars and prestige to be squeezed from the serious and controversial hour-long drama, network executives loaded their schedules with them the following year and scrambled to get more into development. At the start of the 1994–95 season, quality dramas could be seen on prime time six nights a week, occasionally scheduled opposite each other on different networks. *Sisters, Northern Exposure, NYPD Blue, Law & Order, Picket Fences,* and *Homicide: Life on the Street* all returned, and as many new series debuted. The creators of *thirtysomething* introduced *My So-Called Life* to rave reviews, the creator of *Picket Fences* brought out *Chicago Hope, Law & Order*'s Dick Wolf did *New York Undercover* for Fox, and ex-*China Beach*ers John Wells, Carol Flint, Lydia Woodward, and Mimi Leder were among the production staff of Michael Crichton's creation *ER.* With regard to Friday night's *Picket Fences, The X-Files,* and *Under Suspicion, Entertainment Weekly* warned: "Don't turn off your mind yet. Quality dramas crowd a once-dull night."[17] An executive of an ad agency whose job it is to keep abreast of programming trends said in November 1994, "The drama wasn't dead—it was just asleep."[18]

By the middle of the season *NYPD Blue* was regularly scoring in the top ten, and *ER* had become the smash hit of the year, often ranking as high as number one, and earning an average rating that made it the fourth most popular series of the decade to date. Once *Chicago Hope,* which had started the season scheduled opposite *ER* on Thursday nights, was moved to a better time slot, it too could often be found in the top fifteen.

Not surprisingly, the lowest-rated networks were quite active in the quality arena. David Kelley had defected from NBC to do *Picket Fences* and *Chicago Hope* for third-place CBS. In February 1995 Steven Bochco ended a long-standing exclusive agreement with ABC and also signed a deal with CBS, preferring, according to Bill Carter of the *New York Times*, "to work for the oppressed, the downtrodden and the needy."[19] *Under Suspicion*, a cross between *Cagney & Lacey* and PBS's *Prime Suspect*, was also developed and nurtured at CBS. Perpetual also-ran Fox, while known for its neo-jiggle series like *Melrose Place* and *Models, Inc.*, was also airing more cerebral series like *The X-Files*. When announcing the debut of *VR.5*, a "cyber noir"[20] series from John Sacret Young, Fox programmer Dan McDermott said, "We think there's an intelligent audience out there not interested in *Full House*."[21]

All of the shows mentioned above were firmly based in the quality tradition. The innovation-for-innovation's sake that had made *Twin Peaks* a hit as well as a flop had pretty much been abandoned, although Sam Raimi, the quirky auteur of *The Evil Dead* (1983) and *Darkman* (1990), debuted his *Peaks*-evoking *American Gothic* on CBS in the fall of 1995.[22] For the most part, however, the new shows had returned to the meat-and-potatoes franchises of cops, lawyers, and doctors. The most generically innovative of the new series, *My So-Called Life* and *VR.5*, were in fact among the first of this new wave of quality shows to be canceled. As had been the case back in the early 1980s, quality dramas were once again presenting compelling stories in traditional, old-fashioned settings.

## LAW & ORDER, HOMICIDE, NYPD BLUE, CHICAGO HOPE, and ER: BACK TO THE BASICS OF QUALITY

*Law & Order*, as its title suggests, mixes two reliable old genres, the police show and the legal drama. Half the cast spends the first thirty minutes of the show investigating a crime, and then the other half steps in during the second part of the show to prosecute the suspect. Delivering two stories in the time it takes most other shows to tell one, *Law & Order* relies on scripts and performances that are tight, lean, and fast-paced. The personal lives of the cops and lawyers go almost entirely unexplored, leaving time for complex stories that are often based on recent headlines. The emphasis on story over character may also have something to do with the fact that the show has managed to survive perpetual changes in its cast.

*Law & Order's* creator, Dick Wolf, worked on both *Hill Street Blues* and *Miami Vice* before emerging as one of the most important quality producers of this decade. In the manner of television's first golden age, Wolf made most of his series, including *Law & Order,* in New York City, and often cast stage and film actors in principal roles. Near the end of 1994, Wolf had one series for each of the four networks in production in New York.[23] Debuting in the fall of 1990, *Law & Order* received great critical notices, but its low ratings were consistent with the general recession of the hour-long drama. During the 1994–95 season, however, the show suddenly moved up twenty-two notches on the annual Nielsen hit parade and ended the year in the top twenty-five, consistently beating the two newsmagazines it was scheduled against. In February of that year, NBC renewed the show for two full seasons.

*Homicide: Life on the Street* proved that an artsy cinema style created by an artsy cinema director could also be applied to a traditional television genre. Unlike the mixed up generic stew that was *Twin Peaks,* *Homicide* is at its heart a standard cop show. As was the case with *Miami Vice* and *Twin Peaks, Homicide* is the result of a pairing of a respected movie director (Barry Levinson) and an MTM alumnus (*St. Elsewhere's* Tom Fontana). Set and shot in Baltimore, as were Levinson's films *Diner* (1982), *Tin Men* (1987), and *Avalon* (1990), the series is based on *Baltimore Sun* reporter David Simon's book about the city's homicide department. Levinson's auteur status helped attract movie stars and guest stars like Ned Beatty and Robin Williams back to the small screen. As had been the case with *Twin Peaks,* several cinema directors were brought in to make episodes of *Homicide,* including Tim Hunter (*River's Edge,* 1986), Martin Campbell (*Criminal Law,* 1989), Nick Gomez (*Laws of Gravity,* 1991), and Michael Lehmann (*Heathers,* 1989).

Like so many urban shows since *Hill Street Blues, Homicide* employs hand-held cameras and a *vérité* style, but it takes the style to a whole new artistic level. The swishing and slamming camera moves and the jarring jump cuts do more than just give *Homicide* a documentary flavor. They help to underline and emphasize bits of narrative action like little cinematic rim shots. For a series with the subtitle "*Life on the Street,*" *Homicide* spends a lot of time indoors, often in a stark interrogation cell. Like the anthology dramas of the 1950s, these signature interrogation scenes have a cramped, theatrical look to them that perfectly complements the claustrophobic dance that is being performed on screen by the cops and the suspects. In an effort to save money, Fontana wrote one episode that took place entirely within the interrogation room.[24] He won an Emmy for the episode and it remains one of the most memorable installments of the series.

Like so many quality dramas, *Homicide* has had an anomalous scheduling history. After nine episodes aired in the spring of 1993, only four new shows were made for the 1993–94 season. When those episodes performed reasonably well as temporary replacements for *L.A. Law,* the series was finally given a full season order for 1994–95. Against *Picket Fences* and *20/20,* it ranked eighty-second out of 132 series that season.

Of all the new 1990s quality cop shows, *NYPD Blue* was the most successful. Firmly based in the *Hill Street* tradition and created and staffed by several former *Hill Street* employees, *NYPD Blue* was the third show in what could be seen as Bochco's urban police drama trilogy that had begun with *Hill Street* and *Cop Rock.* Two of the show's breakout stars, in fact, had appeared in *Hill Street.* David Caruso had a small recurring role as an Irish gang leader, and Dennis Franz portrayed both Sal Benedetto, a narcotics cop who committed suicide in the 1982–83 season, and Lieutenant Norman Buntz, a sleazy comic character who was eventually spun off into his own short-lived series, *Beverly Hills Buntz,* in 1987.

It is a real testimony to Bochco's power that, in a time when networks and advertisers were shying away from controversial programming, he had finally managed to launch the "first R-rated TV series" that he'd been talking about for nearly a decade. Several stations across the country refused to air the show and a few advertisers refused to sponsor it because of its strong language and partial nudity. The news media enthusiastically reported these defections, in effect providing the series with more publicity than ABC could have ever afforded to give it. High ratings made most reluctant station managers change their minds about carrying the show, which ended the season in the top twenty. A second season controversy surrounding the departure of David Caruso also didn't hurt the program. *L.A. Law*'s Jimmy Smits stepped in as the new star, and that year the series climbed to seventh place.

The doctor show was the other traditional genre to which quality TV turned in the mid-1990s. David Kelley followed the generically diverse *Picket Fences* with *Chicago Hope,* a straightforward medical drama set in a high-tech research hospital. Kelley was no stranger to the territory, of course. He'd co-created *Doogie Howser, M.D.,* with Bochco back in 1989, and *Picket Fences* had frequently featured stories of a medical nature. Like *Picket Fences* and many of Kelley's episodes of *L.A. Law, Chicago Hope* mixes comedy and drama, explores complex ethical and religious issues, and specializes in quirky characters and unexpected situations. The hospital, however, provides a more centralized narrative setting than do the multiple locales of Rome, Wisconsin.

One might have predicted that the always thought-provoking and often very dark stories presented on *Chicago Hope* would be too much for an audience looking to relax before bedtime. Yet the show finished its first season in the top twenty-five. It may have been helped along by the bizarre scheduling coincidence that resulted in two new medical programs set in Chicago airing simultaneously on Thursdays at 10 o'clock. The other of the two shows, NBC's *ER*, became one of the strongest-starting new series of all time, regularly trouncing *Chicago Hope*. When CBS moved *Chicago Hope* to Monday night, however, many of *ER*'s fans decided to check out the show that had so often been compared to *ER*. Furthermore, much of the quality audience that was used to tuning in to *Northern Exposure* during that time period probably found *Chicago Hope* to be a compatible replacement.

Meanwhile, back on Thursday nights, *ER* was providing a model for the new face of quality. By watching nothing more than NBC's 10 o'clock Thursday offerings from 1981 to 1995, one could get a real sense of the evolution of the quality TV drama. Carrying *Hill Street Blues*, with its small but specific audience, then *L.A. Law*, one of the first quality hits, then *ER*, a top-rated blockbuster, this time slot was the site of quality TV's most important victories.

Although it fit very nicely into the quality formula, *ER*, even more than *L.A. Law*, brought quality into the mainstream. Like David Letterman, who subtly transformed his once-fringe style into something that would play to the much larger and more diverse 11:30 audience, the producers and writers of *ER* made a few fine-tuning concessions to make quality attractive to the truly mass audience. The changes did not need to be major ones; in the nearly fourteen years since the debut of *Hill Street Blues*, most viewers had learned to watch programs that were more challenging and complex than those they had been exposed to before the 1980s. *ER* quite shamelessly ripped off story ideas, details, and situations that *St. Elsewhere* had done years ago, and much of the grim, "depressing" feel for which people had blamed *St. Elsewhere*'s low ratings was present in many episodes of *ER*. But the new show had less eclectic main characters, more pretty faces, and an audience 50 percent larger than *St. Elsewhere*'s. Its hit status was greatly helped by its hyperkinetic pacing. *ER* was perfectly designed for the remote-controlled cable era: it moved so fast, you didn't need to change the channel because it kept doing it for you. In retrospect, the leisurely *St. Elsewhere* looks like *ER* unplugged.

*ER*'s visual style was a little cleaner than that of *NYPD Blue* and *Homicide*, but it was just as chaotic. Coming out of a period when television had been flooded with "reality" shows like *Cops* and vérité reenactments on a host of tabloid programs, these dramas responded with an urgency and realism of their own.

In a single season, *ER* had become the second highest-rated series on television, it had tied *Hill Street Blues*'s record by winning eight Emmy awards in one year, and it had celebrity movie directors like Quentin Tarantino lining up to do an episode.

■ ■ ■

It is fairly clear why the networks keep airing quality dramas. They make their money right up front by selling advertisements, and they usually do not pay the program suppliers more than they can make back immediately. Even when these shows don't become big hits, their prime demographics bring in more money than higher-rated shows with less desirable audiences, and the critical acclaim they get provides the network with badly needed prestige. Hour-long blocks are also easier to program and potentially hook an audience for twice as long as a sitcom. Furthermore, network executives are usually willing to risk a few failures in the hope of hitting it big, especially when those failures are part of the price of keeping a hot producer or star happy. Bochco's *Cop Rock* was a lot easier to swallow for ABC when he followed it up with *NYPD Blue,* for example.

It's also no surprise why producers and writers keep creating these shows. The quality dramas of the 1980s had trained a sizable number of new television artists like David Milch, Tom Fontana, and David Kelley who were eager to continue making programs that were admired and taken seriously. As long as the networks keep buying these shows, the people who make them get their salaries while they stay on the air.

The biggest question is why the production companies and studios keep making quality drama. *ER* and *NYPD Blue* may be blockbusters in prime time, but it's hard to imagine them doing as well a few years down the road in the lucrative early evening rerun time slots. *Cagney & Lacey, Miami Vice,* and *L.A. Law* had also been hits, and their stars had once graced the covers of popular magazines. Instead of earning the enormous syndication revenues that went to their contemporaries like *Cheers, The Cosby Show,* and *Family Ties,* however, they had to settle for much less remunerative deals on cable services like USA and Lifetime. And those were the hits. Quickly canceled series like *Going to Extremes* and *The Road Home* are virtually impossible to syndicate and will likely never break even. Tom Thayer, the president of Universal TV, told *Variety* that the rebirth of the drama was an "empty victory." He said, "The networks want us to do quality hours—we have no problem selling product—but they don't want to pay any more than they've been paying for years."[25]

Yet still the quality dramas keep coming, and the reasons why may point to their future. Back in the early 1970s, the small and independent status of MTM allowed its staff to break away from the pack. Leaner and meaner than the major studios, MTM's position on the fringes of Hollywood encouraged them to create programs that were themselves different and on the fringe. It is now impossible for such relatively small independent companies to create quality all by themselves. NBC, after all, didn't cancel *St. Elsewhere;* MTM decided that projected syndication revenues simply didn't justify their continuing to make the show for so much more money than the network was paying them for it.

There are now many more participants involved in most series than there were ten years ago. Most productions now include partners with deep pockets. *Picket Fences* is produced by David Kelley's production company in partnership with Twentieth Century Fox Television. Twentieth Television also helps finance Kelley's *Chicago Hope* and Steven Bochco Productions' *NYPD Blue. ER* sports three production logos at the end of each episode: Constant C Productions, Steven Spielberg's Amblin TV, and Warner Brothers. With backing from major companies, these shows can wait a little longer to break even. Revenues from overseas sales and long-term earnings from more modest cable syndication deals will eventually make up their production deficits, and program equity will always be at a premium in a future hungry for software. If, as predicted, living rooms are eventually wired for five hundred channels, even *Cop Rock* could live again.

In the case of a show like *ER,* of course, some of the problems of deficit financing go away. Production companies that find they have a big hit on their hands can simply demand that the networks pay them a higher license fee up front in subsequent seasons. While NBC wasn't committed enough to *St. Elsewhere* in 1988 to cough up the money it would have taken for MTM to keep making it, one can rest assured that their commitment to their top-rated series is considerably greater. Rather than face the possibility of losing *ER* to another network, NBC will undoubtedly accede to raising its licensing fee. Hoping for another *ER,* production companies have been encouraged to keep giving quality a shot.

Furthermore, by the mid-1990s, the previously noted FCC regulations that had severely restricted ownership of programs by networks were in the process of being lifted as part of a deregulatory plan that had begun years ago. The financial interest and syndication (fin/syn) rules had been issued by the FCC in the early 1970s in an effort to block the networks from effectively dominating both the production and distribution of television programming. The rules greatly limited the networks' right to produce or own the programs they broadcast and barred them from making profits through domestic syndication. Upon the institution of these new rules, the standard model whereby a network would pay a studio or independent production company a license fee for two broadcasts of each show was established. These rules were for the most part repealed in 1993, making it possible for networks themselves to own or partially own the programming they air.

We have yet to see whether the overall effect of the repeal of the fin/syn rules will be good news or bad news for quality drama. During another era, NBC might have been tempted to cancel *Homicide: Life on the Street,* for example, after its first few episodes of lackluster ratings. But NBC Productions is a partner in *Homicide* and the more episodes they make, the higher the price they will be able to demand in the syndication market. When a network has a stake in what happens to a series after it is no longer in production, they may think twice before casually canceling it. Network ownership is by no means a guarantee of protection, however. ABC had a financial interest in *My So-Called Life,* which spent most of the five months it was on the air near the very bottom of the ratings heap. After some aggressive promotions still didn't help much, ABC cut their losses and canceled the show. Once networks become used to producing and owning their own programs, they may elect to steer away entirely from potentially low scoring shows that they'll then feel compelled to hold onto.

Finally, economics alone cannot always fully explain why some of the quality dramas get on the air. For all the talk that commercial television serves only the bottom line, some quality drama may get made because some producers are artists who want to make something good, and they persuade others who also want to be a part of something good to pay for it. Most present-day accounts of how the television business works completely ignore the fact that at the heart of the business are creative people who tell stories for a living. While issues of taste and artistic integrity are by no means the dominant criteria used in decisions about what programs to make, how to make them, and whether to air them, it is misleading to assume that these factors never figure into the commercial television equation.

• • •

The 1995–96 network lineup was an impressive one. The weekly presence on the schedule of such series as *NYPD Blue, ER, Chicago Hope, Law & Order, Homicide, Picket Fences, The X-Files, New York Undercover,* and *Murder One* indicate that the second golden age of television drama isn't over.[26] Fifteen years ago, any one of those series might have been lauded as the best thing on TV. "Television is better now than it has ever been," *Los Angeles Times* TV critic Howard Rosenberg claimed in 1995.[27] Artistically, these series compare favorably not only to any other period in television history, but to what is being done in other media as well. "In terms of dramatic value, relevance and humor," Bernard Weinraub wrote in the *New York Times* in February 1995, "prime-time television—much of it, anyway—is far better than what's on at the movies."[28] In May of that year, University of Houston media professor Garth Jowett said, "If I were looking for quality acting and scriptwriting consistency, I would look to TV rather than movies these days."[29]

Once the season got underway, the praise became even louder. In a span of less that two weeks in October, *Time* ran a piece called "The Real Golden Age Is Now"; the cover of the *New York Times* magazine announced, "Want Literature? Stay Tuned. More than Movies, Plays, and even in Some Ways Novels, Television Drama Is Making Art out of Real Life"; "10 Reasons Why TV Is Better Than the Movies" was blazened across the cover of *Entertainment Weekly;* and a widely syndicated *Chicago Tribune* article carried the headline, "Go on, Admit It: Television Has Become Quality Entertainment."[30]

Quality programming in the 1980s raised overall expectations of commercial television. The number of sophisticated dramas and comedies has grown significantly since *Hill Street Blues* debuted in 1981. Like most series TV, these sophisticated shows fit into a readily identifiable formula. But it is a formula that includes thoughtful writing, innovative stories, and strong performances among its principal characteristics. By institutionalizing "quality" programming into an imitatable formula, the creators of such shows have found a way to make artistically interesting programs that are compatible with prime-time television's demands for predictability.

Anyone still clinging to the old notion that TV is a cultural wasteland has failed to recognize the profound changes that the medium has undergone in the last fifteen years. If you can't find anything good on network TV today, you just aren't looking very hard.

# Notes

## Preface: From "The Golden Age of Television" to Quality TV

1. Howard Rosenberg, "Grace under Pressure in *Cagney & Lacey,*" *The Los Angeles Times,* part 6, p. 1.

2. David Bianculli, *Teleliteracy—Taking Television Seriously* (New York: Continuum, 1992), p. 272.

3. Jane Feuer, Paul Kerr, and Tise Vahimagi, eds., *MTM: "Quality Television"* (London: British Film Institute, 1984).

4. Ken Tucker and Bruce Fretts, "Fall TV Preview," *Entertainment Weekly,* September 16, 1994, p. 66.

5. Ken Tucker, "1992 Best and Worst—Television," *Entertainment Weekly,* December 25, 1992, p. 114.

6. Dorothy Swanson, interview with author, June 27, 1994.

7. Jane Feuer, "The MTM Style," in Feuer, Kerr, and Vahimagi, pp. 32–60; Susan Boyd-Bowman, "The MTM Phenomenon: The Company, The Book, The Programmes," *Screen* 26, no. 6 (1985), pp. 75–87; Betsy Williams, "'North to the Future': *Northern Exposure* and Quality Television," in Horace Newcomb, ed., *Television The Critical View,* 5th ed. (New York: Oxford University Press, 1994), pp. 141–54. Another interesting treatment of what the author calls "class dramas," can be found in Eric Weisbard, "It's 10 P.M. Do You Know Where Your Values Are?" *The Village Voice,* March 22, 1994, pp. 39–41.

8. Quoted in Karen Stabiner, "The Pregnant Detective," *The New York Times Magazine,* September 22, 1985, p. 104.

9. Williams, pp. 148–49.

10. Feuer, p. 56.

11. Carolyn Thompson, "Kennedy Assassination Tops Poll," *The Los Angeles Times,* October 9, 1990, p. P10.

12. "*TV Guide* Presents 40 Years of the Best," *TV Guide,* April 12, 1994, pp. 12, 38.

13. Robert Thompson and Ian Bruce. A survey conducted in the summer of 1994 asked TV critics from the nation's 388 largest circulation daily newspapers to name their choice of the ten best prime-time series in history. The response rate was 24 percent.

14. Feuer, p. 37.

## Chapter 1: The Golden Ages of Television

1. For an extensive discussion of this attitude, see David Bianculli, *Teleliteracy: Taking Television Seriously* (New York: Continuum: 1992).

2. John J. O'Connor, "Television: Golden Ages; When Networks Took Risks, and the High Road," *The New York Times*, April 17, 1994, section 2, p. 36.

3. J. Fred MacDonald, *One Nation under Television: The Rise and Decline of Network TV* (Chicago: Nelson-Hall, 1994), p. 82.

4. Christopher H. Sterling and John M. Kittross, *Stay Tuned. A Concise History of American Broadcasting*, 2nd ed. (Belmont, CA: Wadsworth, 1990), pp. 286, 655.

5. Sterling and Kittross, pp. 341–42.

6. Les Brown, *Les Brown's Encyclopedia of Television*, 3rd ed. (Detroit: Visible Ink Press, 1992), p. 228.

7. Sterling and Kittross, pp. 149, 290.

8. Lynn Spigel, *Make Room For TV: Television and the Family Ideal in Postwar America* (Chicago: The University of Chicago Press, 1992), p. 49–50.

9. Sterling and Kittross, p. 657.

10. Erik Barnouw, *Tube of Plenty: The Evolution of American Television*, 2nd revised ed. (New York: Oxford University Press, 1990), p. 167.

11. Sterling and Kittross, p. 398.

12. MacDonald, pp. 83, 102.

13. Jeff Greenfield, *Television: The First Fifty Years* (New York: Harry N. Abrams, 1977), pp. 109–10.

14. R.D. Heldenfels, *Television's Greatest Year: 1954* (New York: Continuum, 1994), p. 77.

15. Ibid., pp. 77–78.

16. Quoted in Erik Barnouw, *The Sponsor: Notes on a Modern Potentate* (New York: Oxford University Press, 1978), p. 57.

17. Heldenfels, p. 205.

18. All Minow quotes are from his address to the National Association of Broadcasters in Washington, D.C., on May 9, 1961. The speech is reprinted in Frank J. Kahn (ed.), *Documents of American Broadcasting*, 3rd ed. (Englewood Cliffs, NJ: Prentice-Hall, 1978), p. 281–91.

19. Sterling and Kittross, p. 658–59.

20. Quoted in Mary Ann Watson, *The Expanding Vista: American Television in the Kennedy Years* (New York: Oxford University Press, 1990), p. 40.

21. Watson, p. 43.

22. Tim Brooks and Earle Marsh, *The Complete Directory to Prime Time Network TV Shows, 1946-Present*, 5th ed. (New York: Ballantine Books, 1992), p. 729.

23. MacDonald, pp. 166–67.

24. David Marc, *Comic Visions: Television Comedy and American Culture* (Boston: Unwin Hyman, 1989), p. 84.

25. Vince Waldron, *The Official Dick Van Dyke Show Book* (New York: Hyperion, 1994), p. 27.

26. Watson, p. 43.

27. Ibid., pp. 69–70.

28. O'Connor, p. 36.

29. Horace Newcomb and Robert S. Alley, *The Producer's Medium: Conversations with Creators of American TV* (New York: Oxford University Press, 1983), p. 5.

30. Marc, p. 165.

31. Ibid., p. 200.

32. Horace Newcomb, *TV—The Most Popular Art* (Garden City, NY: Anchor Books, 1974), p. 256.

33. These premise-establishing and singable themes are on the wane. Series like *Wings, Frasier, Murphy Brown,* and *Seinfeld* start cold without playing an opening theme. *The Nanny* and *The Fresh Prince of Bel Air,* however, are two examples of the old-style themes.

34. Quoted in Daniel B. Wood, "At Dawn of Television's 'Third Era,' Networks Already Feel the Heat," *The Christian Science Monitor*, May 22, 1995, p. 12.

## Chapter 2: The Causes of Quality

1. Sydney W. Head, Christopher H. Sterling, and Lemuel B. Schofield, *Broadcasting in America: A Survey of Electronic Media,* 7th ed. (Boston: Houghton Mifflin, 1994), p. 77.
2. Nielsen Media Research, *Report on Television, 1990* (New York: Nielsen Media Research, 1990), p. 12.
3. Head et al., p. 199.
4. Ibid., pp. 98 and 409.
5. Steve Morgenstern (ed.), *Inside the TV Business* (New York: Sterling Publishing, 1979), pp. 16–17.
6. *East Side/West Side*'s average share of 26.28 would have placed it in the top ten by the mid-nineties. Share numbers supplied by Nielsen Media Research.
7. Michael Medved, *Hollywood vs. America* (New York: HarperCollins, 1992), p. 277.
8. Christopher H. Sterling and John M. Kittross, *Stay Tuned: A Concise History of American Broadcasting* (Belmont, CA: Wadsworth, 1990), p. 398.
9. Sterling and Kittross, p. 659.
10. Head et al., p. 497.
11. Quoted in R. D. Heldenfels, *Television's Greatest Year: 1954* (New York: Continuum, 1994), p. 141.
12. Sterling and Kittross, p. 659.
13. Ibid.
14. Quoted in Deborah Hastings, "Producers of 'China Beach,' 'Parenthood' Turn up the Heat," *Chicago Tribune,* December 29, 1990, p. C20.
15. Tom Shales, "Dark, Potent 'China Beach'; On ABC, A Drama Series About Women in Vietnam," *The Washington Post,* April 26, 1988, p. B1.

## Chapter 3: The Quality Factory

1. Jane Feuer describes MTM as "an academy for sitcom writer-producers, a prestigious and elite university to be sure, but one from which graduation seemed inevitable." Jane Feuer, "MTM Enterprises: An Overview," in Jane Feuer, Paul Kerr, and Tise Vahimagi (eds.), *MTM: 'Quality Television'* (London: The British Film Institute, 1984), p. 17.
2. Grant Tinker and Bud Rukeyser, *Tinker in Television: From General Sarnoff to General Electric* (New York: Simon & Schuster, 1994), pp. 96–97.
3. Quoted in ibid., p. 97.
4. Ibid., p. 126.
5. Tinker and Rukeyser, p. 94.
6. Ibid., p. 118.
7. Jane Feuer, "The MTM Style," in Feuer, et. al., pp. 32–33.
8. Tinker and Rukeyser, p. 149.
9. Feuer, "The MTM Style," pp. 56–57.
10. Ibid., p. 44.
11. Tinker and Rukeyser, p. 102.
12. It might be argued that *The Mary Tyler Moore Show* was the only TV series with connections in all four of the "golden ages" described in chapter 1. Moore starred in *The Dick Van Dyke Show,* which had been partly inspired by the fifties Golden Age variety show *Your Show of Shows,* for which Carl Reiner wrote and starred and upon which he loosely based "The Alan Brady Show." *The Dick Van Dyke Show* itself was at the center of the Kennedy era blossoming of prime time, and *The Mary Tyler Moore Show* was one of the three series that made the early seventies an especially notable period. *The Mary Tyler Moore Show,* of course, established MTM and inspired the creation of shows like *Hill Street Blues,* which ushered in the "second golden age" described in this book.
13. Vince Waldron, *The Official Dick Van Dyke Show Book* (New York: Hyperion, 1994), pp. 82–83.
14. Tinker and Rukeyser, p. 57.
15. Waldron, p. 297.
16. Tinker and Rukeyser, p. 89.

17. Horace Newcomb and Robert S. Alley, *The Producer's Medium: Conversations with Creators of American TV* (New York: Oxford University Press, 1983), p. 200; Robert S. Alley and Irby B. Brown, *Love Is All Around: The Making of The Mary Tyler Moore Show* (New York: Dell, 1989), p. 2.

18. Waldron, pp. 291–92.

19. Tinker and Rukeyser, p. 86.

20. Quoted in Alley and Brown, p. 3.

21. Quoted in Tinker and Rukeyser, p. 91.

22. Tinker and Rukeyser, p. 22.

23. Alley and Brown, p. 4.

24. Tinker and Rukeyser, p. 115.

25. Ibid., p. 184.

26. Ken Auletta, *Three Blind Mice: How the TV Networks Lost Their Way* (New York: Random House, 1991), p. 88.

27. "Dialogue on Film: Grant Tinker," *American Film*, September 1983, p. 25.

28. Auletta, p. 89.

29. Tinker and Rukeyser, p. 155.

## Chapter 4: *Hill Street Blues*: The Quality Revolution

1. Joyce Carol Oates, "Why *Hill Street Blues* Is Irresistible," *TV Guide*, June 1, 1985, p. 5.

2. Todd Gitlin, *Inside Prime Time* (New York: Pantheon, 1983), p. 277.

3. David Freeman, "Television's Real A-Team," *Esquire*, January, 1985, pp. 77–85.

4. Quoted in Gitlin, p. 274.

5. Gitlin, p. 273.

6. *Hospital* was written by Paddy Chayefsky, author of *Marty* and a long list of anthology dramas from the Golden Age of Television.

7. Paul Kerr, "Drama at MTM: *Lou Grant* and *Hill Street Blues*," in Jane Feuer, Paul Kerr, and Tise Vahimagi (eds.), *MTM: 'Quality Television'* (London: The British Film Institute, 1984), p. 148.

8. Quoted in Gitlin, p. 279.

9. Freeman, p. 80.

10. Michael Kozoll in a 1984 interview with Tise Vahimagi and Paul Kerr, in Feuer, et al., p. 247.

11. Quoted in Richard Levinson and William Link, *Off Camera: Conversations with the Makers of Prime-Time Television* (New York: Plume, 1986), p. 21.

12. Kozoll, p. 247.

13. Quoted in Gitlin, p. 280.

14. Quoted in "Dialogue on Film: Steven Bochco," *American Film*, July/August, 1988, p. 16.

15. Quoted in Gitlin, p. 284.

16. Steven Bochco, "The Censorship Game," in Judy Fireman (ed.), *The TV Book* (New York: Workman, 1977), pp. 55–56.

17. Quoted in Gitlin, p. 280.

18. Levinson and Link, p. 22.

19. Quoted in John Gabree, "Can 'Hill Street Blues' Keep Dodging the Nielsen Bullet?," *TV Guide*, October 31, 1981, pp. 28–29.

20. Gitlin, p. 281.

21. Grant Tinker and Bud Rukeyser, *Tinker in Television: From General Sarnoff to General Electric* (New York: Simon & Schuster, 1994), p. 98.

22. Quoted in Morgan Gendel, "The Battle for the Living Rooms of America," *The Los Angeles Times*, September 4, 1984, part 6, p. 1.

23. Quoted in Levinson and Link, p. 23.

24. Tom Shales, "The 'Hill Street' Zanies and the Boys in Blue," *The Washington Post*, January 15, 1981, D1.

25. "Television Looks at Itself," *Harpers*, March, 1985, p. 44.

26. Michael Pollan, "Can 'Hill Street Blues' Rescue NBC," Channels, March/April, 1983, p. 34.

27. Quoted in "Dialogue on Film: Steven Bochco," p. 16.

28. Documentaries are often shot on 16-millimeter film, but most network shows use 35-millimeter film.

29. Gitlin, p. 296.

30. Pollan, p. 31.

31. For a more detailed discussion of this material, see Robert J. Thompson, "Collective Blindness on American Television," in Gary Burns and Robert J. Thompson (eds.), *Television Studies: Textual Analysis* (New York: Praeger, 1989), pp. 79–87.

32. Quoted in Neal Koch, "Prime-Time Renegade," *Channels*, November, 1989, p. 58.

33. Quoted in Gendel, p. 1.

34. "Playboy Interview: Hill Street Blues," *Playboy*, October, 1983, p. 156.

35. Ken Auletta, *Three Blind Mice: How the TV Networks Lost Their Way* (New York: Random House, 1991), pp. 429–31.

36. Tom Shales, "'Hill Street.' Hail and Farewell," *The Washington Post*, May 12, 1987, p. D1.

37. Gitlin, p. 273.

38. Ibid., p. 274.

39. Ibid.

40. "Playboy Interview: Hill Street Blues," *Playboy*, October, 1983, p. 160.

41. Gitlin, p. 324.

## Chapter 5: Quality—The Next Generation: *St. Elsewhere*

1. Quoted in Todd Gitlin, *Inside Prime Time* (New York: Pantheon, 1983), p. 274.

2. Quoted in Diane Haithman, "Closing the Curtain on 'St. Elsewhere' Operation," *The Los Angeles Times*, May 25, 1988, part 6, p. 1.

3. Grant Tinker, interview with the author, June 2, 1993.

4. Mark Tinker, interview with the author, April 18, 1993.

5. Quoted in Joseph Turow, *Playing Doctor: Television, Storytelling, and Medical Power* (New York: Oxford University Press, 1989), p. 239.

6. Brandon Tartikoff and Charles Leerhsen, *The Last Great Ride* (New York: Turtle Bay Books, 1992), p. 166.

7. Turow, p. 240.

8. Ibid.

9. Quoted in Mark Christensen and Cameron Stauth, *The Sweeps: Behind the Scenes in Network TV* (New York: William Morrow, 1984), p. 119.

10. Mark Tinker, interview with the author, April 18, 1993.

11. Grant Tinker, interview with the author, June 2, 1993.

12. Michele Brustin, "*St. Elsewhere*: Creative Changes through Reexamination," a paper presented at the Third International Conference on Television Drama, Michigan State University, East Lansing, MI, May 20, 1983. Brustin delivered this paper when she was a vice-president of drama development at NBC.

13. Grant Tinker and Bud Rukeyser, *Tinker in Television: From General Electric to General Sarnoff* (New York: Simon & Schuster, 1994), p. 173.

14. Quoted in Daniel Paisner, *Horizontal Hold: The Making and Breaking of a Network Television Pilot* (New York: Birch Lane Press, 1992), p. 52.

15. Howie Mandel, interview with the author, February 27, 1995.

16. Ralph Daniels, interview with the author, March 21, 1993.

17. For a detailed list and discussion of these jokes, see Robert J. Thompson, *Good TV: The St. Elsewhere Story* (Syracuse: Syracuse University Press, forthcoming).

18. Quoted in Morgan Gendel, "The Battle for the Living Rooms of America; Three Producers Who Regularly Push at TV's Boundaries," *The Los Angeles Times,* September 4, 1985, part 6, p. 1.

19. Jane Feuer, "The MTM Style," in Jane Feuer, Paul Kerr, and Tise Vahimagi (eds.), *MTM: 'Quality Television'* (London: The British Film Institute, 1984), p. 44.

20. Quoted in Turow, p. 247.

21. David Bianculli, interview with the author, June 19, 1995.

22. Quoted in Scot Haller, "Good Night *St. Elsewhere,*" *People,* May 23, 1988, p. 40.

23. An excellent discussion of the "yuppie" audience can be found in Jane Feuer, *Seeing through the Eighties: Television and Reaganism* (Durham, NC: Duke University Press, 1995), pp. 25–41.

24. Tom Fontana, one of *St. Elsewhere's* two principal writers, claims to have been a big fan of *Green Acres* and many references to the show can be found in *St. Elsewhere.* Tom Fontana, personal interview with the author, April, 1995.

25. For a detailed discussion of these, see Donna McCrohan, *The Life and Times of Maxwell Smart* (New York: St. Martin's, 1988), pp. 113–15.

26. This episode has been discussed at some length by Scott R. Olson, "Metatelevision: Popular Postmodernism," *Critical Studies in Mass Communication,* September, 1987, pp. 288–89; Alexander Nehamas, "Seriously Watching," *South Atlantic Quarterly,* Winter, 1990, pp. 169–72; and David Bianculli, *Teleliteracy: Taking Television Seriously* (New York: Continuum, 1992), pp. 150–52.

27. Michael Wood, *America in the Movies* (New York: Dell, 1975), p. 10.

28. Ibid., pp. 10–11.

29. Tom Fontana, interview with the author, April 19, 1993.

30. This was the case only from the last episode of the first season through the end of the fifth season.

31. Tom Fontana, interview with author, May 27, 1993.

32. Ibid.

33. Ken Auletta, *Three Blind Mice: How the TV Networks Lost Their Way* (New York: Random House, 1991), p. 449.

34. William Mahoney and Marianne Paskowski, "MTM Breaks 'St. Elsewhere' Silence," *Electronic Media,* March 7, 1988, p. 12.

35. *Donahue,* syndicated, February 23, 1988.

36. Haller, pp. 36–41.

37. *TV Guide,* May 21, 1988, p. A105 (Syracuse, NY edition).

38. Turow, pp. 242–44.

39. Quoted in Diane Haithman, "On Television, There's More Than One Way to Say Goodbye; 'St. Elsewhere' As Seen Through a Glass Darkly," *The Los Angeles Times,* May 26, 1988, part 6, p. 1.

40. Ibid.

41. Quoted in Haithman, "Closing the Curtain on 'St. Elsewhere' Operation," p. 1.

## Chapter 6: The Second Golden Age of Television: *Cagney & Lacey, Moonlighting, L.A. Law, thirtysomething,* and *China Beach*

1. Sydney W. Head, Christopher H. Sterling, and Lemuel B. Schofield, *Broadcasting in America: A Survey of Electronic Media,* 7th ed. (Boston: Houghton Mifflin, 1994), p. 98.

2. Quoted in Richard Turner, "The Curious Case of the Lady Cops and the Shots That Blew Them Away," *TV Guide,* October 8, 1983, p. 57.

3. Julie D'Acci, "Defining Women: The Case of *Cagney and Lacey,*" in Lynn Spigel and Denise Mann (eds.), *Private Screenings: Television and the Female Consumer* (Minneapolis, MN: The University of Minnesota Press, 1992), p. 173.

4. Quoted in Karen Stabiner, "The Pregnant Detective," *The New York Times Magazine,* September 22, 1985, p. 104.

5. Ibid.

6. Quoted in Marjorie Rosen, "*Cagney & Lacey,*" *Ms.,* October, 1981, p. 49.

7. Turner, p. 52.

8. Ibid., p. 52–53.

9. Quoted in Rosen, p. 50.

10. Turner, p. 54.

11. Quoted in ibid., p. 54.

12. Gless was available because of the recent cancellation of *House Calls*, a series in which she had also replaced a fired actress, Lynn Redgrave.

13. Turner, p. 52.

14. Quoted in ibid., p. 57.

15. D'Acci, p. 187.

16. Erich Segal, "Sometimes They Don't Even Catch the Crook," *TV Guide*, March 17, 1984, pp. 20–22.

17. John J. O'Connor, "Date Rape on *Cagney and Lacey*" *The New York Times*, January 5, 1988, section C, p. 18.

18. Barney Rosenzweig, presentation at the Television Critics Association, Los Angeles, July 21, 1994.

19. Jane Hall and Mary Ann Norbom, "*Cagney & Lacey* Creators Barbara Corday and Barney Rosenzweig Mix Cops, Controversy and Marriage," *People*, November 25, 1985, p. 127.

20. Todd Gitlin, *Inside Prime Time* (New York: Pantheon, 1983), p. 89.

21. Rosen, pp. 47–50, 109.

22. D'Acci, pp. 175–78.

23. Gloria Steinem, "Why I Consider *Cagney & Lacey* the Best Show on TV," *TV Guide*, January 16, 1988, pp. 4–6.

24. D'Acci, p. 187.

25. Carolyn McGuire, "*Cagney & Lacey* Detect Strife," *Chicago Tribune*, November 11, 1985, Tempo, p. 6; and Morgan Gendel, "*Cagney & Lacey* Seek Help on Abortion Show," *The Los Angeles Times*, part 6, p. 1.

26. Dorothy Swanson, interview with author, June 27, 1994.

27. Barney Rosenzweig, presentation at the Television Critics Association, Los Angeles, July 21, 1994.

28. David Friedman, "*Cagney & Lacey:* Mixed Results on a Tough Topic," *Newsday*, January 5, 1988, part 2, p, 11.

29. Tim Brooks and Earle Marsh, *The Complete Directory to Prime Time Network TV Shows, 1946-Present*, Fifth Edition (New York: Ballantine, 1992), p. 137.

30. Barney Rosenzweig would do his next series, *The Trials of Rosie O'Neill*, at MTM.

31. Julie D'Acci, *Defining Women: Television and the Case of Cagney & Lacey* (Chapel Hill, NC: The University of North Carolina Press, 1994), p. 207.

32. D'Acci, *Defining Women: Television and the Case of Cagney & Lacey.*

33. An unidentified CBS programmer quoted in "TV Update," *TV Guide*, June 12, 1982, p. A1. Meg Foster had, in fact, portrayed a lesbian in the 1978 film *A Different Story*, but then Sharon Gless, the actor who replaced Foster in the role of Chris Cagney, had portrayed a man stuck in a woman's body in the 1979 NBC sitcom *Turnabout*.

34. "Fiercer Struggle for Shrinking Market; The Battle for Prime Time Television," *Broadcasting*, April 29, 1985, p. 37.

35. Quoted in David Bianculli, "Getting Down to Business, New NBC President Cites 'Hill Street Blues' as Too Complicated," *The Philadelphia Inquirer*, October 24, 1986, p. D1.

36. Ken Auletta, *Three Blind Mice: How the TV Networks Lost Their Way* (New York: Random House, 1991), pp. 105–6.

37. Morgan Gendel, "ABC's 'Hands-Off' Experiment," *The Los Angeles Times*, June 20, 1985, part 6, p. 1.

38. Quoted in ibid., p. 1.

39. Joy Horowitz, "The Madcap Behind 'Moonlighting'," *The New York Times*, March 30, 1986, section 6, p. 24; Morgan Gendel, "New Sitcoms, Dramas on the Light Side; ABC Throws Comedy into the Breach," *The Los Angeles Times*, part 6, p. 9; Steve Daley,

"Writer of 'Moonlighting' Cast in a Different Glow," *Chicago Tribune*, March 11, 1986, Tempo, p. 5; Barbara Siegel and Scott Siegel, *Cybill and Bruce: Moonlighting Magic* (New York: St. Martin's Press, 1987), p. 8.

40. Howard Rosenberg, "Two Risky Shows Light Up Gray TV," *The Los Angeles Times*, December 17, 1986, part 6, p. 8.

41. Siegel and Siegel, pp. 14–15.

42. Ibid., pp. 56, 57.

43. Joy Horowitz, "The Madcap Behind 'Moonlighting'," *The New York Times*, March 30, 1986, Section 6, p. 24.

44. Quoted in Gendel, "New Sitcoms, Dramas On the Light Side," p. 9.

45. Quoted Siegel and Siegel, p. 37.

46. Steve Daley, "Writer of 'Moonlighting' Cast in a Different Glow," *Chicago Tribune*, March 11, 1986, Tempo, p. 5.

47. Aljean Harmetz, "If Willis Gets $5 Million, How Much for Redford," *The New York Times*, February 16, 1988, Section C, p. 15.

48. Susan Faludi, *Backlash: The Undeclared War Against American Women* (New York: Anchor Books, 1991), p. 157.

49. Quoted in Nikki Finke, "Any Sparks Left?" *The Los Angeles Times*, December 6, 1988, part 6, p. 1.

50. Quoted in David Friedman, "Sexy and Naughty Take Two; 'Moonlighting' Goes Back to the Basics This Week to Recapture That Old Sparkle," *Newsday*, December 4, 1988, TV Plus, p. 8.

51. Quoted in Finke, p. 1.

52. *Moonlighting* "production office" employees quoted in Monica Collins, "Farewell to 3 Originals; 'Ties,' 'Vice' and 'Moonlighting' Sign Off; In Their Prime Times, They Were Magic," *USA Today*, May 12, 1989, p. 1D.

53. Horowitz, p. 24.

54. Ibid.

55. Rosenberg, p. 8.

56. Quoted in "News Update: *Moonlighting* to Make Only 20 New Episodes," *TV Guide*, March 15, 1986, p. A1.

57. Horowitz, p. 24.

58. Ibid.

59. Ibid.

60. Ibid.

61. Quoted in Horowitz, p. 24.

62. "News Update: *Moonlighting* to Make Only 20 New Episodes," *TV Guide*, March 15, 1986, p. A1.

63. Lewis Erlicht, personal communication, July, 1987.

64. Barbara Siegel and Scott Siegel. *Cybill and Bruce: Moonlighting Magic* (New York: St. Martin's Press, 1987), p. 24.

65. Horowitz, p. 24.

66. "News Update: *Moonlighting* To Make Only 20 New Episodes," *TV Guide*, March 15, 1986, p. A1.

67. Quoted in Horowitz, p. 24.

68. Tom Shales, "Steven Bochco: A 'Law' Unto Himself," *The Washington Post*, June 8, 1986, section G, p. 1.

69. David A. Kaplan, "L.A. Law, TV-Style," *The National Law Journal*, June 30, 1986, p. 45. According to David Shaw, "The Partner Lay There Dead . . . Face Down in a Dish of Beans," *TV Guide*, October 11, 1986, pp. 34–35, this story began circulating in 1984 and neither Tinker nor Bochco recalls the conversation concerning a show based on *The Verdict* ever occuring. Having read about the idea, however, Tinker apparently decided to pursue it with Bochco.

70. Diane Haithman, "NBC Executive, Fisher Spokesman Trade Shots in 'L.A. Law' Dispute," *The Los Angeles Times*, December 12, 1987, part 6, p. 1.

71. Quoted in Morgan Gendel, "Bochco Renders Opinions on 'Law'," *The Los Angeles Times,* April 25, 1986, part 6, p. 1.

72. Diane Haithman, "Steven Bochco, the $10 Million Man," *The Los Angeles Times,* November 24, 1987, part 6, p. 1.

73. Diane Haithman, "Bochco-ization of the Networks?," *The Los Angeles Times,* December 29, 1987, part 6, p. 1.

74. Quoted in Diane Haithman, "Bochco's Defection Won't Hurt 'L.A. Law'—Tartikoff," *The Los Angeles Times,* November 12, 1987, part 6, p. 12.

75. T. Klein, "A behind the Scenes Look at *L.A. Law,*" *Cosmopolitan,* December, 1987, p. 191.

76. Shales, p. G5.

77. Quoted in Robert Lindsey, "From 'Hill Street' to 'L.A. Law'," *The New York Times Magazine,* August 24, 1986, p. 60.

78. Judy Flander, "Producer's Trials Helped Her Put 'L.A. Law' in Order," *The Los Angeles Times,* October 29, 1986, part 6, p. 1.

79. Michael Orey, "Sex! Money! Glitz! In-House at *L.A. Law,*" *The American Lawyer,* December, 1988, p. 32.

80. Quoted in Shales, p. G5.

81. Harry Waters with Janet Huck, "Lust for Law," *Newsweek,* November 16, 1987, p. 84.

82. Quoted in Flander, p. 1.

83. Diane Haithman, "NBC Executive, Fisher Spokesman Trade Shots in *L.A. Law* Dispute," *The Los Angeles Times,* December 12, 1987, part 6, p. 1.

84. Diane Haithman, "Terry Fisher's Side of the Bochco Split-Up," *The Los Angeles Times,* February 23, 1988, part 6, p. 9.

85. Quoted in Diane Haithman, "Bochco on His Own; . . . And At 'L.A. Law' A New Production Team Takes Over," *The Los Angeles Times,* September 14, 1989, part 6, p.1.

86. Quoted in Patricia Brennan, "'L.A. Law' Faces a Crucial Fourth Season," *The Washington Post,* May 28, 1989, p. Y8.

87. Steve Weinstein, "Steven Bochco On the Case, 'L.A. Law' Co-Creator Returns to Fine-Tune Troubled Series," *The Los Angeles Times,* April 2, 1992, part F, p. 1.

88. *TV Guide,* March 27, 1993, p. 161.

89. Michael McWilliams, "The Biggest Snow Job in Prime Time," *The Village Voice,* October 7, 1986, p. 46.

90. Rick Marin, "80's Trends; Television: The Party's Over," *The Washington Times,* December 21, 1989, p. E1.

91. Clifford Terry, "'Thirtysomething' Is a Real Zero," *The Chicago Tribune,* September 28, 1987, Tempo, p. 7.

92. Tom Shales, "*thirtysomething:* Yup-and-Coming on ABC," *The Washington Post,* September 29, 1987, p. D1.

93. "*thirtysomething,* A Chronicle of Everyday Life," *The New York Times,* February 24, 1988, Section C, p. 26.

94. Michael Bygrave, "Beginning of the End; Michael Bygrave on changes in the American television industry and the declining years of *thirtysomething,*" *The Independent,* April 6, 1991, p. 30.

95. *thirtysomething Stories—By the Writers of thirtysomething* (New York: Pocket Books, 1991).

96. Liberty Godshall, *thirtysomething Stories—By the Writers of thirtysomething,* p. 246.

97. Faludi, p. 162.

98. Quoted in Richard Kramer, "The *thirtysomething* Journal," *Playboy,* December, 1989, p. 154.

99. Paraphrased by Kramer, p. 154.

100. Susan Shilliday, *thirtysomething Stories—By the Writers of thirtysomething,* p. 57.

101. Faludi, p. 161.

102. Quoted in "'Thirtysomething,' A Chronicle of Everyday Life," p. 26.

103. "Interview: The Creators and Cast of *thirtysomething*," *Playboy,* June, 1990, p. 57.
104. Ibid.
105. Faludi, p. 161.
106. "Thirtysomething Ends on Highsomething Note," *PR Newswire,* May 29, 1991. In an attempt to cash in on these viewers, Apparel Resources International, Ltd., licensed the show's title and came out with a mail order catalog of "lifestyle fashions."
107. Quoted in John Lippman, "*thirtysomething* Pair to Produce 3 ABC Series," *The Los Angeles Times,* April 25, 1991, part D, p. 1.
108. Quoted in Howard Rosenberg, "ABC Pulls Plug On a Rerun of 'thirtysomething'," *The Los Angeles Times,* part F, p. 1.
109. Ibid.
110. Writer Richard Kramer discusses this in *thirtysomething Stories—By the Writers of thirtysomething,* p. 291.
111. "Interview: The Creators and Cast of *thirtysomething*," p. 57.
112. Quoted in Matt Roush, "*thirtysomething* Goes Way of '80s," *USA Today,* May 22, 1991.
113. Tom Shales, "The Days of Whines and Neuroses," *The Washington Post,* May 30, 1991, p. D1.
114. *The Tonight Show,* NBC, May 28, 1991.
115. "Interview: The Creators and Cast of *thirtysomething*," p. 57.
116. Randall Rothenberg, "Ad Executives Cheer as Ethics Wins the Day on *thirtysomething*," *The New York Times,* May 16, 1991, section C, p. 17.
117. Episode written by Joseph Dougherty, *thirtysomething,* May 14, 1991.
118. Joseph Dougherty quoted in Rothenberg, p. 17. It is interesting to note the actor Ken Olin went on to work as a director of television commercials.
119. Quoted in Laurie Halpern Berenson, "So-Called Limbo: Now They Really Feel Alienated," *The New York Times,* March 12, 1995, p. H35.
120. Quoted in Berenson, p. H40.
121. A detailed discussion of the presentation of women in *China Beach* can be found in Leah R. Vande Berg, "*China Beach,* Prime Time War in the Postfeminist Age: An Example of Patriarchy in a Different Voice," *Western Journal of Communication,* Summer 1993, p. 349–66.
122. Quoted in Richard Mahler, "*China Beach* Producer Tells 'Story of a Generation,'" *Electronic Media,* May 23, 1988, p. 18.
123. Quoted in David Gritten, "Women at War, *China Beach* Settles into a Different Vietnam," *The Chicago Tribune,* December 4, 1988, ARTS, p. 28.
124. Ibid.
125. Richard Zoglin, "War As Family Entertainment," *Time,* February 20, 1989, p. 84.
126. Henry Allen, Review of *The Weather Tomorrow, The Washington Post,* April 16, 1982, p. B10.
127. William Broyles, Jr., *Brothers in Arms: A Journey From War to Peace* (New York: Knopf, 1986).
128. Mahler, p. 18.
129. Ibid.
130. Brooks and Marsh, p. 533.
131. Oddly enough, *thirtysomething* had also told a story "backward" that year, and in this case it was the episode in which Susannah (Patricia Kalember) gives birth to Gary's baby. Ann Lewis Hamilton, the writer of the episode, claimed in *thirtysomething Stories— By the Writers of thirtysomething* (p. 342) to have been inspired by Harold Pinter's *Betrayal.*
132. Irv Letofsky, "ABC Cites the Losses from Advertiser 'Defections,'" *The Los Angeles Times,* July 24, 1990, p. F12.
133. The final quote was from Tom Shales, "'China Beach;' Going Far beyond Vietnam," *The Washington Post,* September 29, 1990, p. D1.
134. Thomas Tyrer, "'China Beach' Staff Lobbies for 2nd Chance," *Electronic Media,* April 8, 1991, p. 34.
135. Quoted in ibid.

136. Quoted in Art Chapman, "Time to Move on, *China Beach* Finale Stays True to the Spirit of the Series," *The Chicago Tribune,* July 22, 1991, Tempo, p. 7.

137. Steven Herbert, *"China Beach* Winds Up Production . . . ," *The Los Angeles Times,* February 15, 1991, p. F28.

138. Quoted in ibid.

139. Gail Caldwell, "After Four Seasons, ABC's 'China Beach' Says Farewell . . . ," *The Boston Globe,* July 19, 1991, Living, p. 23.

140. Howard Rosenberg, "Advertisers Cooling off to Hot Topics," *The Los Angeles Times,* July 26, 1990, part F, p. 1.

## Chapter 7: Quality Goes Quirky: *Twin Peaks, Northern Exposure,* and *Picket Fences*

1. Jeff MacGregor, "The Importance of Being Quirky (At All Costs)," *The New York Times,* February, 19, 1995, p. 34.

2. Spielberg's other made-for-TV movie, *Something Evil,* was not made at Universal.

3. Alex McNeil, *Total Television: A Comprehensive Guide to Programming from 1948 to the Present* (New York: Penguin, 1991), p. 34.

4. License fee estimate published in *Variety,* September 25, 1985, p. 55.

5. Richard Corliss, "Czar of Bizarre," *Time,* October 1, 1990, p. 84.

6. Bill Carter, "At ABC, Several Motives for Keeping 'Twin Peaks,'" *The New York Times,* May 21, 1990, section D, p. 1.

7. Ibid.

8. Tinker said this in a speech to the NBC affiliates. He quotes himself in, Grant Tinker and Bud Rukeyser, *Tinker in Television* (New York: Simon & Schuster, 1994), p. 201.

9. Howard Rosenberg, "TV You've Never Seen Before . . . ," *The Los Angeles Times,* April 6, 1990, part F, p. 1.

10. Tinker in Grant Tinker and Rukeyser, p. 202.

11. Steve Pond and Marcia Froelke, "You Are Now Leaving *Twin Peaks* . . . ," *Playboy,* February, 1991, p. 104.

12. Quoted in Carter, section D, p. 1.

13. Robert DiMatteo, "The Lynch Mob's Prime-Time Warp," *Newsday,* April 8, 1990, TV Plus, p. 6.

14. Rosenberg, p. 1.

15. Bochco had appeared in NBC advertisements for *Bay City Blues* in 1983.

16. Pond and Froelke, p. 104.

17. David Lavery, "The Semiotics of Cobbler: *Twin Peaks'* Interpretive Community," in David Lavery (ed.), *Full Of Secrets: Critical Approaches to* Twin Peaks (Detroit, MI: Wayne State University Press, 1995), p. 18.

18. Richard Zoglin, "Like Nothing on Earth . . . ," *Time,* April 9, 1990, p. 96.

19. Warren Rodman, "The Series That Will Change TV," *Connoisseur,* September, 1989, p. 139.

20. David Lynch, Mark Frost, and Richard Saul Worman, *Welcome to Twin Peaks: An Access Guide to the Town* (New York: Pocket Books, 1991); Jennifer Lynch, *The Secret Diary of Laura Palmer* (New York: Pocket Books, 1990); Scott Frost, *The Autobiography of F.B.I. Special Agent Dale Cooper* (New York: Pocket Books, 1991).

21. David Bianculli, *Teleliteracy: Taking Television Seriously* (New York: Continuum, 1992), p. 271.

22. Howard Rosenberg, "Who Killed Laura? The Suspense Is Murder," *The Los Angeles Times,* May 17, 1990, p. F12; and "Meanwhile, Back at *Twin Peaks,*" *The Los Angeles Times,* May 23, 1990, p. F10.

23. Steve Weinstein, "New *Twin Peaks* Cliffhanger: Can Loyal Fans Save the Show?" *The Los Angeles Times,* February 23, 1991, part F, p. 11.

24. *"Twin Peaks* Finale Draws Low Ratings," *The New York Times,* June 12, 1991, section C, p. 18.

25. Corliss, p. 84.

26. Marc Dolan, "The Peaks and Valleys of Serial Creativity: What Happened to/ on *Twin Peaks*," in David Lavery (ed.), p. 32.

27. Quoted in Steve Pond, "Shades of Change," *US*, May 28, 1990, p. 24.

28. Quoted in John Leonard, "The Quirky Allure of *Twin Peaks*," *New York*, May 7, 1990, p. 35.

29. Rob Owen, "Peaks Freaks Ensure Cult Series Lives On," *The Richmond Times-Dispatch*, September 3, 1994, p. F32.

30. David Lavery (ed.) *Full of Secrets: Critical Approaches to* Twin Peaks (Detroit, MI: Wayne State University Press), 1995.

31. Bill Carter, "At ABC, Several Motives for Keeping 'Twin Peaks,'" *The New York Times*, May 21, 1990, section D, p. 1.

32. Tom Shales, "'Exposure's' Tasty Encore," *The Washington Post*, April 8, 1991, p. C2.

33. Quoted in John J. O'Connor. "New Doctor Adrift in Alaska," *The New York Times*, July 12, 1990, p. C22.

34. Quoted in Michael E. Hill, "What Is *Northern Exposure* Like?; Funny? Quirky? Or Just Weird?" *The Washington Post*, May 19, 1991, p. Y7.

35. This was all part of a proud CBS heritage that went back to the top-ten days of not only *Green Acres*, but also *Petticoat Junction, The Andy Griffith Show, The Beverly Hillbillies*, and *Gomer Pyle, U.S.M.C. Northern Exposure* and *Evening Shade* debuted within a few months of each other, both offering up a romanticized version of the American small town. Both shows had updated the theme with a heavy dosage of what would soon be called "political correctness."

36. Lance Luria, interview with the author, March 30, 1993.

37. Quoted in Eric Mink, "Setting the Tone for Series' Theme," *The St. Louis Post-Dispatch*, July 19, 1990, magazine, p. 7E.

38. Quoted in Kenneth R. Clark, "CBS Schedule Gives Alaska Some 'Exposure,'" *The Chicago Tribune*, July 8, 1990, TV Week, p. 3.

39. N. R. Kleinfield, "The Networks' New Advertising Dance," *The New York Times*, July 29, 1990, section 3, p. 1.

40. Tinker and Rukeyser, pp. 34–61. See also Paul Kerr, "Drama at MTM: *Lou Grant* and *Hill Street Blues*," in Jane Feuer, Paul Kerr, and Tise Vahimagi, *MTM: 'Quality Television'* (London: The British Film Institute, 1984), p. 136.

41. Daniel Cerone, "The Cast of 'Northern Exposure' Faces a Daunting Prospect, Living through Dozens More Episodes without the Show's Creators," *The Los Angeles Times*, May 10, 1992, Calender, p. 3.

42. Books about or based upon *Northern Exposure* included Louis Chunovic, *The Northern Exposure Book* (New York: Citadel, 1993); Louis Chunovic (ed.), *Chris in the Morning: Love, Life, and the Whole Karmic Enchilada* (New York: Contemporary Books); Scott Nance, *Exposing Northern Exposure* (Las Vegas, NV: Pioneer Books, 1992); Ellis Weiner, *The Northern Exposure Cookbook* (New York: Contemporary Books); and Ellis Weiner, *Letters From Cicely* (New York: Pocket Books, 1992).

43. Cerone, p. 3.

44. Chunovic, *The Northern Exposure Book*, p. 143.

45. Clark, p. 3.

46. Stephen Fried, "Moose Music," *GQ*, November, 1991, pp. 98–103.

47. Quoted in Jeanie Kasindorf, "New Frontier—How *Northern Exposure* Became the Spring's Hottest TV show," *New York*, May 27, 1991, p. 46.

48. Michael Orey, "Sex! Money! Glitz! In-House at *L.A. Law*," *The American Lawyer*, December, 1988, p. 32.

49. Bill Carter, "He's a Lawyer. He's a Writer. But Can He Type?" *The New York Times*, February 7, 1990, section C, p. 15.

50. Marvin Kitman, "Beyond the 'Picket Fences'," *Newsday*, September 17, 1992, p. 69.

51. Thomas Tyrer, "Producer Carving Niche in CBS's 'Picket Fences,' *Electronic Media*, October 19, 1992, p. 3.

52. Quoted in Steve Pond, "*Picket Fences* and the Man Behind Them," *The New York Times*, September 13, 1992, section 2, p. 47.

53. Quoted in Jill Gerston, "This Season, They've Rebuilt Picket Fences," *The New York Times*, November 21, 1993, p. H36.

54. Howard Rosenberg, "Kiss of the Teenage Girls Impales CBS on Its *Picket Fences*," *The Toronto Star*, April 29, 1993, p. F7.

55. Quoted in Gerston, p. H36.

56. Quoted in Tyrer, p. 3.

57. Kitman, p. 69.

58. Quoted in Steve Weinstein, "When in Rome . . . ," *The Los Angeles Times*, March 28, 1993, TV Times, p. 2.

59. Quoted in Manny Mendoza, "*Picket Fences* Plots and Cast Stand Up," *The Dallas Morning News*, April 28, 1994, p. 1C.

60. Ibid.

61. Quoted Weinstein, "When in Rome . . . ," p. 2.

62. Kelley grew up in Maine, Jessica Fletcher's stomping grounds. Though *Picket Fences* is set in Wisconsin, Kelley claims to have modeled Rome after the Maine towns he'd experienced as a child.

63. Norman Lear, whose quality family tree fizzled out after *All in the Family* and its offspring left the air, tried something along these lines in his sitcom *Sunday Dinner*, which came and went in 1991.

64. Quoted in Gerston, p. H36.

65. MacGregor, p. 34.

66. Ibid.

## Chapter 8: The Future of Quality

1. *Equal Justice* was executive produced by Thomas Carter, another MTM alumnus who had costarred in *The White Shadow* and had gone on to direct for series like *St. Elsewhere* and *Miami Vice*.

2. Quoted in Matt Roush, "Season Flashback; A Look at TV's Good, Bad, and Departed; Innovation is Going Way of Dinosaurs," *USA Today*, June 4, 1991, p. 1D.

3. Quoted in Michael Bygrave, "Beginning of the End," *The Independent*, April 6, 1991, ARTS, p. 30.

4. Quoted in "Cheers 'n' Jeers," *TV Guide*, January 29, 1994, p. 8.

5. Quoted in Lee Goldberg, "Where to Put Brainy Shows?" *Electronic Media*, January 12, 1987, p. 90.

6. In the fall of 1995, the cable channel Nick at Nite announced that they would be launching a new classic TV channel called TV Land which would concentrate on reruns of hour-long programs.

7. Grant Tinker and Bud Rukeyser, *Tinker in Television: From General Electric to General Sarnoff* (New York: Simon & Schuster, 1994), p. 256.

8. *Seinfeld's* Michael Richards and *Mad about You's* Helen Hunt had both played recurring roles on *St. Elsewhere*.

9. Paul Reiser, quoted in Mark Goodman and Craig Tomashoff, "Groom with a View," *People*, May 23, 1994, p. 74.

10. The Children's Television Act of 1990 became law without President Bush's signature. President Reagan had vetoed an earlier version of the legislation. See Sydney W. Head, Christopher H. Sterling, and Lemuel B. Schofield, *Broadcasting in America: A Survey of Electronic Media, Seventh Edition* (Boston: Houghton Mifflin, 1994), pp. 527–28.

11. Quoted in J. Fred MacDonald, p. 227.

12. Mona Mangan, executive director of the Writers Guild of America, East, predicted that realistic and creative programs will suffer along with those that employ gratuitous violence as a result of these measures. Violence monitoring will, she claimed, "make television much less realistic than it should be." Quoted in Neil Hickey, "Networks Set for Violence Monitor," *TV Guide*, June 11, 1994, p. 37.

13. Edmund L. Andrews, "F.C.C. Joining A Move to Curb Violence on TV," *The New York Times*, July 7, 1995, pp. A1-A16.

14. Quoted in Eric Schmuckler, "The News Is Good for NBC," *Mediaweek*, February 28, 1994, p. 17.

15. Steven Bochco, "How I'd Fix Network TV," *The Los Angeles Times*, August 16, 1992, Calender, p. 7.

16. Ibid.

17. Ken Tucker, "Don't Turn off Your Mind Yet. Quality Dramas Crowd a Once-dull Night," September 16, 1994, p. 66.

18. Steve Sternberg, senior partner at BJK&E Media Group, as quoted in A. J. Jacobs, "Tales of the Gritty," *Entertainment Weekly*, November 4, 1994, pp. 18–20.

19. Bill Carter (*New York Times* News Service), "Bochco Shuffles Networks, Again," *The Syracuse Herald-American*, March 12, 1995, TV Cable Guide, p. 3.

20. John Saret Young used this term to describe his new show in Benjamin Svetkey, "The Next X," *Entertainment Weekly*, March 10, 1995, p. 26.

21. Mike Hammer and Ileane Rudolph, "Nets Shuffle Schedules in Battle for Spring Audience," *TV Guide*, March 4, 1995, p. 54.

22. The series was created by Shaun Cassidy, costar of the 1970s ABC series, *The Hardy Boys Mysteries*.

23. J. Max Robins, "Dick Wolf's Gotham Grand Slam," *Variety*, October 31, 1994, p. 27.

24. Tom Fontana, interview with the author, March, 1995.

25. Quoted in J. Max Robins, "New Power for Hour," *Variety*, October 31, 1994, p. 1.

26. PBS, in fact, aired a restaging of Paddy Chayefsky's classic 1954 Golden Age drama "The Mother," as the October 24, 1994, installment of *Great Performances*. Back in March 1993, Fox debuted a short-lived anthologylike drama *TriBeCa* that was shot entirely in New York City.

27. Quoted in Daniel B. Wood, "At Dawn of Television's 'Third Era,' Networks Already Feel the Heat," *The Christian Science Monitor*, May 22, 1995, p. 10.

28. Bernard Weinraub, "In Sheer Quality, TV is Elbowing Hollywood Aside," *The New York Times*, February 14, 1995, p. B1.

29. Quoted in Wood, p. 12.

30. Bruce Handy, "The Real Golden Age Is Now," *Time*, October 30, 1995, pp. 84–90; Charles McGrath, "The Triumph of the Prime-Time Novel," the *New York Times* magazine, October 22, 1995, pp. 52–59, 68, 76, 86; Bruce Fretts, "TV Saves the World," *Entertainment Weekly*, October 20, 1995, pp. 22–30; Steve Johnson, "Go On, Admit It: Television Has Become Quality Entertainment," *Chicago Tribune*, November 1, 1995, p. E5.

Tom Shales responded to these articles in his *Washington Post* column on November 5, 1995 (p. G01). "See It Then: TV's Real Golden Age," celebrated the live anthology dramas of the 1950s under a headline that announced "Some say that network television has never been better. They're wrong."

# Select Book Bibliography

See notes for articles, interviews, and other book sources.

Altman, Mark A. *Twin Peaks: Behind the Scenes.* Las Vegas, NV: Pioneer Books, 1990

Anderson, Christopher. *Hollywood TV: The Studio System in the Fifties.* Austin, TX: The University of Texas Press, 1994

Auletta, Ken. *Three Blind Mice: How the TV Networks Lost Their Way.* New York: Random House, 1991

Alley, Robert S., and Irby B. Brown. *Love Is All Around: The Making of The Mary Tyler Moore Show.* New York: Dell, 1989

Barnouw, Erik. *The Sponsor: Notes on a Modern Potentate.* New York: Oxford University Press, 1978

———. *Tube of Plenty: The Evolution of American Television* (2nd revised edition). New York: Oxford University Press, 1990

Bianculli, David. *Teleliteracy: Taking Television Seriously.* New York: Continuum, 1992; New York: Touchstone, 1994

Boddy, William. *Fifties Television: The Industry and Its Critics.* Urbana, IL: The University of Illinois Press, 1990

Brooks, Tim, and Earle Marsh. *The Complete Directory to Prime Time Network and Cable TV Shows, 1946-Present* (6th edition). New York: Ballantine, 1995

Brown, Les. *Les Brown's Encyclopedia of Television* (3rd edition). Detroit: Visible Ink, 1992

Buxton, Frank, and Bill Owen. *The Big Broadcast, 1920–1950.* New York: Avon, 1972

Caldwell, John Thorton. *Televisuality: Style, Crisis, and Authority in American Television.* New Brunswick, NJ: Rutgers University Press, 1995

Castleman, Harry, and Walter J. Podrazik. *Watching TV: Four Decades of American Television.* New York: McGraw Hill, 1982

———. *The TV Schedule Book: Four Decades of Network Programming from Sign-On to Sign-Off.* New York: McGraw-Hill, 1984

———. *Harry and Wally's Favorite TV Shows.* New York: Prentice Hall Press, 1989

Chunovic, Louis. *The Northern Exposure Book: The Official Publication of the Television Series.* New York: Citadel Press, 1993

Christenen, Mark, and Cameron Stauth. *The Sweeps: Behind the Scenes in Network TV.* New York: William Morrow, 1984

D'Acci, Julie. *Defining Women: Television and the Case of Cagney & Lacey.* Chapel Hill, NC: The University of North Carolina Press, 1994

Dunning, John. *Tune in Yesterday: The Ultimate Encyclopedia of Old-Time Radio 1925–1976.* Englewood Cliffs, NJ: Prentice-Hall, 1976

Eisner, Joel, and David Krinsky. *Television Comedy Series: An Episode Guide to 153 TV Sitcoms in Syndication.* Jefferson, NC: McFarland, 1984

Faludi, Susan. *Backlash: The Undeclared War Against American Women.* New York: Crown, 1991

Feuer, Jane, Paul Kerr, and Tise Vahimagi (eds.) *MTM—'Quality Television.'* London: The British Film Institute, 1984

Feuer, Jane. *Seeing through the Eighties: Television and Reaganism.* Durham, NC: Duke University Press, 1995

Gianakos, Larry James. *Television Drama Programming: A Comprehensive Chronicle* (6 volumes). Metuchen, NJ: Scarecrow, 1978, 1980, 1981, 1983, 1987, 1992

Gitlin, Todd. *Inside Prime Time.* New York: Pantheon, 1983

Goldberg, Lee. *Unsold Television Pilots, 1955–1988.* Jefferson, NC: McFarland, 1990

Greenfield, Jeff. *Television: The First Fifty Years.* New York: Crescent Books, 1981

Gripsrud, Jostein. *The Dynasty Years: Hollywood Television and Critical Media Studies.* London: Routledge, 1995

Gross, Edward. *The LA Lawbook.* Las Vegas, NV: Pioneer Books, 1991

Hamamoto, Darrell Y. *Nervous Laughter: Television Situation Comedy and Liberal Democratic Ideology.* New York: Praeger, 1989

Head, Sydney W., Christopher H. Sterling, and Lemuel B. Schofield. *Broadcasting in America: A Survey of Electronic Media* (7th edition). Boston: Houghton Mifflin, 1994

Heide, Margaret J. *Television Culture and Women's Lives:* thirtysomething *and the Contradictions of Gender.* Philadelphia: The University of Pennsylvania Press, 1995

Heldenfels, R. D. *Television's Greatest Year: 1954.* New York: Continuum, 1994

Herskovitz, Marshall, Edward Zwick, Susan Shilliday, Joseph Dougherty, Jill Gordon, Liberty Godshall, Richard Kramer, Ann Lewis Hamilton, and Winnie Holtzman. *thirtysomething Stories by the Writers of thirtysomething.* New York: Pocket Books, 1991

Kahn, Frank J. (ed.). *Documents of American Broadcasting* (3rd edition). Englewood Cliffs, NJ: Prentice-Hall, 1978

Knickelbine, Scott. *Welcome to Twin Peaks: A Complete Guide to Who's Who & What's What.* Lincolnwood, IL: Publications International, 1990

Lavery, David (ed.). *Full of Secrets: Critical Approaches to* Twin Peaks. Detroit, MI: Wayne State University Press, 1995

Levinson, Richard, and Wiiliam Link. *Off Camera: Conversations with the Makers of Prime-Time Television.* New York: Plume, 1986

MacDonald, J. Fred. *One Nation under Television: The Rise and Decline of Network TV.* Chicago: Nelson-Hall, 1994

Marc, David. *Demographic Vistas: Television in American Culture,* revised edition. Philadelphia: The University of Pennsylvania Press, 1996

————. *Comic Visions: Television Comedy amd American Culture.* Boston: Unwin Hyman, 1989

————and Robert J. Thompson. *Prime Time, Prime Movers.* New York: Little, Brown, 1992

Marill, Alvin H. *Movies Made for Television: The Telefeature and the Mini-Series 1964–1986.* New York: Zoetrope, 1987

McNeil, Alex. *Total Television: A Comprehensive Guide to Programming from 1948 to the Present* (3rd edition). New York: Penguin, 1991

Medved, Michael. *Hollywood vs. America.* New York: HarperCollins, 1992

Milch, David, and Bill Clark. *True Blue: The Real Stories Behind* NYPD Blue. New York: Morrow, 1995

Moore, Mary Tyler. *After All.* New York: Putnam, 1995

Morgenstern, Steve (ed.). *Inside the TV Business.* New York: Sterling Publishing, 1979

Nance, Scott. *Exposing Northern Exposure.* Las Vegas, NV: Pioneer Books, 1992

Newcomb, Horace. *TV—The Most Populat Art.* New York: Anchor, 1974

————and Robert S. Alley. *The Producer's Medium: Conversations with Creators of American TV.* New York: Oxford University Press, 1983

Paisner, Daniel. *Horizontal Hold: The Making and Breaking of a Network Television Pilot.* New York: Birch Lane Press, 1992

Perry, Jeb. *Universal Television: The Studio and Its Programs, 1950–1980*. Metuchen, NJ: Scarecrow, 1983

Pourroy, Janine. *Behind the Scenes at ER*. New York: Ballantine, 1995

Selnow, Gary W. and Richard R. Gilbert. *Society's Impact on Television: How the Viewing Public Shapes Television Programming*. Westport, CT: Praeger, 1993

Siegel, Barbara, and Mark Siegel. *Cybill & Bruce: Moonlighting Magic*. New York: St. Martin's, 1987

Spigel, Lynn. *Make Room for TV: Television and the Family Ideal in Postwar America*. Chicago: The University of Chicago Press, 1992

Stempel, Tom. *Storytellers to the Nation: A History of American Television Writing*. New York: Continuum, 1992

Sterling, Christopher H., and John M. Kittross. *Stay Tuned: A Concise History of American Broadcasting* (2nd edition). Belmont, CA: Wadsworth, 1990

Tartikoff, Brandon, and Charles Leerhsen. *The Last Great Ride*. New York: Turtle Bay Books, 1992

Taylor, Ella. *Prime-Time Families*. Berkeley, CA: The University of California Press, 1989

Terrace, Vincent. *Encyclopedia of Television: Series, Pilots and Specials* (3 volumes). New York: Zoetrope, 1986

Tichi, Cecelia. *Electronic Hearth: Creating An American Television Culture*. New York: Oxford University Press, 1991

Tinker, Grant, and Bud Rukeyser. *Tinker in Television: From General Electric to General Sarnoff*. New York: Simon & Schuster, 1994

Turow, Joseph. *Playing Doctor: Television, Storytelling, and Medical Power*. New York: Oxford University Press, 1989

Waldrom, Vince. *The Official Dick Van Dyke Show Book*. New York: Hyperion, 1994

Watson, Mary Ann. *The Expanding Vista: American Television in the Kennedy Years*. New York: Oxford University Press, 1990

Weissman, Ginny, and Coyne Steven Sanders. *The Dick Van Dyke Show: Anatomy of a Classic*. New York: St. Martin's, 1983

Wicking, Christopher, and Tise Vahimagi. *The American Vein: Directors and Directions in Television*. New York: E. P. Dutton, 1979

Wilk, Max. *The Golden Age of Television: Notes from the Survivors*. New York: Dell, 1976

Woolley, Lynn, Robert W. Malsbary, and Robert G. Strange, Jr. *Warner Bros. Television*. Jefferson, NC: McFarland, 1985

# Home Video Sources

Most of the ten series profiled in this book are available on home video from the following sources:

*Hill Street Blues*
United American Video Corporation
P.O. Box 7647
Charlotte, NC 28241
803-548-3335

*China Beach*
Warner Home Video
4000 Warner Blvd.
Burbank, CA 91522
818-954-6000

*St. Elsewhere*
United American Video Corporation
P.O. Box 7647
Charlotte, NC 28241
803-548-3335

*Twin Peaks*
Republic Pictures Home Video
5700 Wilshire Blvd., Suite 525
Los Angeles, CA 90036
213-965-6963

*Moonlighting*
Warner Home Video
4000 Warner Blvd.
Burbank, CA 91522
818-954-6000

*Northern Exposure*
MCA/Universal Home Video
70 University City Plaza
Los Angeles, CA 91608
818-777-4300

*L.A. Law*
Foxvideo
P.O. Box 900
Los Angeles, CA 90067
310-203-3900

Movies Unlimited, 1-800-4MOVIES, distributes all of the above titles by mail order.

# Index of Television Titles

# Index of Names